EVALUAT
FOR
SOCIAL WORKERS

Tony Tripodi
University of Michigan

Prentice-Hall, Inc., Englewood Cliffs, N.J. 07632

Library of Congress Cataloging in Publication Data
Tripodi, Tony.
　Evaluative research for social workers.

　Bibliography: p.
　Includes index.
　　1.-Social service—Research.　2.-Evaluation research
(Social action programs)　I. Title.
HV11.T743-1983　　361.3'0723　　82-12204
ISBN　0-13-292326-2

Editorial/production supervision
　and Interior design by Virginia Livsey
Cover design by Zimmerman/Foyster Designs
Manufacturing buyer: John B. Hall

© 1983 by Prentice-Hall, Inc., Englewood Cliffs, N.J. 07632

All rights reserved. No part of this book
may be reproduced in any form or
by any means without permission in writing
from the publisher.

Printed in the United States of America

10　9　8　7　6　5　4　3　2　1

ISBN 0-13-292326-2

Prentice-Hall International, Inc., *London*
Prentice-Hall of Australia Pty. Limited, *Sydney*
Prentice-Hall of Canada Inc., *Toronto*
Prentice-Hall of India Private Limited, *New Delhi*
Prentice-Hall of Japan, Inc., *Tokyo*
Prentice-Hall of Southeast Asia Pte. Ltd., *Singapore*
Whitehall Books Limited, *Wellington, New Zealand*

*To the memory of
my parents
Christina Grandinetti Tripodi
and
Nick Tripodi*

ACKNOWLEDGMENTS

Thanks are due to Deans Phillip Fellin and Harold Johnson of the University of Michigan School of Social Work for their support and provision of time and clerical assistance. I am indebted to friends, colleagues, and students with whom I have exchanged ideas about evaluative research; in particular, I benefited from the sound advice of Irwin Epstein, Srinika Jayaratne and Jesse Gordon. In addition, I appreciate Roxanne Loy's work on the original manuscript. Thanks to Dr. Alan Siman and Dr. Wallace J. Gingerich for their suggestions in reviewing the manuscript. Finally, I thank Roni, Rachel, David, and Stephen for their patience and forbearance while I was writing this manuscrpt.

Tony Tripodi

CONTENTS

PREFACE ix

Chapter 1   PLANNING EVALUATIVE RESEARCH   1

    Evaluative Research   1
    The Process of Evaluative Research
    and the Format of This Book   2
    Major Focuses of Evaluative Research   3
    Knowledge Gained from Evaluation   6
    Consumers of Evaluative Research   10
    Deciding to Evaluate   12

Chapter 2   CONCEPTUALIZING SOCIAL WORK   15
             PROGRAMS, PRACTICES, AND OBJECTIVES

    Programs   15
    Practices   16
    Social-Work Tasks   17

vi *Contents*

       Stages of Development in Programs   19
       Stages of Development in Practice   21
       Program and Practice Objectives   24
       Unanticipated Consequences   25
       Choosing among Objectives   26
       Criteria for Detailed Objectives   27
       Writing Specific Objectives   30
       Examples of Social-Work Objectives   31

Chapter 3   VARIABLES FOR EVALUATIVE RESEARCH   33

       Criteria of Evaluation   33
       Locating Variables   34
       Choosing Variables   42
       Properties of Useful Variables   43

Chapter 4   SECONDARY DATA RESOURCES   50
                       AND AVAILABLE INSTRUMENTS

       Location of Secondary Data Resources   51
       Types of Secondary Data Resources   52

Chapter 5   DEVELOPING NEW INSTRUMENTS   64
                       FOR GATHERING DATA

       Questionnaires   65
       Interviews   71
       Rating Scales   76
       Observations   79

Chapter 6   THE LOGIC OF EVALUATIVE RESEARCH DESIGN   83

       The Process of Formulating
       Research Designs   83
       Criteria for Developing Knowledge   84
       Criteria for Generality   89
       Procedures for Inferring Generality   91
       Selecting an Evaluative Research Design   97

Chapter 7 RESEARCH DESIGNS FOR EVALUATING SINGLE-CASE INTERVENTIONS — 100

Level 1: Hypothetical-Developmental Designs   100
Level 2: Quantitative-Descriptive Designs   104
Level 3: Correlational Designs   108
Level 4: Cause-Effect Designs   114

Chapter 8 RESEARCH DESIGNS FOR EVALUATING PROGRAMS — 121

Level 1: Hypothetical-Developmental Designs   122
Level 2: Quantitative-Descriptive Designs   126
Level 3: Correlational Designs   130
Level 4: Cause-Effect Designs   139

Chapter 9 INTERPRETING AND REPORTING RESULTS — 145

Research and Statistical Procedures   145
Statistical versus Practical Significance in Measuring Change   149
Uses of Data for Program Evaluation   150
Uses of Data for Evaluating Individuals   152
Communication   154
Timing of Information Feedback   156
Implementation   157

REFERENCES   161

INDEX   171

PREFACE

This book is for students and practitioners who are interested in concepts, strategies and procedures for evaluating social-work programs and practices. It emphasizes the methodology of evaluative research and illustrates applications in social-work settings.

The book introduces and integrates notions of evaluative research within a conceptual framework based on levels of knowledge and stages of development for social-work programs and practices. It is assumed that the reader has been introduced previously to basic concepts of research—descriptive statistics and statistical inference—as discussed in such texts as *Social Work Research and Evaluation* (Grinnell 1981), *Social Work Research Methods for the Helping Professions* (Polansky 1975), and *Introduction to Social Research* (Labovitz and Hagedorn 1981). Although this book is primarily an introduction to basic ideas about evaluative research, there are a few brief sections in chapters 3 and 6 that are more heavily theoretical and geared to advanced students and practitioners of evaluative research. These sections are asterisked so that beginning students can recognize them as optional reading.

Unique to this book are the presentation of research designs in relation to four levels of knowledge: hypothetical-developmental, quantitative-descriptive, correlational and cause-effect. It also examines procedures for evaluating practice with individual clients in social-work programs with aggregates of clients.

x   *Preface*

A logic for constructing evaluative research designs is developed for the evaluation of programs and practice interventions targeted for individual clients. Basically, chapter 6 presents a strong argument for differentiating research designs by the levels of knowledge sought in evaluative research. Research designs in chapters 7 and 8 illustrate that issues of knowledge development are similar for both evaluating programs and single-case interventions.

The purposes of chapter 1 are to present an introduction to conceptions of evaluative research, an outline of succeeding chapters based on the process of evaluative research, and a working conception of levels of knowledge that is basic to the understanding of frameworks discussed in subsequent chapters.

EVALUATIVE RESEARCH FOR SOCIAL WORKERS

CHAPTER ONE
PLANNING EVALUATIVE RESEARCH

EVALUATIVE RESEARCH

Evaluative research is the application of research methods to the production of knowledge that is useful in appraising the effectiveness of technologies and programs (Suchman 1967, ch. 1; Rossi, Freeman, and Wright 1979, ch. 1). It is applied research. In social work it basically provides knowledge about the extent to which practitioners have achieved their objectives in both programs and individual treatment, as well as information about the consequences of social-work activities (Mullen, Dumpson, and Associates; Fischer 1968).

Principles of evaluative research are used, for example, in situations such as the following: A group worker wishes to assess the extent to which a film on birth control devices is more or less effective than group discussion in increasing knowledge of birth control among teen-agers; a social caseworker is interested in evaluating the extent to which changes in the anxiety of a particular client are associated with her or his treatment activities; a program director of a substance-abuse clinic wants to know whether group therapy is as effective as individual therapy in reducing drug intake among clients; an administrator is concerned about whether a new information and referral service is, in fact, leading to more referrals to his or her social agency.

Evaluative research is most useful when it provides information that can be taken into consideration by social workers prior to making decisions that affect their clients and programs (Tripodi, Fellin, and Epstein 1978, ch. 6). Individual cases are terminated, programs are altered or abolished, techniques are abandoned or modified, program or client objectives are changed, and so forth. All of these decisions are influenced by the feedback of information from evaluative research.

Since evaluative research is applied research, it takes place within the sociopolitical context in which social work is practiced. It is affected by individuals and groups in the social environment, just as social-work practice is. Factors that influence the operation of programs, such as staff turnover, budget cuts, and personal conflicts, also affect the conduct of evaluative research (Weiss 1972, ch. 5). It is therefore important for evaluative researchers to understand the setting and the sociopolitical context in which social work is practiced. In planning an evaluative research study, the researcher should understand the factors that influence individuals and programs, such as vested interests, demands of competing persons or groups, decisions of sponsors, and changes in available resources.

THE PROCESS OF EVALUATIVE RESEARCH AND THE FORMAT OF THIS BOOK

The process of evaluative research is a dynamic one in which there are interacting phases ranging from decisions on the type of evaluation and the program or individual practice objectives to the selection of variables, choice of research design, analysis of data, and feedback of results to the evaluation consumer (Shortell and Richardson 1978, ch. 1). Suchman shows that evaluative research can be regarded as a device for gathering information that helps determine decisions on social programs and the development and refinement of social policies (1967, chaps. 1-4). He also argues that decisions about social and health programs are imbedded in systems of social values, and the results of evaluative research are interpreted in view of the social values of program personnel.

Included in the process of evaluative research are sets of decisions that are really steps or procedures in the conduct of an evaluation and that are generally described as follows:

1. *Planning for the research.* Make a decision as to whether or not evaluative research should be conducted. Consider the focus of evaluation (comprehensive or particular, summative or formative, program or individual practice) and determine the level of knowledge desired.
2. *Specifying objectives and activities.* Delineate the social-work objectives, whether they are concerned with programs or with individual practices, so that the expectations of social workers are clear, specific, and comprehensive. Indicate activities and social-work tasks for the purpose of conceptualizing consequences that may not have been planned by the social workers.

3. *Selecting variables for evaluative research.* Specify reliable and valid measures relevant to social-work tasks and objectives. Decide on the use of those variables that provide the best measures for the research.
4. *Determining available resources, data and instruments.* Decide about the feasibility of using available data and about the possibility of using existing instruments. Use existing sources of data, if available and pertinent to the objectives of the research.
5. *Deciding whether to construct original instruments.* Construct original instruments when there are insufficient sources of available data and existing instruments are not relevant to the purposes of the research. Decide on the type of instrument to construct (such as questionnaires or observational forms) and follow the principles for construction of reliable, valid devices.
6. *Choosing appropriate research designs.* Determine which research designs to use for evaluating practice (such as single-case designs) or programs (such as quasi-experimental research designs). Select designs according to their potential for producing evidence related to desired levels of knowledge.
7. *Interpreting, analyzing, and using the results of evaluative research.* Make appropriate decisions regarding analyses of the data, distribution of research results, and possible implementation of those results.

The preceding seven steps in the process of evaluation are interrelated. The evaluator needs to know about data analysis for planning research, research designs depend on the selection of variables, and so forth. In other words, the process of evaluation may not follow the neat sequential order depicted here and in most textbooks on evaluation. However, in order to clearly present the process, the chapters in this book follow the same order as these seven steps. The student should read the chapters sequentially, bearing in mind that they are interrelated. Planning for the research is considered in this introductory chapter. Chapter 2 focuses on concepts and procedures for specifying the objectives of social-work interventions, activities, and programs; while chapter 3 concerns the selection of appropriate variables geared to stages of practice and program development. Chapters 4 and 5 treat the uses of available data, available data-gathering instruments, and development of original instruments. Chapters 6, 7, and 8 examine the development of research designs geared to knowledge development about interventions with individuals, groups of people, and organizations exposed to social-work programs. And chapter 9 deals with interpretation, analyses, and uses of data generated from evaluative research.

MAJOR FOCUSES OF EVALUATIVE RESEARCH

There are three major focuses that distinguish the concerns of evaluative researchers:

1. Object of analysis
2. Extent of desired generalizability
3. Degree of comprehensiveness

The object of analysis can be an individual client, a group, a program, or an organization. Texts on "evaluative research" are typically geared to the evaluation of programs and organizations but not to individuals (Rossi, Freeman, and Wright 1979). Books dealing with the evaluation of individuals or groups use the concepts of empirically-based (proven by experience) practice, single-subject designs, and evaluation rather than those of evaluative research (Gottman and Leiblum 1974; Hersen and Barlow 1976; Jayaratne and Levy 1979). If evaluative research is regarded as the systematic use of research concepts, techniques, and strategies to provide information related to the objectives of social-work programs and practices (Tripodi, Fellin, and Epstein 1978, ch. 1), then it can logically be extended to single objects of analysis such as individuals and groups. Throughout this book evaluative research will be divided into research that focuses on the evaluation of individual practice and research that focuses on programs, organizations, or both. This choice is partly arbitrary and partly conventional, due to the fact that a great deal of literature and experience have been concentrated on single-subject design and program evaluation. The basic reason, however, is that research design, data collection, and analytic strategies vary as a function of these two primary units of analysis. Moreover, evaluation in social work typically focuses on assessment of practitioners' work with individuals or appraisal of agencies or programs that involve the combined efforts of practitioners with many clients (Pincus and Minahan 1973).

A second major focus of evaluation concerns whether the information from evaluative research is used for *formative* or *summative* purposes (Scriven 1967). In analysis of an individual, formative evaluation is the information provided to the social worker while she or he is developing the intervention strategy with the client. Formative evaluation of a program provides information related to the development of that particular program. Hence, formative evaluation, either for individuals or groups, supplies information directly pertinent to a particular practice or program; it is not intended to be generalized to other practitioners or programs.

The purpose of summative evaluation, in contrast, is to provide generalizable information. Rather than evaluating a particular program or practice, it evaluates a population of practices or programs, on the basis of a sample of them. Since summative evaluation is concerned with generalizability, it concentrates most on strategies and issues dealing with representative sampling, replications, and rules of inference. These issues will be dealt with in subsequent chapters on the logic of research design.

The extent of generalizability has implications for the consumer of evaluation. On one hand, administrators, clients, and direct-service workers are more likely to be interested in formative evaluative research. On the other hand, sponsors and policy formulators need information that can be generalized from program to program. And social-work practice theoreticians and supervisors of direct practice require information that can be generalized from one client to another (Tripodi and others 1977).

The third major focus of evaluative research is on comprehensiveness. Evaluative research is comprehensive when it provides the following sets of information:

1. Data on the efforts, effectiveness, and efficiency of the program or practice with respect to all of its objectives
2. Data regarding unplanned efforts, effectiveness, and efficiency
3. Data about the relationship of effectiveness to the need for the program or practice

A program or practice may have few or many objectives. The larger the number of objectives being studied, the more extensive and complicated the evaluative research. More than one research design and many data collection strategies may be required. Information on efficiency includes cost information regarding resources and time expended by the practitioners as well as data on the achievement of objectives (Tripodi, Fellin, Epstein 1978; Rossi, Freeman, and Wright 1979). Procedures for securing data about social need are different from techniques for obtaining information about unplanned consequences, that is, results not planned for by social-work administrators or direct-service practitioners. For example, survey and census strategies are used to obtain data on social needs, while case studies and participant observation are used to observe the occurrence of unplanned results.

Evaluative research that is not *completely* comprehensive is partial. Partial evaluations focus on one or more, but not all, objectives of a practice or program. The evaluation consumer might prioritize objectives, and only those designated as most important would be studied. All evaluative criteria are not used for each objective. For example, a practitioner may be more interested in ascertaining whether or not his or her client has become less depressed and is more satisfied in her or his work with colleagues than in learning the total costs involved in the treatment.

Any partial evaluation leaves out information that could be viewed as important. The basic task of the evaluator is to ascertain who the appropriate consumers are and to ensure that the evaluative research produces results that those consumers regard as important.

There are four basic reasons for partial evaluation:

1. Consumers and evaluator are not interested in all the possible information that could be obtained.
2. Some information is already available, and it is regarded as trustworthy and reliable.
3. Limited resources are available for the evaluation.
4. Results of the research are requested within a limited amount of time.

KNOWLEDGE GAINED FROM EVALUATION

The type of knowledge available from evaluative research depends on the specific substantive (essential) concerns of a program or practice, as well as on the objectives chosen for analysis. Substantive knowledge varies from program to program; yet there is no all-encompassing classification for categorizing knowledge from evaluative research of programs and practices in social work (Tripodi 1974, p. 44). Knowledge should be classified into categories that are relevant to social-work practice; but what is "relevant" is subject to change, and a classification scheme that is useful now may soon be outdated. This is due to changes in social problems, priorities in social work, financial support for social programs, client needs and demands, and society.

A relatively stable basis for classifying knowledge is that of knowledge levels. Knowledge from evaluative research, irrespective of substantive considerations, can be specified in a sequence that has four distinct levels: (1) hypothetical-developmental, (2) quantitative-descriptive, (3) correlational, and (4) cause-effect (Tripodi 1981). Level 4, cause-effect knowledge, contains the knowledge in levels 1, 2, and 3; level 3, correlational knowledge, includes the knowledge in levels 1 and 2; and level 2 contains knowledge from level 1. Hence, hypothetical-descriptive is the lowest level and cause-effect is the highest level in this progressive sequence of knowledge.

Each of the knowledge levels can be directed to the major focuses of evaluation. For example, hypothetical-developmental knowlege can be obtained for the evaluation of practice with one client as well as of an entire program. Quantitative-descriptive knowledge can be particular to a specific program or generalizable to other programs. And correlational and cause-effect knowledge can be comprehensive or partial depending on a social worker's practice or program objectives. Moreover, the desired knowledge level in an evaluative research project can be regarded as an objective of the evaluation itself. As chapters 6, 7, and 8 illustrate, designs for evaluative research can be logically related to these knowledge levels.

Level 1:
Hypothetical-Developmental
Knowledge

In this level of knowledge, the evaluative researcher seeks to develop concepts and variables, to generate questions and formulate hypotheses or both. Concepts are verbal labels for organizing and succinctly summarizing experiences. They are the basic ingredients of communication, and their specification is necessary for the formulation of hypotheses and the development of higher levels of knowledge. There are two ways to define concepts: nominally or operationally. Whereas a *nominal definition* is a verbal definition like those in a dictionary, an *operational definition* specifies all the procedures required for defining a concept so that it can be measured. An example of an operational definition of the variable "depression" for a particular client who is receiving intervention from a social worker is as follows: the extent to which, when queried by the social worker, the client indicates he or she is depressed on a scale that ranges from no depression (0) to mildly depressed (3) to very depressed (5).

Operational definitions are arbitrary, but they allow evaluators to translate concepts into variables, which are measurable dimensions of a concept (Labovitz and Hagedorn 1971, p. 18). Measurement is necessary to achieve higher levels of knowledge. Further, operational definitions help evaluators make systematic observations that can be communicated and repeated by different observers.

It is important that pertinent questions and relevant hypotheses be formulated about the effectiveness of programs and practices. Otherwise the quest for higher knowledge levels cannot be satisfied. The purpose of questions is to seek simple facts. For example, policy developers may be interested in the answers to questions such as these: what is the proportion of public assistance clients who would work if there were jobs available; would low-income, minority persons participate in health education programs; what proportion of clients who have received services from community mental health centers use the resources of other social agencies in the community?

Hypotheses are statements of predicted relationship between two or more variables. One of the variables in evaluative research studies is a program, practice, or technology (independent variable), while the other variable is the expected results of the independent variable (dependent variable). A partial evaluation of the effectiveness of a practice technology with many clients might include, for example, the hypothesis that clients who are taught how to be assertive by a teaching machine are more likely to be assertive in public encounters than clients who are not taught this. For this hypothesis there is a predicted relationship between the variables of "teaching" and "assertiveness." If there is a prediction about the existence of a relationship, the hypothesis is correlational. However, if it is predicted that changes in the independent variable are solely responsible for changes in the dependent variable, the hypothesis is cause-effect.

Hypotheses are neither true nor false. They are queries, which await empirical verification. Depending upon the empirical evidence gathered in evaluative research studies, they may be refuted or verified. They may be particular to a specific program or practice, or be generalizable, or be used for purposes of a partial or comprehensive evaluation.

Level 2: Quantitative-Descriptive Knowledge

Quantitative-descriptive knowledge is information in the form of facts, which are answers to simple, descriptive questions. Facts provide information about frequency counts and proportions within one variable that is identified by another. For example, in a particular social-work agency a social worker observes that the proportion of handicapped clients is 20% or that she or he uses behavioral technology with all of her or his clients 30% of the time.

Quantitative-descriptive knowledge can be specific to workers, programs, practices, or clientele or it can be generalizable. "There are more nonminority social workers than minority social workers in the social agency" is a simple, nongeneralizable fact; there may or may not be more minority workers in other social agencies. A greater degree of generalizability is expressed in this fact: "There are more nonminority than minority social workers in family service agencies."

When facts can be generalized to other situations (such as programs, social workers, and clients), they are regarded as low-order empirical generalizations. Examples of these empirical generalizations are:

> the largest proportion of patients in mental hospitals are schizophrenic; there are more male juvenile offenders than female juvenile offenders; 80 percent of the clients seen by social workers receive fewer than five interviews; citizens identified as belonging to lower social classes are less likely to vote in state and county elections than citizens identified as belonging to middle and upper classes. (Tripodi 1981)

Generalizable facts are useful data for sponsors interested in developing new programs. They may refer to the needs of a potential client population or to the potential utliization of new social programs. When facts are obtained from a variety of sources directly and indirectly related to a social program, they can contribute to a comprehensive evaluation. That is, facts can be gathered regarding program efforts, effectiveness and efficiency, side effects (i.e., unplanned-for results), and social needs of program recipients.

Level 3: Correlational Knowledge

Correlational knowledge exists when there are empirical data indicating a quantitative relationship between two or more variables. The statistical significance of a relationship is expressed by statistics, such as chi square and F, that test for differences between proportions and means of distributions; the magnitude of relationship is indicated by correlation coefficients that range from $r = 0$ or no relationship, to $r = 1.0$, a perfect relationship (Winer 1971; Hays 1973). For example, the correlation between the amount of contact with social caseworkers and the expressed degree of client satisfaction might be $r = 0.7$, a strong relationship. In addition, the average degree of satisfaction may be much greater for those who receive more casework contact than for those who receive less, and that difference may be statistically significant, as shown by a t test for two independent samples (Blalock 1972).

Correlational knowledge can be focused on a program such as the one just mentioned, or it can be directed to a smaller unit of analysis such as to the client of one social caseworker. For example, there may be a relationship of $r = 0.8$ between the number of reinforcing comments made by a caseworker and the client's expression of self-esteem. The client's average degree of self-esteem, furthermore, may be significantly greater in interviews in which the caseworker maintains a high level of reinforcement activity than in those interviews in which he or she maintains a low level of reinforcement.

Correlational knowledge can also be expressed in terms of the directionality of the relationship. A positive (+) or direct relationship refers to a relationship in which increases in one variable, x, are associated with increases in another variable, y; whereas, a negative (−) or inverse relationship exists when increases in x are associated with decreases in y, and increases in y are associated, correspondingly, with decreases in x. In the example in the previous paragraph, the relationship between the worker's reinforcing comments and the client's self-esteem is direct. If the client's self-esteem decreases as a result of the worker's increased level of reinforcement, an inverse relationship is obtained, that is, $r = -0.8$.

Correlational knowledge can be particular to a specific worker, client, group, family, program, organization, community, and so on, or it can be generalizable. For example, one component of a social program is a film on uses and abuses of drugs. The purpose of the film is to provide knowledge about drugs to uninformed teen-agers and adults. It is demonstrated that the average knowledge of drugs is higher for those who saw the film than for those who didn't, and this positive relationship is generalizable to a variety of different settings and target populations.

Two variables that are correlated are not necessarily causally related. A significant correlation is necessary for determining a causal relationship, but it is not sufficient. However, one could infer the absence of a causal relationship if there is no relationship between variables. Suppose one is investigating the extent to which a job counseling program is effective for a designated client population by studying the relationship between exposure to the program and the percentage of clients who obtain and stay in jobs for longer than six months. If the correlation is of the magnitude of $r = 0$, it can be inferred that the program is not causally related to "employment." Hence on the criteria of employment, the program can be regarded as ineffective.

Level 4: Cause-Effect Knowledge

Cause-effect knowledge is the highest knowledge level that can be obtained by evaluative research procedures. It is produced when evidence of the following items appears:

1. A strong correlation between one or more independent variables and one or more dependent variables
2. Changes in the independent variable or variables that precede observed changes in the dependent variable or variables
3. No other variables are responsible for changes in the dependent variable or variables (Blalock 1967; Susser 1973)

In evaluative research for social work the independent variables are typically components of practices, programs, or technologies. The dependent variables reflect expected changes that are results of the independent variables. In terms of evaluation criteria, the independent variables refer to the efforts made by social workers, and the dependent variables refer to the extent to which objectives are achieved—effectiveness. Comparing the relative effectiveness of different programs or technologies in relation to the same dependent variables leads to knowledge about efficiency.

For example, it is shown that social-work interviews about medical facts and future planning with women awaiting abortions are responsible for reducing the degree of postabortion depression. The interviews are effective in terms of reducing depression. It is further demonstrated that group counseling is more efficient than individual interviewing, since the social-work costs are cheaper and the same degree of reduced postabortion depression is accomplished. If this knowledge is produced with the workers and clients of one hospital, then there is no evidence for its generalizability to other hospitals or clinics. Thus, there may be cause-effect knowledge for a particular situation, but it may not be generalizable. With no evidence that it can be applied to other situations, the knowledge reverts back to the level of a cause-effect hypothesis awaiting further verification.

Cause-effect knowledge contains the knowledge included in all of the lower knowledge levels. It is based on verification of a researchable hypothesis. Descriptive information within variables is available, and empirical relationships between the independent and dependent variables are specified.

Causal relations can be relatively simple, delineating a relationship between one independent and one dependent variable; or they can be complex, in that there are multivariate relationships. For example, there may be a causal connection showing that workers of the same ethnic status and gender as their clients are more likely to be effective in teaching child-rearing skills, other things being equal, than workers of a different ethnic status and gender. Multivariate relationships can be investigated in either partial or comprehensive evaluations; many variables are interrelated to assess the extent to which two or more variables are involved in causal relationships (Cohen and Cohen 1975).

CONSUMERS OF EVALUATIVE RESEARCH

A consumer of evaluative research is a person, group, or collectivity that calls for an evaluation or uses the results of evaluative research. Consumers are program sponsors, administrators or managers, staff, and clients (Riecken et al. 1974, ch. 7). All of these consumers make decisions and use information from evaluative research, but each type makes different decisions and focuses on different aspects of social-work programs and practice. What is relevant for one consumer is not necessarily relevant for another.

Sponsors want to know if their monies are being spent wisely in achieving program and practice objectives. They are interested in promoting social programs that will be regarded as helpful and effective, as well as efficient. Often they need to choose recipients of their funds from among competing programs, and they must find out about each program's relative effectiveness. When there are decreasing resources and budgets, they use information that indicates where cuts can be made with the least amount of reduced effectiveness in a program or organization. Sponsors are also interested in information that bears on policies affecting the programs and organizations they finance.

Program managers and agency directors are concerned with the implementation of policy and the survival of their organizations. So they are interested in developing and maintaining resources, as well as in proper management of the budget, existing resources, and agency personnel. Administrators are responsible to program sponsors, boards of directors, their own staffs, and other constituencies. They must provide information to the groups to which their agencies are accountable, and they strive to maintain good public relations within the communities where their agencies are located.

The line workers or staff of an organization are interested in providing direct services to their clientele—individuals, families, groups, neighborhoods, organizations, and communities. They need to comply with administrative requirements in addition to solving problems that arise in the delivery of services. In comparison with managers and sponsors, they care most about the relative efficacy of specific techniques of intervention used in their practices.

Sponsors, administrators, and staff also have personal goals that may be compatible or in conflict with those of their organization (Etzioni 1964). They may view their jobs as stepping-stones to other jobs, or they may be more interested in job security than in delivery of effective services to clientele.

Clients are interested in services and the extent to which they are consistent with their demands and social needs. They may worry about relevant referral sources or their rights, privileges, and eligibility for social programs and individual treatment.

Clients, sponsors, administrators, and staff are all potential consumers of evaluative research. They all have their vested interests, which often show in the social interactional context of evaluative research. The evaluative researcher's basic objective is to provide valid, reliable information that can be used by consumers. Because there are potentially different consumers whose basic interests may or may not be harmonious with either each other or an evaluative research staff, the evaluative researcher should identify the appropriate consumer, that is, the sponsor of the evaluation. If there are several consumers, the researcher should determine whether the demands of those consumers can be met in a single evaluation or whether more than one evaluation is necessary. He or she can accomplish this by specifying each consumer's objectives (see chapter 2), determining the extent to which they are compatible, and estimating the resources available for the evaluative research.

In some instances there may be conflict between the evaluator and the program personnel. Not only might they emphasize different program and personal goals, but fear of losing a job or making undesired changes and distrust and suspicion of the researcher's motives may get in the way of effective cooperation with each other (Weiss 1972, ch. 5; Rodman and Kolodny 1977). Although such threats cannot be entirely eliminated, they can be minimized by the professional manner of the evaluator, by clear definition of the purpose of the evaluative research, by administrative support, and by use of a contract (Tripodi, Fellin, and Epstein 1978, ch. 6). The contents of the contract, which should be negotiated between the consumers of evaluative research and the researcher, should clearly specify the mutual obligations and responsibilities of program personnel and researcher. Contents such as the following might be included: expected date of completion; resources provided for the evaluative research; accessibility of the results; publication rights; extent of staff cooperation in terms of available time, data, and so on; and projected uses of information. The specific items of a contract help to clarify expectations and to increase the chances that the results of evaluative research will be used. An advisory body composed of representatives of different consumers and other evaluators can also be created to facilitate the conduct of evaluation and to provide a sounding board where potential grievances of evaluators and practitioners can be discussed.

In many instances conflicts among evaluative researchers and program staff do not exist. For example, a social caseworker may evaluate his or her own work with a single client, or a program manager may assign his or her own staff to evaluate a social program. Hence a social worker can be the consumer as well as the producer of evaluative research results. Of course, this is consistent with the notion of an empirically-based practice in social work (Jayaratne and Levy 1979).

DECIDING TO EVALUATE

The decision to evaluate or not can be made easier by consideration of the following interrelated factors:

1. Desires of evaluation sponsors
2. Focuses of evaluation
3. Clarity and specificity of programs and practices
4. Evaluation objectives
5. Available resources, time, and expertise
6. Potential for using the results of evaluative research

Sponsors of the evaluation can be identical to or different from the sponsors of a practice or program. For example, a sponsor can be a direct practitioner who desires to evaluate his or her practice with a single client and who is willing to devote part of his or her practice time to evaluating. Or a sponsor may be a funding agency such as the National Institute of Mental Health, which has financial responsibility for a demonstration project. Sponsors can require evaluations at specified periods of time. When an evaluation is mandatory there is obviously no choice as to whether or not there should be an evaluation, although there may be some flexibility regarding the type of research procedures used.

Sponsors of a program or practice can also be the evaluation sponsors, depending on their notions of accountability. Accountability, for example, can be seen as the provision of knowledge about the effectiveness and efficiency of programs and practices to relevant consumers (Tripodi, Fellin, and Epstein 1978). This conception of accountability would lead program sponsors to call for routine, periodic evaluations, with the presentation of results to the various program constituencies. On the contrary, program sponsors who don't believe in this idea of accountability or program, or who don't practice responsibility to their consumers, are less likely to demand evaluative research.

Sponsors can be accountable to the profession of social work. If evaluation is seen as a necessary part of good practice (Compton and Galloway 1975; Tripodi and Epstein 1980), then it is probable that routine evaluations will be conducted.

Sponsors can demand evaluations with different focuses. Some may desire formative evaluations, while others are interested in summative evaluations. Some may want evaluation of specific workers with particular clients, a social program, or both. And, the requested evaluation can be comprehensive or partial. Sponsors who can focus their needs, either independently or with the aid of evaluators, are more likely to be supportive of evaluative research efforts than those who can't.

The program or practice that is to be evaluated should be specific and identifiable. The object of evaluation should be carefully described, so that it is clearly understood what is to be evaluated. An evaluator cannot improve a practice or program, or make generalizations about it, if it is not described sufficiently enough to be replicated. Hence lack of program clarity (Weiss 1972, ch. 2) and specificity would probably not produce an effective evaluation of a fully-implemented program. However, evaluative research can be concerned with providing information related to the development of a program or practice, especially a nonimplemented program (see the stages of development discussed in chapter 2).

A program or practice can be specified in terms of its objectives. It is obvious that evaluation defined as the feedback of information related to the achievement of program or practice objectives requires a clear definition of objectives. Thus, to evaluate a program that is fully operational, the evaluator must first clearly outline the program objectives. For example, a social caseworker interested in evaluating the effectiveness of what she or he does with a client needs to specify what she or he does in practice, as well as her or his objectives with the client.

Evaluation objectives can be considered with respect to knowledge levels, program or practice objectives, and program or practice decisions. If there is uncertainty about the knowledge level, then there is need for an evaluation to reduce the uncertainty. However, if there is certainty about the knowledge, then evaluative research need not be pursued. Correlational or cause-effect knowledge is a premature evaluation objective if a program or practice is not fully implemented, while the pursuit of quantitative-descriptive knowledge is unnecessary for a program that is operational and about which there is sufficient information concerning its setting, operations, and clientele.

Evaluation objectives should seek information pertinent to program objectives (see chapter 2 for a description of program objectives). Otherwise, the data are not as useful for making decisions. For example, an insufficient evaluation of an educational program with the objective to change the knowledge of its clientele is one that doesn't produce information about whether or not the program is associated with, or causes, such changes. This is not to say that other information shouldn't be produced; for, in addition to data about the social workers' objectives, information can be obtained about unplanned-for effects on the relationship of programs to community need.

If it is possible to identify decisions that need to be made regarding practice, programs, or policy, evaluative research can be helpful. Information can be gathered that can be fed back to the decision makers prior to their decisions. A caseworker may need to know whether a client is making progress or deteriorating before switching to another intervention technique. A program funder may want to know whether psychotherapy programs being sponsored are effective before deciding to sponsor similar programs. An administrator who knows that he or she needs to reduce the budget may decide to do so in those program areas where the staff is least effective, and an evaluation providing information about the relative efficacy of different program areas provides a useful set of information pertinent to this decision.

To conduct evaluations it is necessary to have resources, time, and one or more qualified evaluators. Resources include necessary equipment (e.g., computer time, typewriters and tape recorders), funds (e.g., money for evaluators' salaries), facilities (e.g., office space), and staff. There must be a sufficient amount of time to conduct the evaluation. In view of this, the estimated schedule for the evaluation must be clearly spelled out in the negotiations between evaluator and sponsor.

Qualified evaluators are located within a program or practice, or outside of it. If the evaluation is formative, then inside staff are appropriate because they are in a position to understand the program or practice in great detail, to facilitate feedback, and to enhance the use of evaluation results. For summative evaluation, evaluators not located within the program or practice are preferable. In general, outside evaluators provide a greater degree of perspective and objectivity than inside evaluators. (Weiss 1972, ch. 6; Tripodi, Fellin, and Epstein 1978, ch. 6). Moreover, outside evaluators are preferable when the knowledge level sought is cause-effect; while inside evaluators are the better choice to produce data for lower levels of knowledge. Inside evaluators who don't have the appropriate degree of evaluation skills can use consulting and technical assistance from outside evaluators.

Evaluative research should not be conducted if its results cannot be utilized. In order for evaluation to be useful, sponsors and other relevant consumers must view the results as important information related to potential changes in policies, programs, or practices (Davis and Salasin 1975; Coursey, Mitchell, and Friedman 1977).

CHAPTER TWO
CONCEPTUALIZING SOCIAL WORK PROGRAMS, PRACTICES, AND OBJECTIVES

An evaluator cannot provide generalizable information on the effectiveness and efficiency of social-work programs and practices unless she or he can describe the programs or practices being evaluated. No one can change a program or practice unless she or he knows what it is that needs to be changed. Similarly, the evaluator must know the objectives of a program or practice in order to provide information about achievement of those objectives. Hence, an evaluator of social-work programs should know about, or at least be able to describe, their contents and be adept in defining program and practice objectives.

This chapter provides some useful concepts for describing the contents of social-work programs and defining program and practice objectives. The purpose is not to provide an introduction to social-work practice, for this has been covered extensively in other volumes (e.g., Pincus and Minahan 1973; Compton and Galloway 1975; Tripodi and others 1977). Rather, the object here is to illustrate kinds of tasks and objectives that can be located and specified.

PROGRAMS

Programs for social work have the broad goal of enhancing individual and social change by providing services that meet individual and community needs (Tripodi,

Fellin, and Epstein 1978). The services may be welfare, educational, health, economic, and so on; and they are provided by social workers and other professionals in a variety of settings.

Etzioni (1964) discusses several identifying features for studying organizations, and some of these can be used to describe differences in programs: single goals versus multipurpose goals, complexity, size, duration of the organization, and type of physical plant (Tripodi, Fellin, and Epstein 1978, ch. 2). A department of social services can be composed of a large number of units, such as protective services, adoptions, and aid to families of dependent children, which have many goals. Another program may have the sole purpose of delivering hot food to elderly, low-income persons once a day. The administration of a program can be complex, with many persons and departments involved in decision making, or it can be relatively simple, with one social worker providing information and referral services in a particular neighborhood. A program can be vast in scope, (e.g., national) and it can be comprised of hundreds of personnel who serve thousands of clients; or it can be smaller, as for example, a residential treatment center aimed at a population of ten to sixteen persons for an average length of stay of two years. A program may have been in existence for a short period of time, like a demonstration project of one to three years; or it may be a long-standing, family service agency funded by United Way. Finally, a program can be housed in a large structure such as a hospital or prison, or its physical plant can consist solely of a rented office.

PRACTICES

Within programs there are many different techniques involved in the delivery of services. These technologies, although overlapping and interrelated with programs, can be called practices. More specifically, a social-work practice is defined in this text as a set of principles for achieving social-work objectives. As with programs, practices can be simple or complex, single-purpose or multipurpose, large or small. Moreover, practices vary in their objects, modalities, and theoretic orientations.

Objects of practice refer to the units of the target populations, from individuals and families to groups, neighborhoods, and communities. *Modalities* include major divisions of social work such as casework, group work, and community practice (Pincus and Minahan 1973; Tripodi et al. 1977). *Theoretic orientation* is the specific set of principles and assumptions that serve as a prescription and proscription for a social worker. The orientation can be that of transactional analysis within a group work setting, for example, or it can be a combination of different perspectives such as therapeutic, custodial, and humanitarian for social workers practicing in reformatories.

Description of the contents of practices and programs is a complex undertaking and is the subject matter of methods courses in schools of social work. Ideally, an evaluator of social-work programs should have experience in some aspect of social-work practice and should have studied the subject matter appropriate to the practice being evaluated. At the very least, the evaluator should attempt to understand basic principles and assumptions relating to the particular practice under scrutiny, for this will provide guides to what social workers actually do, and lead to a more specific definition of the contents of social-work programs and practices.

SOCIAL-WORK TASKS

Social workers deal with individuals, groups, and communities in a diversity of settings, from hospitals and mental health clinics to citizens' planning councils and "grass-roots" community organizations. Direct-service workers provide the contents of social-work practices and programs; while, in general, other social workers, such as supervisors, administrators, and planners, develop policies and manage the activities of direct-service workers.

Pincus and Minahan (1973) indicate a number of activities that direct-service workers perform. Among them are the following:

1. Providing advice to clients
2. Seeking and providing facilities for the nurturance and care of deprived groups
3. Providing treatment for the purposes of changing attitudes, behaviors, knowledge, and moods
4. Teaching clients about societal needs and problems and the location of social, health, and economic services pertinent to their needs
5. Advocating for clients' rights and formulating plans for and with clients to change policies, legislation, and social conditions
6. Assessing needs of clients and developing community organizations.

Social workers involved in indirect service engage in activities such as these:

1. Supervising direct-service workers
2. Preparing program budgets
3. Providing information about programs and practices to sponsors
4. Evaluating programs
5. Hiring staff
6. Organizing and planning programs
7. Developing networks of community relationships (Tripodi and others 1977)

There are such a large number of social-work activities that it is virtually impossible to catalog all the possible tasks of social workers in order to give evaluators a ready-made list of tasks to describe. It is possible, though, to provide a way of thinking that helps in specifying relevant tasks for a particular program or practice. The approach advocated here is to think of the program or practice in terms of a model in which programmatic or practice decisions can be located and to describe the tasks necessary at key points within the model. For example, much of social-work practice can be thought of in terms of a problem-solving model which includes five interrelated components of practice: assessment, formulation of intervention plans, implementation of intervention, evaluations of progress, and termination (Tripodi 1974, pp. 122-31). Social-work tasks can be specified for a particular program or practice within each component.

Assessment includes all the tasks in which a social worker engages for the purpose of determining whether there is a problem or need and what its nature is. Community organizers may be interested in assessing the extent to which a community is responsive to programs for minority persons. Caseworkers may assess the needs and goals of a particular client in relation to the services they can provide within the constraints of their organization.

Formulation of intervention plans is the process of specifying practice goals that can solve the problems or meet the needs identified in the assessment phase. For example, an administrator formulates a plan that includes a program for educating teen-agers about the effects of drugs. This can be in response to an assessment that revealed that an increasing number of teen-agers use heroin and that the community residents desire a program that will lead to reduced heroin usage. Tasks involved would be locating a program site, outlining an educational program, hiring appropriate staff, determining the extent of community participation, and so on.

Implementation of intervention refers to all the procedures involved in the implementation of a program or practice. A caseworker attempts to develop a practice plan that is compatible with his or her clients' desires, and for which contractual agreements can be maintained. In a group work program with the purpose of educating parents in child-rearing skills, part of the intervention may require that the parents do homework exercises with their children. If they don't, the practice is not fully implemented, so the social worker monitors the extent to which the parents complete their homework, in addition to holding meetings for a specified number of sessions, organizing the contents of the sessions, engaging the active participation of the parents, and so forth.

Evaluations of progress involve the observations that a social worker makes to form judgments about whether or not his or her intervention program or practice is working. The reasons for these evaluations are to decide when, and if, other strategies should be used; to plan for termination if the client's problems are solved and needs are met; and to plan for possible referrals to other helping persons and programs. Since these evaluations are made during the conduct of social-work practice, they are formative evaluations for the purpose of feeding back information to social workers about their practice.

Termination "...refers to the conscious planning of the social worker to discontinue working with his clientele. It may be a result of problem solution or of a determination that the social work intervention is not helpful" (Tripodi 1974,

p. 130). In the termination phase, decisions are made about the disengagement of clients, whether there should be follow-up or maintenance activities, and so on. For example, a settlement house or neighborhood center provides a sex-education program, and the center's staff decides to periodically reassess the needs and demands of their clientele.

STAGES OF DEVELOPMENT IN PROGRAMS

A related way to describe the tasks of social workers in programs is to think of stages of program development and to locate tasks within each stage of development. This model of social-program development identifies three sequential phases: initiation, contact, and implementation (Tripodi, Fellin, and Epstein 1978, ch. 2). Each stage includes tasks necessary for the development of social programs, and the location of these tasks is helpful as a frame of reference for specifying useful information to program administrators. Hence evaluative efforts can be geared to different stages of program development.

The stages of program development are often overlapping in social programs. It is possible for some programs to be in all three stages simultaneously, and some multipurpose programs may have different components of their programs in different stages of development at the same time. Nevertheless most programs are predominately in one stage, operationally defined as that stage in which more than 50% of the program activities, time, and effort are deployed.

> Program initiation is the first stage of program development. It is during this stage that necessary material, social and technological resources are secured. Although initiation activities vary from program to program, all social programs must deal with the problems of procuring or developing competent staff, financial and physical resources, and social legitimation. Also included in this stage is the planning process: determining a need for the program; specifying program objectives and appropriate technologies for reaching those objectives; identifying a target client population of individuals or organizations, and establishing eligibility criteria; spelling out staff functions, personnel policies and practices; and so forth. (Tripodi, Fellin, and Epstein 1978, p. 26)

Here is an example of a program in the initiation stage. Within a hospital section for infants under intensive care, a medical social worker believes there is a need to provide group therapy for the infants' parents. A program is conceived in which parents are to be oriented to the hospital by films, pamphlets, and large discussion groups. This is followed by several small group sessions in which parents share and discuss their concerns and feelings with other parents under the guidance of one or more social workers, nurses, and physicians. The initiation of this program requires at least the following:

1. Resources to allow time for appropriate staff to be involved in the program
2. Physical space to be used for meetings and group sessions
3. Queries to parents regarding their willingness to participate in such a program
4. Development of the factual contents of the pamphlets and films
5. Legitimation of the program within the hospital's sociopolitical environment
6. Schedule of meetings and list of the groups' composition

The second stage of program development is program contact. This refers to all those resources and procedures necessary to engage potential program recipients in the program. It involves all the tasks that take place in the delivery of services in the first contact with clientele. Contacts are made in different locations such as offices, satellite clinics, clients' homes, social organizations, churches, and elsewhere. Often the locations are varied, to make the services more accessible and available to clientele, for in this stage, administrators are most concerned with determining those factors that make contact easier or harder. Once applicants for a program are recruited, the program staff devotes much of its time to establishing the eligibility of those applicants.

Referring to the previous example of a group therapy program for parents of hospitalized infants, the contact stage involves these tasks:

1. Requesting the parents' participation and deciding when participation should be solicited
2. Locating several different meeting places to help out the parents from different cities
3. Resolving any transportation problems
4. Stating precise criteria for eligibility in the program and making sure that only persons meeting those criteria participate
5. Determining whether there should be a fee for the service or whether it should be included in the total costs for infant care, depending on insurance provisions and hospital policies
6. Providing program services in the orientation meeting and the first group therapy sessions.

The third stage of program development is program implementation. This is the stage in which a program is operational. The problems of initiation and contact have been solved, and services are now provided in accordance with the planning objectives and the clients' needs. In this stage, it is important to decide how many services should be provided, how frequently, and for how long. Just as engagement of clientele is a concern in the contact stage, disengagement is a focus in the implementation stage. Hence administrators need to decide when clients should be terminated from services or referred to other programs.

When a program is in the implementation stage, the evaluator can seek to ascertain whether the program's ultimate objectives are being attained. Questions of the program's effectiveness and efficiency are raised, and data related to the achievement of program objectives are gathered. With respect to the preceding illustration of group therapy for parents of hospitalized infants, questions such as these are asked:

1. Is there a reduction in parents' anxiety (and to what degree) and an increase in factual knowledge about the illness of their infants?
2. Do the parents feel relieved to engage in discussions with other parents and with hospital personnel?
3. Are the parents' reactions to group therapy directly related to the severity of their infants' illnesses?
4. Would it be as effective, but more costly, to engage each set of parents with one social worker in individual therapy?

In the implementation stage for the group therapy program for parents of hospitalized infants, the social-work staff are involved in tasks such as these:

1. Providing program services, (group therapy) to parents
2. Deciding on termination criteria (e.g., ten sessions) or the parents' desire to leave
3. Determining whether there should be follow-up services for the parents after the group therapy is completed
4. Concluding whether or not to refer the parents to other community agencies, depending on their needs
5. Supplying information on program costs and achievements to appropriate hospital staff

STAGES OF DEVELOPMENT IN PRACTICE

The concepts of initiation, contact, and implementation are used to distinguish developmental phases in practice. This means that the notion of differential evaluation, which has been applied to social-work programs (Tripodi, Fellin, and Epstein 1978), is also applicable to the evaluation of practice with individual clients. The basic idea of differential evaluation is that different types of evaluation should be conducted for different phases of program or practice development. For example, evaluation of initiation involves need assessment procedures; in the contact stage, questionnaires for monitoring treatment activities; in the implementation stage, follow-up surveys and single-subject designs.

The initiation stage in social-work practice with an individual (or with other units such as a couple, family, or group) is the same as program initiation stage and is roughly comparable to the assessment or diagnostic phase of the problem-solving process. It refers to all those procedures and resources necessary for deciding whether or not there will be intervention or treatment with a specific client or group. Indeed, the purposes of assessment in an initiation stage of practice are to decide: (1) whether there is a problem that can be dealt with within the constraints of the agency or organization where the social worker works; (2) who the appropriate clients are; and (3) the extent to which each client is motivated to pursue the kind or kinds of intervention or treatment offered.

To achieve these aims the social worker must obtain information from the potential client, significant others in the client's psychosocial environment, or both. She or he attempts to discern the nature of the pretreatment contact—whether the client is self-referred, mandated to show up for "treatment" as in probation and parole, or referred by other persons or agencies. Not only must the social worker assess the nature of the problem, but she or he also needs to diagnose its severity and duration. Depending on the type of practice (e.g., school social work, psychiatric casework) and its setting, the social worker often seeks and uses additional information from other relevant persons or groups. Information on problems in child management may be sought from teachers, parents, and psychologists. In a correctional setting, information is available from police records, case studies, and other sources.

An example of an initiation phase in social-work practice is as follows: A potential client phones a family service agency for marital counseling. The agency agrees to see the client in an intake interview. In that interview, the participants discuss the problem from the client's point of view, and consider whether the "client" is the individual in the interview, the married couple, or the couple and their children as a family unit. They talk about fees for service and the client's desire, and possibly that of other family members, to be involved in a treatment process. They may realize that the husband wishes to pursue help for his marital relationship and prefers that his wife go with him for treatment sessions.

The initiation stage in practice also requires the deployment of appropriate personnel and references. For example, an intake worker in a social agency refers a couple for marital counseling to an available social worker, who appears to have the relevant experience and be most suitable to provide intervention. Moreover, some practice involves actively reaching out to clients, as in aggressive casework (Tripodi and others 1977, pp. 74-80) or door-to-door canvassing to organize a neighborhood around a particular issue. This is comparable to recruiting clients and assessing their needs for social programs.

The contact stage of development in practice involves interaction with a client, after it has been agreed that treatment will be conducted. An intake interview to decide whether treatment will take place is not necessarily regarded as "contact." However, initiation and contact stages in some forms of practice are overlapping, and contact may take place during an intake interview when a contract between a worker and client are negotiated. During the contact stage of practice development, the social worker negotiates a working relationship with the client and develops an appropriate treatment plan or strategy. Essentially, the social worker formulates hypotheses about effective modes of interaction. For example, in the treatment of a couple with a marital problem of communication, the worker develops a plan of reinforcement, based on learning therapy, for positive communications in simulated social interactions between the spouses. The worker hypothesizes that practice in positive communications under simulated conditions in therapy leads to increased positive communications for the couple in other, nontherapy situations.

After a treatment plan has been formulated and the client or clients have engaged in the initial contact of treatment, the practice advances to the implementation stage. The practitioner monitors treatment to make sure it is carried out in accordance with his or her plans. For example, as part of a treatment plan for increasing positive communication between spouses, the worker instructs the clients to tape-record two segments of interaction between themselves and to indicate positive and negative instances of communication. This instruction may have been given as a "homework assignment" between sessions. Therefore, for the treatment to be implemented, the homework assignment must be completed.

Having fully implemented the treatment, the worker looks for signs of progress or deterioration, gathering this information from the clients themselves, as well as by other means (Tripodi and Epstein 1980). In the example of marital counseling, the clients report changes in communication patterns, the worker observes changes in tape-recorded interactions, and the worker and client observe possible changes in simulated interactional conditions. Depending on whether or not there is progress, the worker and client make decisions regarding the continuation or modification of treatment.

Multiple objectives can be treated simultaneously or serially. If they are treated in sequence, it is possible for one aspect of the treatment to be in the implementation phase while another is in the initiation phase. The social worker and the couple may have chosen to work on the problems of communication, but there may be other problems such as relationships with their children. The treatment for this problem may be different from the treatment for communication, and if it is, it requires its own practice development.

The stages of initiation, contact, and implementation are interrelated and overlapping; yet the concepts serve to alert the evaluator to differential developments in practice and to different tasks of concern to social workers. An evaluation of the effectiveness of treatment in terms of client change would be premature if the treatment had not been fully implemented. Formative evaluative information can be provided differentially at different predominant stages of practice. Whereas data regarding problem location, needs assessment, and client motivation are crucial in initiation, the formulation of treatment hypotheses and the monitoring of treatment plans are important in the contact stage. Ultimately, the extent to which the objectives are accomplished is evaluated in the implementation stage.

PROGRAM AND PRACTICE OBJECTIVES

To evaluate social-work programs and practices it is necessary to clearly specify social-work objectives. Then the evaluator can set up methods to determine the extent to which these objectives have been achieved, as well as the degree to which other unintended results have occurred.

Prior to specifying criteria for writing comprehensive and specific objectives, it is instructive to consider the following: the relationship between program and practice objectives, the location of objectives, the conceptualization of unanticipated consequences, and the choice of objectives. Although "goals" is sometimes used to refer to "...broad generalizations, reflecting the attitudes and values that give direction to human enterprises" (Isaac 1971, p. 164) or to abstractions of one or more objectives, this text will refer only to "objectives," primarily to avoid the confusion that often results from mixed use of "goals" and "objectives."

Objectives are relatively concrete and specific; they spell out observable behaviors in programs and practices and in their end products. Program objectives are broader and more encompassing than practice objectives. Whereas practice objectives can be restricted to the aims of one social worker working with one client, program objectives typically involve more than one social worker and more than one client. When the practice objectives and the program objectives are identical, they are called *common* objectives; nonequivalent objectives are *unique to either* a program or practice. For example, one program objective in an alcoholic rehabilitation center is to reduce the consumption of alcoholic beverages. This may be a common objective for all of the social-work practices in that organization. A unique objective for one social worker and his or her client, a teen-aged high-school dropout, is for the client to return to school and complete his or her education. It is apparent, therefore, that practice and program objectives that are common are overlapping and that the evaluations of individual practices can be combined to form program evaluations—so long as the objectives are *common.*

Objectives are discovered in existing programs or practices by a combination of devices such as the following: describing tasks; finding written statements of sponsors, contracts, or other documents, and interviewing significant persons. Having described the social-work activities and tasks involved in programs by referring to the written items, the evaluator then asks key persons what the purposes of the activities were. Answers to questions of purpose should reveal the expected consequences of a program. Sometimes, there are explicit statements of objectives that are mandated by sponsors or that have been delineated by program staff. Those practitioners who use written contracts with clients may include objectives or expectations of treatment, as well as mutual obligations of worker and client, in their contracts. The evaluator can even ask what the program or practice objectives are, and this may yield information in some settings. As Weiss points out, an evaluator may find that social-work objectives are vague and unclear (1972, pp. 26-30); but, the evaluator, in consultation with social workers, may be able to clarify and specify program or practice objectives. Program objectives are frequently multipurpose and much more complex than practice objectives. Practice objectives can be more completely defined by interviewing the client and asking him or her what the treatment objectives are, thus discovering to what extent the perceptions of objectives by social workers and their clients are compatible.

UNANTICIPATED CONSEQUENCES

Unanticipated consequences are those results of a program or practice that are not planned; they are the side effects of social-work interventions and may be desirable or undesirable. Participants in a drug-education program may increase their intake of some drugs after discovering that they aren't excessively harmful. A client aiming to be self-assertive may become overly so, becoming a very obnoxious person. Birth control pills may prevent the conception of children, but they may also result in poor kidney functioning.

Shortell and Richardson (1978, p. 24) indicate that the following strategies can be used to project "unanticipated consequences":

1. Becoming thoroughly familiar with the organization in which the program exists
2. Paying particular attention to those departments and programs that supply information or resources to the program under evaluation or that depend on it
3. Talking with intended clients or recipients of the program
4. Talking with people who honestly believe the program will fail
5. Communicating with kindred organizations
6. Contacting agencies which may have launched similar programs
7. Brainstorming
8. Contacting other program evaluators to get their thoughts and suggestions.

The basic idea is to locate possible effects of a program or practice not thought of by the social-work administrator or practitioner.

A practical procedure is to imagine the results of social-work tasks and activities and consider them in relation to social-work objectives. For example, a social-work program has the objective of getting information about social agencies to prospective clientele in a particular neighborhood. The social worker who is transmitting the information is brusque, rude, and disrespectful to potential clientele. The information was received, but the prospective clients won't use the services because of the negative image of social workers projected by this one particular worker in the delivery of services.

Hyman, Wright, and Hopkins suggest two other procedures that are helpful in visualizing unanticipated consequences: (1) include open-ended questions at the end of an evaluation study, and (2) imagine the extreme quantitative values of intended effects (1962). Etzioni indicates that a systems perspective is useful in visualizing the context in which programs take place, which may help the development of ideas about unanticipated consequences (1964). As a routine procedure in an evaluation study, the evaluator asks program or practice personnel and clients about the extent to which changes (planned or unplanned) occurred as a result of the intervention. An extreme quantitative value of an intended effect is pertinent, depending on the measurement employed. If the measurement of program success is obtaining jobs, the extreme value is 100% success, which is certainly desired. However, if the measure is one of activity, extreme values may be unanticipated. A school social worker wants to reduce hyperactivity in a child; the extreme value of the measure would, of course, be no activity or possibly depression, which might not have been anticipated. A systems perspective is useful for thinking of other environmental factors that may bear directly on clients in a social program. For example, a worker works with one delinquent street gang, with the purpose of reducing its delinquent activities. A systems approach would reveal that there are other gangs in the neighborhood. If the worker provides rewards to the group with whom she or he is working, the other gangs may start fights with that group to take their "share" of the rewards. The unplanned consequence is that the delinquent gang is getting into more trouble.

CHOOSING AMONG OBJECTIVES

Weiss specifies several dimensions that an evaluator should consider in choosing among specific objectives: (1) usability and practicality, (2) relative importance, (3) incompatibility, and (4) short-term or long-term objectives (1972, pp. 30-31). Usability refers to the extent to which information pertaining to objectives relates to decisions to be made, while practicality refers to the time, costs, and available staff and equipment for studying the objectives.

Since not all objectives can be studied, it is useful, as previously indicated, to rank them in terms of their relative importance. The perceptions of importance should be primarily those of the principal consumers of the evaluation. Sometimes different consumers have incompatible objectives, and even one consumer may have incompatible objectives. It is important that an evaluator identify these incompatibilities. For example, one co-therapist may attempt to encourage group participation by positively reinforcing comments made by group members, whereas the other co-therapist may engage in negative reinforcement. Thus, there is incompatibility in the methods of practice, making it difficult to study the effects of either positive or negative reinforcement.

Short-term objectives are essentially those that are restricted to earlier stages of program development, while long-term objectives are those that are expected in follow-up studies on the effectiveness of programs or practices that have been implemented. Hence an evaluator can specify the location of objectives in terms of program development, considering with the consumers of evaluations what initial decisions need to be made.

CRITERIA FOR DETAILED OBJECTIVES

Program or practice objectives are detailed when they include relatively specific statements about their operations and their expected consequences. Each objective in a program or practice can be detailed by using a frame of reference derived from the following writers: Suchman (1967, pp. 37-45), Hiebert (1974), Shortell and Richardson (1978, pp. 16-23), Hersen and Barlow (1979), Jayaratne and Levy (1979), and Tripodi and Epstein (1980). The framework poses this question: *Who* does *what* to, for, or with *whom* with *what expected change or changes*? Within each of the categories, who, what, whom, and expected changes, there are a series of defining principles to be considered. This chapter will next illustrate dimensions for each category, discuss writing specific objectives, and conclude with examples of detailed program and practice objectives.

Who refers to the number, qualifications, and personal characteristics of the staff that are providing services to social-work clientele. There may be many different persons offering services and managing social programs or there may be only one professional engaging in a particular practice. To provide services requires some degree of qualification. The psychiatric social worker in a mental hygiene clinic needs an M.S.W. degree plus two years of experience. If she or he is working with a Chicano population, knowledge of Spanish is essential. On the other hand, a volunteer worker needs no educational requirements but should be mature, interested, and available for work on a project. Different types of practice (e.g., transactional analysis, behavioral modification) require certain amounts of training for the services to be rendered appropriately. Hence, it is important to identify the qualifications necessary for delivering program or practice services and to include them in the defined objectives.

Personal characteristics are demographic, physical, psychological, economic, and other variables necessary for the provision of services. These variables include social class, age, gender, race, intelligence, personality, nationality, and so forth. For example, part of a program objective may be to have female social workers work with female clients and male social workers work with male clients.

What refers to the contents of contacts with clients, the site of contacts, and the frequency and duration of contacts. The contents of a program or practice are difficult to specify in advance, for often the contents are dependent on the interactions between workers and clients. Nevertheless, there are aspects of practices and programs that can be specified from the beginning. For example, a worker shows a particular film or presents a set of standard facts. If the contact depends on the quality of social interaction, he or she plans to record or film the interaction so the contents can be preserved and specified after they have taken place. Moreover, the social worker outlines in detail the general strategies of his or her role in the interaction. A caseworker wishes to reinforce positive, self-referring statements made by a client in an effort to enhance the client's self-esteem; an administrator offers incentives for increased staff productivity; and so forth.

The site, frequency, and duration of service contacts is also specified. The site of contacts is the location or locations in which they occur. In some programs, there is little variation in location; contacts occur in the offices of social workers, in hospital wards, or elsewhere. For other programs, the specification of the site is crucial. For example, the location of satellite clinics in low-income areas, the use of home visits, and mobile offices are all devices to bring services closer to clients.

The frequency of contacts is the number of separate contacts that are planned in order to achieve the change objective. One showing of a film on sex education might be thought sufficient to achieve the objectives of increasing knowledge. The number of contacts necessary for psychotherapy with a particular client may be indeterminate in advance, but a range may be specifiable (e.g., from a minimum of fifteen to a maximum of fifty contacts).

Whereas frequency refers to the number of contacts, duration is the length of time each contact involves. Thus a training film and discussion of the film may cover 1½ hours in one session; a psychotherapy interview may last for forty-five minutes; a group session may extend for two hours; and so forth.

Whom is the intended target population—that person or those persons to whom the social work intervention is directed. Typically, there are certain requirements for eligibility to receive services from different social-work agencies or programs. In one agency the clients need to be of a certain age (programs for children, teen-agers, and the aged); in public welfare, the clients must prove a lack of economic resources. Veterans can receive services from the Veterans Administration. A special project may be set up for the children of low-income migrant farm workers within a particular geographic area.

To specify the whom, the evaluator thinks of whether there are any personal characteristics of the client that are essential for participation in the program. In addition, the evaluator considers whether the client's experiences are necessary for program eligibility (e.g., a program geared to high school dropouts), whether the program is to take place only within a specified geographic area, and whether there is to be a time limit.

The category of *expected change* can be considered in relation to four interrelated questions: (1) What are the contents of the expected change? (2) What is the degree of change? (3) Where is the change expected to occur? (4) If expected changes occur, how long will they last?

Suchman indicates that the contents of expected change refer to possible changes in knowledge, attitudes, skills, and behaviors (1967, p. 39). Knowledge changes are increases in facts about a particular phenomenon; the client learns about the location and availability of social, health, and economic resources; the effects of drugs; the advantages and disadvantages of family planning devices; the facts of a particular disease; and so forth. Attitude changes refer to changes in a set of beliefs or values. A client accepts his or her homosexuality as a function of psychotherapy; delinquent children learn to favor antidelinquent activities; parents become less rejecting of their retarded children; and so forth. Skills are acquired abilities. Unemployed persons learn new job skills (e.g., typing). Family members increase the amount of shared communication activities, as an index of increased communication skills.

Changes in behaviors are directly observable and are, therefore, easier to measure than changes in knowledge, attitudes, or skills. The behaviors may be decreased drug usage, increased weight, increased homework, decreased gambling, increased visiting of relatives, increased participation in political activities, and on and on. In addition to aspects of the contents of change that Suchman delineates, one can also refer to a change of state or condition. Much of social work involves environmental manipulation, where, for example, a child is placed in adoption or with a foster family and elderly persons are placed in nursing homes, hospices, or other alternatives. Hence, the changes of many programs are changes of condition in persons or institutions, rather than behavioral changes. The recipient of a hot meal receives a different kind of meal than she or he ordinarily would have had; spouses who continually argue and are unpleasant with each other simply change their environment by separating or divorcing; a delinquent who gets into trouble in one neighborhood is moved to another.

The contents of a particular program or practice may aim to achieve changes in knowledge, attitudes, skills, behaviors, and conditions, but it is not necessary to achieve changes in all areas; change in one area can be sufficient for a particular program objective.

The evaluator must be careful to note that changes in one area are not necessarily related to changes in another area. For example, a program or practice may assume that changes in knowledge, attitudes, or both will lead to behavioral changes. This is an hypothesis, and data must be provided to demonstrate the extent to which it can be supported. It might be a program assumption that changes in attitude about drinking liquor will lead to a reduction in drinking behavior. Whether or not this hypothesis is supported has obvious implications for program development. Therefore, to the extent possible, the evaluator indicates whether these are program assumptions or hypotheses that assert relationships among knowledge, skills, attitudes, behaviors, and conditions.

The degree of change refers to the amount of change in variables selected as measures of change (see chapter 3 for a discussion of variables and measurement). The amount of change can be specified in terms of fixed quantities, as in predetermined frequencies and proportions. For example, it is expected that 50% of the applicants in a job-counseling program will obtain a job or that a particular client will eat three meals per day instead of five and will lose twenty pounds. When the precise degree of change cannot be specified, the evaluator should at least indicate whether an increase or decrease is sought. Evidence for change then consists of statistical significance in the increases or decreases of the change variables (Henkel 1976). For example, a program has the objective of increasing the number of persons in the program who obtain jobs. A statistically significant increase in the number of jobs is evidence of goal attainment in the event there is no fixed quantity of persons who were expected to be employed.

A program is more specifically planned if the administrator indicates when expected changes are to take place; moreover, such information informs the evaluator when measurement should occur. An employment program that expects to have 50% of its applicants employed two months after program completion should be evaluated two months after program completion! Of course, additional measures can be taken over time. These measures provide information about whether the time period for expected change in the program objective is realistic. The program may have expected a fixed amount of change in two months, but it may not have occurred, if at all, until six months later.

When the expected length of time before change occurs cannot be specified, social workers and evaluators must use their best judgment as to which points in time are useful for assessing progress. Sometimes there are program or agency constraints that prohibit extensive measurement activities; so it is important that judgments, even though arbitrary, be made and that they be based on the best knowledge available regarding the particular measures employed and the social-work clientele.

If the expected changes occur, the evaluator considers how lasting these changes are, in other words, what the expected duration of change is. This informs them about minimum requirements for follow-up data and provides information to social workers about the impact of a program or practice. A caseworker and client may expect a change such as weight loss to last indefinitely, but they might agree that six months after the social-work intervention is a reasonable time for follow-up measurements. Certainly, a client who achieves the change in one day but reverts to the previous condition the following day would be mistakenly regarded as a success if there weren't planned follow-up measurements.

These criteria for detailed objectives are illustrative of the types of information to consider in delineating program or practice objectives. Most social workers will not be able to indicate from the beginning all the expectations involved in their programs and practices. This is because there are often many unknown elements and intangible qualities that cannot be foreseen. Nevertheless, it should be emphasized that more pertinent data from evaluative research are provided for purposes of program or practice development when more detailed objectives are outlined.

WRITING SPECIFIC OBJECTIVES

Every objective for a program or practice can be described in detail, as discussed above. Within each category, such as "who" and "what," the practitioner and the evaluator should be careful to be precise and specific. This means that objectives should be written so that independent practitioners and evaluators conceive of the objectives in the same way. (Isaac writes that objectives should be clear-cut, specific, and tied down to concrete, visible behaviors as much as possible (1971, pp. 162-63). He lists the following characteristics for behaviorally defined objectives:

1. They describe the terminal behavior for a client who has achieved the objective. As examples, a client will answer correctly 70% of the items on a knowledge test of agency resources, a married couple will reduce the number of arguments they have at dinner from seven to two per week.
2. They specify "...any qualifying conditions or restrictions that must exist for the terminal behavior to be acceptable" (Isaac 1971, p. 162). For example, the knowledge test will be administered to all clients attending the program at the end of their first week and the end of their third week of program participation; the number of arguments at dinnertime will be monitored by the couple's oldest child every evening from 6:00 P.M. to 7:00 P.M. for two weeks.
3. They include criteria necessary for the attainment of the objective. For example, acceptable performance is 70% or higher for knowledge attainment and two arguments or less for reduction in the number of arguments.
4. They use words that are concrete and unambiguous, and hence are open to fewer rather than many interpretations. For example, "To increase the number of positive self-references of a given child in weekly counseling sessions by at least 50 percent over a six week period, based on evaluation of authorized tape recordings," is much more concrete and specific than "To improve the self-concept of every child" (Isaac 1971, p. 163).

The writing of objectives should be detailed and specific. Behaviorally-defined objectives clarify the expectations of programs and practices. Along with a description of program and practice activities, they provide a basic context for the development of measures for evaluative research.

EXAMPLES OF SOCIAL-WORK OBJECTIVES

Here is an example of a program objective. In a drug-abuse clinic located in a low-income area of a town of fifty thousand persons, there is a staff of one physician, two secretaries, and six social workers. Each social worker has an M.S.W. degree, is a member of the academy of certified social workers, has three years' experience working with drug addicts, and is between twenty-five and thirty-five years old. There are three male and three female social workers. The social workers will use group psychotherapy techniques and a contingency-based contracting system in which clients are awarded points for reductions in drug intake. The social workers are supervised by the psychiatrist, who has extensive experience in group psychotherapy. Points received by clients are cumulative and can be traded in for prizes such as radios, clocks, and so on. Arrangements are made to tape-record each group session so the precise contents can be determined afterwards. There will be one two-hour session at the clinic at the same time each week for approximately twelve weeks.

There will be thirty-six clients twenty-five to thirty-five years old who are white-collar, male workers employed in an automobile plant, and who are self-referrals desirous of reducing their drug intake. Each client uses drugs several times a week.

There will be six groups, each comprised of six clients and each assigned to one social worker. It is expected that the average intake of drugs will be reduced by 50% by the end of the twelfth group session, and that the reduction of drug intake will be maintained for at least three months.

Within that same program there can be objectives for individual clients. For example, one client has difficulty interacting with his child. His social worker will see him individually to work on an objective in this area. The female social worker, age twenty-eight, with five years experience in social casework, plans to see the client, a thirty-year-old male lawyer, once a week for fifty minutes for a minimum of five and a maximum of twelve sessions. The purpose of the sessions is to discuss the client's relationship with his ten-year-old daughter and to increase his skills in child management. The worker will use role playing in her sessions to enable the client to understand the functioning of a ten-year-old and will follow notions of positive reinforcement in a behavior modification approach.

The client argues with his child three times a day over clothes, house rules, and other items. The expectation is that the number of arguments, as reported by the client and verified by the child's mother, will be reduced from twenty-one to five or less per week. This is expected to occur between the fifth and the twelfth sessions. Once the change occurs, it is expected to be maintained for at least three months.

CHAPTER THREE
VARIABLES FOR EVALUATIVE RESEARCH

An evaluative research study can only be as good as the variables used to measure program or practice activities and change. Irrelevant or inaccurate measurement makes evaluative data useless. Hence it is important that the evaluator be careful in locating and relocating variables for evaluative research. This chapter focuses on a scheme for locating variables for formative and summative evaluation within and between program and practice stages of development. It then considers them in relation to social and client need. It also discusses the criteria for selecting and specifying variables such as operationalism, reliability, and validity.

CRITERIA OF EVALUATION

There are four criteria that are applied to formative and summative evaluation, derived from the works of Hyman, Wright, and Hopkins (1962); Suchman (1967); Shortell and Richardson (1978); and Tripodi, Fellin, and Epstein (1978). They are *efforts*, *effectiveness*, *unanticipated consequences*, and *efficiency*. *Efforts* refer to the amounts and kinds of program or practice activity necessary for the achievement of planned objectives. Efforts include staff time, activity and commitment; allocation and use of financial and material resources; and planned participation of clients.

Effectiveness is the extent to which program or practice objectives have been achieved, while *unanticipated consequences* refer to desirable or undesirable changes that were not planned but result from program or practice efforts. A more comprehensive way of judging effectiveness is to observe the net changes that result from combining the achievement of planned objectives with the occurrence of desirable unanticipated consequences, while taking into consideration the presence of undesirable unanticipated consequences (Rossi, Freeman, and Wright 1979). For example, a medical social worker plans for an overweight client with high blood pressure to lose weight. The client loses weight and also adheres more carefully to his or her medical regimen regarding the regular intake of medication; however, the client increases his or her smoking activity, which is an undesirable, unplanned consequence.

Efficiency is the relationship of effectiveness to efforts, and basically reflects the costs of a program or practice relative to the extent of achieved, desirable change.

LOCATING VARIABLES

Variables for evaluative research are identified by referring to the preceding evaluation criteria, which are specified to stages of program or practice development. For purposes of providing feedback to program administrators and practitioners, it is important to specify variables that are pertinent to different stages of development.

Within Stages of Development

Initiation As discussed in chapter 2, there are three sequential, interrelated stages of development in social practices and programs: initiation, contact, and implementation. In the initiation stage, *efforts* refer to all those program or practice activities carried out for the purpose of attaining the objectives for that stage. Hence within a social program at the initiation stage of development, efforts refer to such activities as the amount of time expended by staff in recruiting clientele; in determining eligibility requirements; in securing funds, equipment, staff, and physical space; in hiring staff; in formulating personnel policies; and in developing plans for an accounting and information processing system. *Effectiveness* is the extent to which clientele are recruited; eligibility requirements are specified; funds, equipment and space are secured; staff are hired; and all the rest. *Unanticipated consequences* are any unexpected changes that occur as a result of staff effort, and *efficiency* is the relationship of effectiveness to efforts, such as the number of hours of staff time expended in recruiting clientele who are potential program participants.

In the initiation stage of practice, *efforts* refer to the activities of the social worker who is involved in assessment or diagnosis. Essentially time is expended to decide if there is a problem, its nature and severity, and the client's willingness to participate in social-work treatment. *Effectiveness* is the extent to which the social-work objectives are realized. For example, effectiveness might be a decision about the client's desire to discuss treatment possibilities; an indication of the severity of the problem; or a decision regarding the prospective client's eligibility for social-work services. *Unanticipated consequences* can be desirable or undesirable. An example of a desirable consequence is the perception of the social worker-client interaction as positive, which is transmitted by the prospective client to significant others in his or her life and which can result in a greater number of clientele for the social agency. In contrast, the social worker may be perceived negatively, and this may result in a reluctance of prospective clientele to go to the agency for assistance, which is undesirable. *Efficiency* is assessed by relating the achievement of objectives to the expenditure of the social worker's time, energy, and resources.

Contact The contact stage of practice development involves the specification of a contract or understanding for the client and worker to engage in the process of social-work intervention. It includes all those tasks and decisions related to the engagement of a client in social-work intervention. *Efforts* include activities such as the following:

1. The social worker plans appointments in relation to the client's work schedule (e.g., evening appointments).
2. The worker takes into consideration any transportation difficulties, which may result in home visits as well as office visits.
3. The worker and the client discuss treatment objectives and their mutual obligations.
4. The worker and the client consider the possibility of the client's close relatives attending sessions.

Effectiveness is the extent to which both people negotiate and put into operation a contract; both maintain initial appointments, the client cooperates with contractual obligations, and so on. An index of *efficiency* might be the number of hours, or fractions thereof, it takes for the social worker and the client to negotiate a contract, while an *undesirable consequence* might be the lack of client participation in treatment due to the social worker's adherence to a rigid, overly legalistic format for a written contract.

The following questions from Tripodi, Fellin, and Epstein (1978, pp. 51-53) illustrate the identification of variables of effort, effectiveness and efficiency for the contact stage of development in social programs:

EFFORT

1. What amount of time and program resources are devoted to making program contacts with intended beneficiaries; number of interviews, and so on?
2. If a referral system is used, what is the amount of time and effort involved in referrals?

3. What efforts are devoted to the compilation of records pertaining to program activity?
4. What amounts of time and activity are devoted to finding resources that could increase the number of program contacts?
5. To what extent are alternative program strategies sought and used, if program efforts do not appear sufficient to reach all the intended target population?

EFFECTIVENESS

1. To what extent is the intended target population represented in those who are designated as program beneficiaries?
2. What are the opinions of the intended target population regarding the extent to which the content of the program is reaching them and the reasons why program contacts are or are not made?
3. What is the number of appropriate services used, out of the possible number of available referral services; what are the reasons for the use (or lack of use) of referral services?
4. What happens to prospective clientele who are referred to other programs; how many persons actually receive services from the programs to which they are referred?
5. What is the extent of unsuccessful completions of service or premature terminations, that is, drop-outs?

EFFICIENCY

1. What are the relative proportions of staff time devoted to program objectives, and to what extent is the use of staff time related to the achievement of those objectives?
2. What are the relative costs of using different means for contacting clientele?
3. Are staff functions and roles structured to maximize program consistency for the achievement of program goals?
4. Are certain client characteristics more related to program contact than others; for example, do whites receive more or less program contact than blacks?
5. Are certain staff characteristics more related to program contacts than others?
6. Are certain staff or client characteristics related to program drop-outs?

Unanticipated consequences in program contact are often a result of the social interactions between social workers and other allied professional and supportive staff and prospective clientele. This is especially true when recruiting minority and lower-class groups of clientele, whose values may be different from those of social workers. Lack of client participation, inadequate representation of client populations, and poor program utilization are undesirable program consequences.

Implementation This stage involves the achievement of, or failure to achieve, ultimate objectives. It is the stage in which a program or practice is fully operational. *Efforts* in program implementation include variables that indicate the amount of time, energy, or resources devoted to the following: selecting criteria for program termination and follow-up; considering policies regarding the re-entry and follow-up of program dropouts; modifying, expanding, or contracting program objectives; and so forth (Tripodi, Fellin, and Epstein 1978, pp. 53-55). Program *effectiveness* is the extent to which the ultimate program objectives have been achieved without negative or harmful side effects (unanticipated consequences). While efforts refer to variables that indicate *who* does *what* to, for, or with *whom* in *what places*, effectiveness is the extent to which expected changes regarding attitudes, knowledge, behaviors, skills, and conditions are realized (see criteria for detailed objectives in chapter 2). Thus, variables of effectiveness are variables that depict changes. For example, variables such as these may be used to reflect change in social programs:

1. Amount of money earned
2. Proportion of persons employed
3. Incidence and prevalence of disease
4. Severity of psychosis
5. Degree of self-esteem
6. Knowledge of birth control devices
7. Knowledge of social agencies that provide financial assistance
8. Attitudes toward authority figures
9. Frequency of headaches
10. Ounces of alcohol consumed per day
11. Speed and accuracy of typing
12. Willingness to place a child for adoption

Program *efficiency* raises questions about the accomplishment of program objectives at varying rates of program effort. Variables of efficiency are combinations of effectiveness and efforts. They may be in the form of ratios, that is, the amount of funds expended to achieve one unit of change for program recipients, or they may refer to differences between effectiveness and efforts in relation to costs. Hence, efficiency variables reflect program accomplishments as a function of different types and amounts of program interventions, as a result of differential costs, or both.

Unanticipated consequences in social programs cannot be completely foreseen. Hence, it is important for the evaluator to plan to ask questions during the conduct of evaluative research that could uncover unanticipated consequences. "Are there any changes you believe you made, either desirable or undesirable, as a result of program intervention?" might be asked of recipients who have recently completed a social program. As Hyman, Wright, and Hopkins indicate, an extreme value of a desired social change may be undesirable, and this phenomenon could occur in a social program (1962). For example, a social program with a basic objective of reducing anxiety by medication may induce extreme apathy in its recipients; or a birth control program may be so successful that there is no growth in a population, with fewer children attending school, and a resulting increase in the unemployment rates of primary-school teachers.

Practice *effectiveness* refers to the extent to which one or more planned objectives are achieved with one or more clients. It may refer to the terms of a written contract or to the oral perceptions and understandings of the social worker and his or her client. For a particular client, it may refer to weight loss or weight gain, increased self-confidence, increased self-acceptance, job changes, and so forth. *Efforts* are time, energy, and resources that are expended or used by the social worker to achieve effectiveness. In practice, efforts are directed toward the achievement of client objectives, as well as toward the critical tasks and decisions necessary to achieve effectiveness, such as the decision to terminate or to make a referral to another agency. Variables of effort, therefore, are expressed in time (e.g., percentage of interview time devoted to particular topics, total amount of time per week devoted to a specific client); energy or activity (e.g., number of questions, clarifying statements, empathic remarks, and interpretations made by a social worker in one interview; number of telephone calls or visits made to significant others in a client's life); resources (e.g., number of referrals made to other workers or agencies for specific services); and costs (e.g., total amount of monies spent on a client, including direct financial outlays and costs such as those for the social worker's time and the resources she or he uses).

Practice *efficiency* is the relationship of effectiveness to efforts and is most easily assessed in terms of the ratio of changes in effectiveness per worker's activity or costs. Efficiency is most useful when it reflects relative differences between workers and clients in relation to the same change objectives. Hence the social worker may note that she or he is more or less efficient with one type of client (e.g., male or female, child or adult, same or different ethnic group) than with another.

In addition to exaggerated changes that result in different, undesirable behaviors or attitudes for a client, a major *unanticipated consequence* may be the extent to which a client becomes dependent upon the social worker. Of course, some clients who have borderline character disorders benefit from a degree of dependence on the social worker, for it may help keep them out of a mental institution. But for those clients who need temporary assistance to help them in crises, an increased amount of worker dependency is undesirable. Moreover, it most certainly leads to a reduction in practice efficiency.

Table 3-1 summarizes variables within program on practice stages of development.* It is important to note that inputs, thruputs, and outputs are not exactly the same as independent, intervening, and dependent variables. *Inputs* are the dependent variables of the initiation stage; *thruputs*, the contact stage; and *outputs*, the implementation stage. Moreover, they represent achieved objectives within each stage. For example, in the development of a program to treat drug abusers, objec-

*This section is intended for advanced students of evaluative research.

TABLE 3-1 Variables within Program or Practice Stages of Development

		CRITERIA OF EVALUATION		
	EFFORTS	EFFECTIVENESS	EFFICIENCY	UNANTICIPATED CONSEQUENCES
Developmental Stages				
Initiation	E_N	I (Inputs)	I/E_N*	$\cup C_N$
Contact	E_C	T (Thruputs)	T/E_C	$\cup C_C$
Implementation	E_M	O (Outputs)	O/E_m	$\cup C_M$

*A slash (/) indicates relationship; hence I/E_N symbolizes the relationship of inputs to the efforts expended to achieve those inputs in the initiation stage of development.

tives for the initiation stage are to obtain staff who can provide treatment and social services in a location convenient to drug abusers. If those objectives are accomplished, they become inputs, and serve as independent variables for the delivery of services to drug abusers in the contact stage. If the planned number of drug abusers becomes engaged in the treatment process, there is effectiveness in the contact stage. Effectiveness in terms of the accomplishment of objectives in the contact stage is depicted by thruput variables. Hence, achieving the desired number of treatment contacts is an example of a thruput variable. Thruputs become, in turn, the independent variables for the output variables in the implementation stage. Outputs are objectives achieved as a result of the programmed inputs and thruputs. In this instance, an output variable is the proportion of clients who significantly reduce their drug intake.

Referring to Table 3-1, one can observe that the first row of initiation has the symbols of E_N, I, I/E_N and $\cup C_N$. E_N refers to variables indicating efforts at the initiation stage; I refers to effectiveness which is program or practice inputs; $\cup C_N$ symblizes unanticipated consequences that can occur; and I/E_N is an index of efficiency that indicates the relationship between inputs (I) and efforts (E) expended in the initiation stage. For example, an administrator advertises for staff (efforts), and, if she or he is successful, obtains the desired number (inputs). T refers to achieved objectives at the contact stage and O is the program or practice outputs. It should be noted that input variables are similar to structural variables; thruputs, to process, instrumental, and service delivery variables; and outputs, to outcome, result, and impact variables (Suchman 1967; Donabedian 1969; and Riecken, and others 1974). Combining effectiveness variables with those representing unanticipated consequences, the *net inputs* can be symbolized as $I \pm \cup C_N$ (inputs plus desirable consequences and minus undesirable consequences); *net thruputs*, as $T \pm \cup C_c$; and *net outputs* as $O \pm \cup C_M$.

For example, net outputs for a drug-abuse program would include the proportion of drug abusers who have reduced their drug consumption and those who have reduced their dependency on state-supported financial assistance. Negative consequences might include the protests of property owners who do not want "junkies" in their neighborhood and who consequently attempt to abort or sabotage the program.

Between Stages of Development*

Variables can be located which show the interrelationships between stages of development. One can study the relationships between outputs or thruputs and inputs as an index of program or practice efficiency; the relationships between outputs and thruputs as an index of successful program or practice planning; and inputs, thruputs, and outputs with respect to client needs.

Between-Stage Efficiency**

Variables that show relationships among effectiveness at different stages of program or practice development provide useful information for program planners and formulators of practice interventions. The relationship between thruputs and inputs (T/I) indicates the efficiency of planning efforts (e.g., the average costs of achieving a specified number of group sessions or individual interviews, the amount of time required by a social worker to achieve a certain number of contacts with a particular client).

Cost effectiveness of social programs or practices basically refers to the relationship of desirable outcomes to costs, time, energy, and resources. Hence, cost effectiveness is equivalent to the relationship represented by O/I—program or practice outputs as a function of inputs. When net outputs are considered in relation to net inputs, and both inputs and outputs are translated into monetary units, the relationships between outputs and inputs are described by benefit-cost analyses (Andriew 1977). For example, an objective of a social-service program is to reduce the public-welfare rolls. Outputs in terms of monies saved for the welfare program, as well as monies contributed in taxes for those newly employed, are compared to the costs involved in providing inputs.

Within a certain program or practice, cost effectiveness and benefit-cost analyses can show cost ratios. But those ratios may be deceptive unless there are standards to which they can be compared. With a particular standard, for instance, 50% effectiveness for a specified amount of staff time and resources, a social worker can estimate the efficiency of his or her work in a program or for a particular client.

When standards are not agreed on, the relationships of thruputs to inputs and of outputs to inputs can be used on a relativistic basis between programs or practices. For example, for the same types of clients with similar problems, one social program, A, may have greater thruputs or outputs per unit of program input than another program, B. All other factors being equal, program A would be regarded as more efficient than B.

*This section is intended for advanced students of evaluative research.
**For clarity of presentation the discussion is limited to T/I and O/I; net effectiveness for inputs, thruputs, and outputs can be simply substituted for the symbols I, T and O.

Program and practice planning* Programmers and social workers involved in direct practice formulate intervention strategies that are practice hypotheses. They try to specify inputs that result in a certain amount of thruputs; in turn, they hypothesize the attainment of thruputs as leading to desirable outcomes. For example, a social worker devotes time, energy, and collateral resources to involving a client in psychosocial therapy (inputs). After fifteen or more sessions (thruputs), she or he hypothesizes that the client's problematic behavior will change (outputs).

The success of program or practice planning is proportional to the number of outputs per unit of thruputs. The greater the number of outputs per unit of thruputs, the greater the success of social-work planning. For example, social workers hypothesize that whether or not clients of job-counseling programs obtain employment depends on the number of job-counseling sessions they receive. Hence a job-counseling program that shows 40% of its recipients as employed indicates more program-planning success than another job-counseling program that indicates a 20% employment rate—given that both programs have equal numbers of job-counseling sessions and that all other pertinent factors are equivalent. This is due to the fact that the ratio of outputs to thruputs is greater for the program with the 40% employment rate.

Information regarding the effectiveness of program or practice planning is useful for comparing programs or practices. Such data can be used in summative evaluation for choosing between intervention strategies. For example, a social worker who uses one type of intervention for several different clients finds that she or he obtains relatively more outputs per thruput than with any other intervention. As a consequence, she or he uses that intervention much more often.

Variables that indicate the effectiveness of planning for social-work practices or programs are also useful for formative evaluation. Within a social program, a program planner hypothesizes that the greater the number of contacts (thruputs) with the target population, the greater the number of outputs. For example, it was posited that increased contacts with a low-income, female population would lead to a greater utilization of birth control devices. If the same number of birth control devices are used regardless of the number of staff thruputs with the target population, the hypothesis can be rejected, and it can be assumed there is a planning failure, since the hypothesized relationship between thruputs and outputs was rejected.** Obviously, if there were complete inefficiency between thruputs and inputs, there would be no thruputs; in that event the planning hypothesis could not be adequately tested.

Relation to need Social programs take place in communities that are bounded by geographic areas. Within those areas, referred to as *catchment areas* in community mental-health planning and research, there are a specifiable number of residents who have particular needs. Some persons may want jobs, others may

---

*This section is intended for advanced students of evaluative research.
**What is regarded here as a planning failure for either practice or social programs is referred to as a theory failure for social programs by Weiss (1972, p. 38).

hope to reduce their intake of narcotics, and still others may desire to engage in marital counseling. Needs are assessed by such research strategies as sample survey techniques, census statistics, and concepts from epidemiology such as the incidence and prevalence of disease (Rossi, Freeman, and Wright 1979). The assessment of needs often occurs before rational policy and planning strategies for social programs (Kahn 1969; Mayer and Greenwood 1980). In other words, a rationale for creating, expanding, or contracting programs depends upon the estimated number of persons who could benefit from these programs.

Variables that show the relationship of program effectiveness to social need are useful for summative evaluation because they represent the magnitude of social programs; they may reach a sizable portion of the estimated target population, or be merely nothing but a ripple in an ocean of social need. Suppose there is a catchment area in which estimates from an epidemiological survey indicate there are two thousand drug addicts who profess a desire to kick their drug habit. A social program is planned to accommodate one hundred drug addicts. Two hundred drug addicts are contacted and one hundred enroll. Of those one hundred persons, fifty remain in the program and twenty-five are drug-free one year later. This hypothetical example illustrates the relationships between program efficiency and program magnitude. The magnitude of program planning—inputs in relation to social need—is 100/2000 or 5%; the magnitude of thruputs to social need is 50/2000 or 2.5%; and the magnitude of outputs to social need is 25/2000 or 1.25%.* While this program is 1% effective in terms of total need, it is 25% efficient in considering outputs with respect to inputs. Another program may be less efficient between stages of development, but it may reach a greater proportion of the target population. For example, the program may be able to accommodate one thousand addicts, two hundred of whom become drug-free, with a resulting magnitude of 10% with respect to the population in need, or "at risk."

CHOOSING VARIABLES

It would be too difficult in terms of cost and time for an evaluator to choose variables that represent all of the relationships discussed in the preceding section. An evaluator should know what information it is possible to gather and then base the choice of variables on the evaluation of consumers' informational needs and the time and resources available for the evaluation. He or she specifies priorities of information and criteria of evaluation with respect to potential variables located within or between stages of development, in relation to social need, or both. The evaluator considers whether the evaluation will be comprehensive, partially comprehensive, or restricted to specific criteria. One evaluator and his or her consumers may be interested in deriving information pertinent to a summative evaluation of a

---

*The magnitude of outputs to social need is regarded as impacts by Rossi, Freeman and Wright, 1979, and as comprehensiveness by Suchman, 1967.

social program, especially of its between-stage efficiency, and the magnitude of outputs with respect to social need. Another evaluator may be primarily concerned with the extent to which outputs are achieved with a minimum of undesirable unanticipated consequences for one particular client.

Although it may be desirable to study the relationships between program outputs and social need, data on social need may not be available. Furthermore, the time and effort required to obtain adequate estimates of social need may be far greater than the resources available for evaluation. If the evaluation is to be used for formative purposes, data on need are not necessary. A summative evaluation, however, would be incomplete without such information, as well as data comparing the relative effectiveness and efficiency of two or more programs.

For any evaluation, it is essential to produce data regarding the variables of efforts, effectiveness, and efficiency. Ultimately all programs and practices should produce information about the achievement of intervention objectives. But these data may not all be provided in any one evaluation. As programs or practices develop, new information is required. Hence evaluations can be continuous, with more than one being carried out at different intervals throughout the life of a program or practice.

PROPERTIES OF USEFUL VARIABLES

Useful variables for evaluative research have these characteristics (described below): pertinence, measurability, operational definitions, reliability, validity, sensitivity, and feasibility.

Pertinence

A variable is pertinent when it can represent data related to the evaluative criteria of efforts, effectiveness, efficiency, or a combination of these three and when it provides information useful to consumers of evaluation, either for programs or practices.

Variables that are directly related to program or practice objectives and to evaluative criteria are obviously pertinent. For example, if an objective for a client is to increase weight, the number of pounds gained within a specified time period is pertinent. Variables that represent unanticipated consequences are pertinent to the extent that they provide information that adds to or subtracts from program or practice effectiveness.

Whereas some variables may be pertinent to evaluations of practice, they may not be appropriate for program evaluation. Pertinent variables for program evaluation refer to all those individuals combined together in the program. For example, if the attainment of jobs is a program variable, *every* program participant should be assessed in terms of that variable. On the other hand, one client may be interested in weight loss, which can be regarded as a practice variable unique to that client, but not necessarily pertinent to the other clients in the job attainment program.

Measurability

A variable can be defined as a measurable dimension of a concept that takes on two or more values (Labovitz and Hagedorn 1971, p. 18). It becomes measurable when it is operationally defined so that data can be gathered and categorized into measurement scales. The most common classification of measurement scales includes these levels: nominal, ordinal, interval, and ratio (see Kogan 1975 for a more extensive classification).

A *nominal scale* has mutually exclusive and exhaustive categories. Mutual exclusivity means no object can be assigned to more than one category and exhaustiveness means that all objects to be classified can be assigned to the available categories on the scale. For example, males and females are two categories in a nominal scale of gender. Persons categorized as males are not regarded as females (mutual exclusivity), and all persons can be assigned to one of the two categories (exhaustiveness).

An *ordinal scale* has the properties of a nominal scale, plus the characteristic of order between the categories. Although there are "greater than" or "less than" relations between categories, the differences in amount cannot be assessed. For example, program participants may rate the extent to which they learned about existing social services on an ordinal scale with these categories: learned a great deal, learned something, learned little, and learned nothing. The category "learned something" signifies less learning than "learned a great deal" and more learning than "learned little." The distances between each category are not the same.

In an *interval scale* there is an equal distance between categories next to each other, and there are also the characteristics of mutual exclusivity, exhaustiveness, and order. However, there is no true zero point or defined point of origin (Shortell and Richardson 1978, p. 74). Thus, the difference between 98°F. and 99°F. is one degree, which is equivalent to the difference between 10°F. and 11°F. but the 0°F. reading is not a true zero point since there are thermometer readings below 0°F.

A *ratio scale* has a true zero point as well as all of the characteristics of an interval scale. Income, number of interviews, time devoted to job seeking, and group size are examples of ratio measurement scales.

Operational Definitions

To transform dimensions of concepts into measurement scales it is necessary to use operational definitions. An operational definition specifies all of those procedures necessary to define dimensions of a concept so they can be measured (Nunnally and Wilson 1975; Mayer and Greenwood 1980). Four steps can be identified in forming operational definitions. First, define verbally the dimension of the concept being measured. For example, if the concept is political affiliation, this definition might be used: "In the United States, political affiliation is one's preference for voting for political parties such as democratic, republican, communist, socialist, and so on. List all of the parties and define each one so that they can be distinguished from each other. Second, specify an indicator of the concept. An indication of political affiliation might be a person's self-report on which political party she or he prefers. Third, specify procedures for gathering data (see chapters 3 and 4 for a more detailed discussion of data gathering). Devise an interview schedule in which respondents are asked to indicate which, if any, of the several political parties they prefer. Also specify the time and place for the interview. Finally, provide rules for the evaluator and his or her staff on how to categorize the data. For this nominal scale of political affiliation, the party that the respondent prefers is checked to represent his or her political affiliation.

Reliability

Reliability is the extent to which repeated measurements are correlated, and assuming that the value of the variable itself does not change during the time intervals between repeated measures. The greater the degree of correlation between repeated measurements, the higher the reliability (Nunnally and Durham 1975, p. 311). Reliability of variables is assessed with respect to time intervals, either at the same point in time or at different points (Shortell and Richardson 1978, p. 76). At the same point in time, *inter-rater or inter-observer reliability* is assessed when different observers make ratings of the same phenomenon on the same measurement scale. *Split-half reliability* is determined when there are many persons responding to a test, questionnaire, or interview in which the variable is comprised of many items. *Test-retest reliability* or stability is assessed for either observers or respondents over two or more time periods.

Inter-rater reliability Consistency of two or more independent raters in their observations or judgments constitutes inter-rater reliability. Empirical indications of reliability are either percentage agreement or correlation. An adequate degree of reliability is obtained when there is 70% agreement or a correlation of 0.8 or higher.

This type of reliability is especially important when the evaluator desires dependable judgments and the observations are recorded on rating scales, classification schemes, or both. For example, judgments are being made about hospitalized psychiatric patients as to whether or not they should be released from a hospital to the community. Suppose two psychiatrists are making judgments about one hundred patients. Each psychiatrist, without consulting the other, decides whether or not each patient should be released; both psychiatrists have the same amounts and kinds of information at their disposal. Inter-rater reliability is determined by two different results in this instance: (1) exact percentage agreement for each of the one hundred patients, or (2) percentage agreement of the frequencies for each category (release-not release). Exact percentage agreement is determined by counting the number of exact agreements, dividing by the number of possible agreements, and multiplying by one hundred. If the two psychiatrists agree in their judgments for seventy-five of the patients, there is an inter-observer or inter-rater reliability of 75%. Percentage agreement of frequencies doesn't require exact agreement for each patient because it refers to the agreement of raters in the numbers of objects assigned to the available categories on a measurement scale. To illustrate, each psychiatrist may indicate that fifty patients should be released and fifty should stay; this is 100% agreement since there are one hundred out of one hundred possible agreements in their assignment of frequencies.

Exact percentage agreement is more precise, particularly if an evaluator is interested in using the judgments for decisions about specific individuals. This type of reliability is also useful for generalizing about groups. In contrast, percentage agreement of frequencies is only useful for making generalizations about groups of subjects, and, although easier to obtain, it is less precise than inter-rater reliability.

Split-half reliability This is the type of reliability obtained when the responses to one-half of the items in a measurement instrument, such as a test or questionnaire, are highly correlated with responses to the other half. It provides an index of the perceived uniformity of a measurement instrument at one point in time. It is most useful when an evaluator needs an instrument to measure an abstract concept that has many indicators. For example, an evaluator devises a questionnaire to measure the degree to which clients indicate they are depressed. The questionnaire has thirty questions, each referring to different indicators of depression such as insomnia, excessive crying, weight loss, and feeling "down in the dumps." At some point in time the questionnaire is distributed to a given number of respondents, say fifty. The responses to fifteen questions (drawn either randomly or systematically from the thirty questions) by the fifty respondents are correlated to their responses to the other fifteen questions. A correlation coefficient (e.g., a Pearson *r* for interval scales, Spearman's *rho* for ordinal scales, or *phi* for nominal measurement scales) is computed, and if the correlation is 0.80 or higher, the questionnaire is regarded as reliable. For more computational detail, refer to Nunnally and Durham (1975), who provide a thorough discussion of the theory of reliability and of the calculation of other reliability coefficients such as the Kuder-Richardson formula for split-half reliability and coefficient alpha for the average correlation among items in a test or questionnaire.

Test-retest reliability Reliability over time is referred to as test-retest reliability or stability. The correlation of judgments made by the same person at two different points in time is either intra-rater or intra-observer reliability (Shortell and Richardson 1978, p. 76), which is a special case of test-retest reliability.

Test-retest reliability occurs when there is a high correlation between responses made by one or more persons at one point in time and their responses at a subsequent point in time, given that there are no basic changes in the variables being measured. For example, one rater (intra-rater reliability) observes a video-taped interview of a social worker and her or his client at two different times, one week apart. The rater may classify the intervention methods used by referring to each sentence uttered by the social worker to her or his client during a ten-minute interview segment. Hollis's system (1972) for categorizing interventions as direct advice, sustaining procedures, and so on might be used. The higher the degree of correlation between the classifications of the social worker's sentences, the higher the intra-rater or test-retest reliability.

Validity

Validity is the degree to which a measurement of a concept corresponds to what is intended by the concept. It can be assessed by two different strategies: (1) content validity, or a sampling of items related to the concept, and (2) empirical validity or empirical evidence of predicted relationships with other variables.*

Content validity The type of validity that is based on the judgment and expertise of investigators about a particular variable is known as content validity. It refers to the extent to which the measurement of a concept adequately samples the content domain that is perceived as relevant to the concept. For example, the variable "degree of anxiety" is operationally defined as the number of anxietylike items out of a specified number, say fifty, that a person would agree are characteristic of him or her. Each item refers to different indications of anxiety, for instance, "I feel nervous when I talk in a group," "I often perspire for no apparent reason," "I have a recurring feeling of 'butterflies in my stomach.'" In this example, there is content validity if those familiar with the concept of anxiety agree that the fifty items are sufficiently representative of symptoms, thoughts, and feelings related to the concept of anxiety. Whereas the items mentioned are related to the concept of anxiety, items about the circumference of the moon, baseball batting averages, and type of perfume used are obviously not relevant.

Although an evaluator can obtain quantitative measures of the empirical agreement among judges on the relevance and adequate sampling of the content domain of possible indicators (i.e., content validity), she or he cannot be sure that those measures are accurate indications of validity. The measures may be based on the biases of the judges as well as on an inadequate idea of the concept being measured. The judges themselves may not constitute a representative sampling of the possible range of "experts" that could rate the contents of a particular measuring device. Hence evaluators seek variables that appear to be relevant to the concept being measured, as a necessary condition for good measurement. Yet this doesn't usually involve quantitative data about expert agreement regarding the representativeness of the items in a measuring instrument. A sufficient condition for validity is one in which empirical evidence is obtained that support theoretical and methodological expectations.

*The reader should note that empirical validity as used here refers to any empirical evidence of predictions made, whether past or future, or to other variables that are theoretically or methodologically related. It refers to any association that could be made to other variables; hence it encompasses such notions as construct validity, concurrent validity, and predictive validity. See Nunnally and Durham (1975) and Shortell and Richardson (1978) for other classifications of validity.

Empirical validity The basic idea of empirical validity is that a variable is measuring what it's supposed to be measuring when it correlates highly with other variables that are considered methodologically or theoretically relevant. A variable that is methodologically relevant is one that measures the same concept with a different measurement device. For example, one measurement of anxiety might be obtained by persons' responses to questionnaire items while another measurement of the same concept might be physiological including heart rate, hand tremors, and degree of perspiration. If there is a high correlation between these two measures, there is evidence of empirical validity. There are as many methodological predictions as there are different ways of measuring a concept; thus, there may be more than one source of evidence for methodological, empirical validity.

Empirical validity is also demonstrated by obtaining evidence of theoretical expectations. Persons who are anxious are expected to have greater difficulty in learning than persons who are not; the proportion of anxious clients in a mental-health center can be expected to be higher than the proportion of anxious persons in the general population.

Empirical evidence is shown by correlation coefficients and by statistically significant differences between the distributions of measurements on known groups. A self-reported measure of drug abuse could be theoretically empirically validated if there is a high inverse correlation between those who say they use drugs in comparison with those who say they don't use them, other factors being equal. Those who experience weight loss should, on the average, show they have less caloric intake than those who don't. Persons in reformatories should score higher on a scale showing a tendency toward delinquency than those who have never been to reformatories.

Just as with empirical validity based on comparing different methods of measuring the same concept, there are as many theoretical empirical validities as there are predictions. A concept is empirically validated to the degree that there is cumulative evidence supporting the possible methodological and theoretical predictions. Hence, there are degrees of validation based on the available empirical evidence for a particular measure. The greater the degree of validation for the measure, the more accurate it is.

Sensitivity

A variable is sensitive if it has a sufficient number of categories for making reliable distinctions among objects assigned to those categories. A measurement scale with k reliable categories is less sensitive than one with $k + 1$ reliable categories. For example, a nominal scale for making judgments of psychiatric impairment consists of two categories: impaired and not impaired. If all psychiatric patients are classified as impaired, that scale is less sensitive than one that has more categories of impairment, such as an ordinal scale with these categories: no impairment, slight impairment, quite a bit of impairment, a great deal of impairment. Sensitivity increases directly as a function of reliable discrimination among categories and the level of measurement. Hence, an interval scale with the same number of categories is more sensitive than an ordinal scale.

Sensitivity in variables means that there is a range of possible responses among respondents, that is, heterogeneity. With variation in responses, there is a greater likelihood that an evaluator can study individual and subgroup differences. For example, different degrees of change may be associated with interventions administered by male and female practitioners. Variables used to register change are sufficiently sensitive if potential male and female differences can be examined.

Feasibility

Finally, a variable is useful if it has the property of feasibility, which refers to practical aspects in obtaining measurements. Feasibility applies to the costs of measurement including time and finances, the extent to which an evaluator or an evaluation team can afford these costs, and the potential availability of data necessary for measurement.

Whether an evaluation is of a complex program or geared to appraising the effectiveness of a particular practice with one individual, the costs of time and of monies to offset the expenses of data gathering are most important. When information is needed relatively quickly for making decisions about practice or program development, a variable that requires a great deal of effort for measurement is obviously less useful than one that takes less time, other factors being equal.

The next two chapters examine the wide variety of procedures for using available data and for constructing procedures for collecting original information. Those data are categorized into the measurement scales for evaluation—the evaluation variables. To the extent that appropriate data can actually be collected for categorization, the evaluation variables are useful. Since an evaluator is bound by ethical and legal constraints, those variables formed by data without such constraints are regarded as feasible.

In summary, the task of an evaluator is to locate and specify variables that are relevant for evaluative research. Evaluations require useful variables, whose properties should be carefully considered.

CHAPTER FOUR
SECONDARY DATA RESOURCES AND AVAILABLE INSTRUMENTS

Evaluators use two basic resources for obtaining variables in evaluative research: primary and secondary data. *Primary data* are gathered by the evaluator during the conduct of an evaluation, but *secondary data* are already available (Tripodi 1974, p. 33; Shortell and Richardson 1978, pp. 84-87). This chapter focuses on secondary resources that evaluators use, and chapter 5 examines issues involved in the collection of original data. Obviously it is more efficient for the evaluator to use available resources if they are compatible with the purpose and scope of the evaluation. However, existing data may be inaccurate as well as irrelevant. Accordingly, the purpose of this chapter is to discuss the location of data, the various types of data, and criteria for their potential use. It should be noted that the intent of this chapter is not to discuss the techniques of data analysis involved in secondary analysis. For a discussion of this subject, secondary analysis, refer to "Secondary Analysis of Existing Data" by Hoshino and Lynch (1981). They discuss analytic techniques and present a detailed case study involving secondary data from a large social services agency in a metropolitan area.

LOCATION OF SECONDARY DATA RESOURCES

Secondary data resources refer to data, records, documents, and instruments that can be used for purposes of measurement. *Data* are found in previous research studies or in statistical series published by governmental and private agencies. For example, statistical data are given in volumes and statistical abstracts published by the National Center of Social Statistics, the National Center for Health Statistics, the Department of Labor Handbook of Basic Economic Statistics, Statistical Abstract of the United States, County and City Data Book, and so forth. National, state, and county censuses may contain useful data. Research centers within universities and agencies concerned with mental health, welfare, education, recreation, corrections, juvenile delinquency, and so on also provide statistical series and data from surveys. Data from published research and evaluation studies are located in professional journals, monographs, periodicals, and books. Journals such as the following include reports of evaluative research studies:

Evaluation and Program Planning,
Social Work Research and Abstracts,
Social Work,
Crime and Delinquency,
American Journal of Orthopsychiatry,
Evaluation,
Journal of Social Service Research,
Journal of Consulting Psychology,
Social Casework,
American Journal of Public Health,
Evaluation Research Quarterly,
Behavioral Research and Therapy,
Child Welfare,
Social Service Review,
Administrative Science Quarterly.

Quantitative data are available from the original investigators, often stored on computer tapes or in IBM files. Some data have been collected and filed but not analyzed. They are most likely to be filed with governmental departments, social agencies, research departments, or individual investigators.

Records in social agencies are an excellent source of potential data. They are often collected and filed but not codified for data analyses. Schools contain records and files of attendance patterns, school performance, and health; hospitals and social service departments have records of client contacts which include such information as diagnoses, medication, and treatment goals; police departments and courts keep data regarding the number of arrests, the nature of offenses, the sentences administered, and so forth. Many records contain qualitative, narrative data that can be transformed to quantitative data (e.g., by procedures such as content analysis). These are case records or narrative responses to questions or previously administered questionnaires and interview schedules.

Qualitative data are also found in *agency documents* such as minutes of meetings, agency policies and personnel practices, and organizational planning and position papers. In addition, useful data are available in mass-media resources. Newspapers often contain stories and editorials that reflect the community's attitudes toward a particular social program. Books, magazines, and films provide information about the historical context in which a social program is placed; they can also stimulate the conceptualization of unanticipated consequences that may affect the evaluations of programs and of interventions for specific clients.

Although the data may not have been collected, the use of available instruments can save a great deal of time and expense in evaluative research. *Instruments* are data collection devices such as tests, questionnaires, interview schedules, and observation forms. Instruments that have already been constructed are a resource for the collection of data to the extent that they facilitate the conduct of evaluative research. They are found by referring to social agencies and organizations and research and evaluation departments and libraries.

Social agencies routinely use questionnaires or forms to obtain agency statistics that are required by program funders, sponsors, and administrators. Some organizations have developed specific instruments for internal evaluation and research. Within agencies, supervisors or social workers may have located or may have developed their own instruments for evaluating their practice.

Research departments of federal and state agencies have developed instruments and have published volumes about their potential use. For example, the National Institute of Mental Health published a *Handbook of Psychiatric Rating Scales* (Lyerly and Abbott 1966), and the University of Michigan Institute for Social Research published *Measures of Social Psychological Attitudes* (Robinson and Shaver 1969). Research departments also contain instruments that are not available in published form, but copies of them can be obtained with the permission of the investigators and their departments.

Instruments can also be located in good libraries with such practice journals as *Social Casework* and *Behavior Therapy*, as well as problem-focused journals such as *Federal Probation* and the *Journal of Alcoholism and Drug Abuse* (Tripodi and Epstein 1980, p. 39). Published guides to research and evaluation that cite studies by subject matter or by the basic concepts of interest are *Reader's Guide to Periodical Literature*, *Psychology Abstracts*, *Sociology Abstracts*, *Social Work Research and Abstracts*, and *Human Resources Abstracts*. Also available are collections of research instruments such as the volumes on mental measurements and personality tests by O.K. Buros (1972, 1975), the measurement of human behavior by Lake, Miles, and Earle (1973), and Strauss's *Family Measurement Techniques* (1969).

TYPES OF SECONDARY DATA RESOURCES

Secondary data resources can be classified into two major types: (1) Data that have been categorized and tabulated and (2) Data that have not been categorized.

Type I: Categorized
and Tabulated Data

This type refers to data published in research reports and monographs, census studies, statistical reports of a variety of social agencies, and so forth. Data may be cross-sectional, describing results of a survey or statistical study at one point in time, or they may be longitudinal, reporting trends over time.

POTENTIAL USES

1. Identification of Clients Eligible for Social Programs and Services. Basic to any program or practice administered in social agencies is a determination of who is eligible. Once criteria are specified, practitioners and administrators screen referrals and applicants for their program and services. For example, some services are geared to populations below a fixed income level, others to clients who have been institutionalized in mental hospitals, and still others to children enrolled in public schools. Programs are devised for clients in particular groups, for instance, physically handicapped persons or minority groups.

Published data on characteristics of populations and subpopulations provide estimates of the number of persons eligible for programs and services. These data indicate whether the number of clients receiving services and program benefits is small or large with respect to the potential program population. They can also be used to support program planning efforts or to show that programs for a specific population are not justified. For example, an educational program is planned in a community for children of migrant workers. If the number of children available for the program is far less than that which was planned, the planning efforts are regarded as inappropriate or unjustified. The planners might have proceeded more efficiently if they had first studied the available population.

2. Needs Assessments and Diagnoses. Assessments of communities, neighborhoods, and other geographic areas involve the collection and tabulation of data from indicators of economic, educational, health, and other needs (Posavac and Carey 1980, pp. 86-90). Available statistics include housing density, incidence and prevalence of disease, plumbing facilities, unemployment, and so forth. These statistics can be assembled from different sources to form need profiles of subpopulations which are estimates of social need. When evaluative research is focused on the size of the program, these data are compared with the amount of effectiveness achieved within a specific program (see chapter 3 for a discussion of size as a criterion of effectiveness).

Social workers who make diagnoses in their practice with individuals use available data that pertain to those clients. School social workers, as an illustration, may have information about a child's school performance, test achievements, and psychological test results. An evaluative study that focuses on the effectiveness of a school social worker uses available information to validate the worker's diagnoses, as well as other variables developed for the evaluation.

3. Baseline Measures. When evaluators locate available data in the form of baseline measures, they can efficiently use research designs that are variations of interrupted time-series designs (see chapters 7 and 8). Baseline measures involve repeated measures taken over relatively fixed time intervals. For example, within correctional settings there may be data over time for average recidivism rates, numbers of escapes, aggressive incidents within institutions, and so on. Program evaluators use those data as bench marks against which to compare the effectiveness of new programs with the same or similar clients.

A practitioner interested in using single-subject designs (or variations of time-series designs) to evaluate his or her practice with an individual can use available baseline measures. In so doing, time-series designs become relatively feasible. For example, a social worker in a correctional facility is directing an intervention toward the modification of an inmate's "aggressive behavior." If data are available on the number of aggressive acts committed by the inmate over time, a baseline rate of aggressive behavior (e.g., hitting other inmates in the presence of custodial personnel) can be observed. The practitioner can subsequently compare the baseline rates to the rates of aggressive behavior after intervention.

4. Change Data. In some instances measurements made before and after a program or practice intervention are available, and the difference between before and after measures can be used as change data. A hypothetical illustration follows. Average attendance data for students in a particular class is available throughout a school year. The average proportion of students attending class for the month of January was 70%. During the month of February a token economy system was introduced as a program intervention, and throughout March the average proportion of class attenders increased to 90% and stabilized at that value. The difference of 20% (90% minus 70%) serves as a change datum for this analysis.

5. Checking Representativeness of Samples. In program evaluation, samples are often drawn that are supposed to be representative of a population. Even when random-sampling procedures are used, the evaluator checks as much as possible the representativeness of the sample, following these steps:

    a. Specify the variables that are regarded as important. An important variable is relevant to the program or empirically related to effectiveness variables. If a social program is concerned with changing public attitudes on public assistance, for example, important variables might be age, social class, education, and ethnic and religious identity.

    b. Determine the distributions of important variables in the population. If data are available, calculate population averages and dispersions.

    c. Determine the distributions of relevant variables for the sample. Calculate averages and dispersions in the same way as for the population.

    d. Compare the distribution of this sample and of the population. Use statistical tests such as *chi square*, the *binomial*, and *t* tests, to decide whether the sample and the population averages are similar or different. Statistically significant results, for example, at or beyond the 0.05 level of statistical inference, indicate the sample is nonrepresentative; whereas, nonstatistically significant differences signify a representative sample.

The second step (b.) is critical. If the data are not available, it is unlikely that representativeness can be checked. This is due to the fact that the basic reason for sampling is for efficiency, that is, to reduce the need to gather data from the entire population.

6. Formulation of Intervention Hypotheses. Data from program evaluations and evaluations of practice with individual clients may or may not be internally valid and generalizable to other programs and practitioners. However, data from previous evaluation studies can be a source of hypotheses for programs and practice. If a particular intervention in an evaluation is regarded as successful in changing the attitudes of a handicapped person toward seeking a job, that intervention might also be successful for another social worker. The social worker hypothesizes that the intervention will also be effective for him or her, recognizing that he or she will test it in practice.

7. *Knowledge about Unanticipated Consequences.* Previous evaluations that are similar or identical to the programs or practice that an evaluator wishes to evaluate can be instructive. Information is obtained about the program and its strengths and weaknesses, and the evaluator develops ideas about the practicality of various research designs and data-collection procedures. In particular, there may be data that show quantitative relationships between program or practice interventions and outcomes, some of which may not have been expected. Correlated with the program interventions in a weight reduction program, for example, may be an increased amount of smoking in program recipients. The increased smoking, as pointed out before, is an unanticipated consequence.

Case histories compiled by social workers may include quantitative relationships. For example, a social worker sets the objective of decreasing anxiety and depression in a client. She or he compiles ratings of depression and anxiety for every casework session. As part of the intervention strategy, the worker plans to influence the client to increase his or her participation in social activities. As the number of activities increases, depression decreases, but anxiety increases—an unexpected result. An evaluator could benefit from that experience. She or he could plan to collect information on both anxiety and depression, rather than on just one of those two variables. The purpose would be to show that desirable decreases in one variable are not associated with undesirable increases in the other.

Criteria for use Available data should not be used simply because they *are* available. They may be distorted, inaccurate, or inappropriate to a specific evaluation. There are four basic criteria to assist the evaluator in determining whether to use Type I data: consistency of definitions, reliability, validity, and accessibility.

1. *Consistency of Definitions.* Definition of variables should be consistent in terms of the concept being measured, the geographical area, and the time assigned to the program or practice (Shyne 1960). Data that are assembled and categorized can be misleading if different definitions of the same concept are used. To illustrate, delinquents are defined by one jurisdiction as those persons under age sixteen who commit offenses that can result in their going to jail; another region has a different age limit as well as another definition of what does and does not constitute an "offense." Obviously, this concept can be operationalized in many ways. In view of this, the evaluator determines to his or her satisfaction whether the operational definitions of the concepts being measured are consistent, and whether the collection of those data is justified.

Definitions of the basic concepts can be consistent, but there can be variance in the geographic areas covered. Delinquency rates can be determined for neighborhoods, cities, counties, and other areas. Combining rates for a city from one state with a county from another state, for example, can lead to selective sampling with overestimation or underestimation of delinquency rates.

Definitions should be consistent over time if the data are used to represent trends. Suppose that conceptions of the variable being measured change from time to time, and this is reflected in the classification of data. Within a social agency, clients who were once labeled as manic depressives may currently be labeled as having affective disorders. Hence in observing data, it is inappropriate to make inferences about the prevalence of manic depressive disorders over time unless the definition of the illness is consistently used.

An evaluator should locate information about the operational definitions of the variables. If there are no discrepancies in definition, then she or he can use the data. If there are discrepancies, the evaluator should determine whether or not they can be resolved. For example, data have been compiled on delinquency rates for two states. Definitions are identical, but one state has an age limit of sixteen, and the other, eighteen. If there is access to the original data for the state that reports delinquency up to eighteen years, and if age is recorded by year, the evaluator can remove the data on the seventeen-year-olds and eighteen-year-olds from that state and combine the results with the other state's. The evaluator, in effect, transforms the data to make the definitions consistent. This requires much effort; however, it may be less costly than collecting original data, especially if these data are reliable and valid.

2. *Reliability.* An evaluator should not use data that are unreliable. There are three strategies to follow when estimating the reliability of available data: (1) examine empirical evidence of reliability, (2) review procedures for gathering data, and (3) consider the possibility of conducting reliability tests on the data.

The first strategy involves a consideration of the kinds of reliability appropriate for the evaluator's study and an appraisal of the empirical evidence. While test-retest reliability is appropriate for repeated measures, inter-rater reliability is more appropriate for observed data at one period of time. Estimates of reliability for the internal consistency of tests are based on split-half methods or on *coefficient alpha* (Nunnally and Durham 1975).

Empirical evidence of reliability should be in published form, either in agency or statistical reports, published literature, or notes or papers of those originally responsible for gathering data. If no empirical evidence is traceable, the evaluator should examine the procedures for gathering data. These include consistent application of very precise operational definitions and standardization of the conditions for data collection. For example, research schedules are used to gather information from a sample of clients in an evaluation of a social agency. Interviewers are extensively trained to provide the same interviewing format for all respondents and to refrain from imposing their biases. Supervisors arrange for spot checks, in which interviewing methods are periodically reviewed. And role-playing sessions are held for all interviewers, to further standardize the interviewing process.

It is through procedures like those above that the potential reliability of data is assessed. The evaluator can be confident in the data in spite of the fact that no empirical evidence regarding reliability is produced. To further increase his or her confidence, the evaluator can also review the original data collection form and judge its adequacy. He or she reviews the question and response alternatives for clarity and lack of bias, following the rules of well-constructed questionnaires (Isaac and Michael 1971). Hence the evaluator makes a judgment as to whether or not procedures that he or she regards as appropriate were used in the construction of data collection instruments and the gathering of data.

Sometimes an evaluator can make empirical estimates of reliability. There are two basic ways to do this. First, determine whether there are quantitative data that pertain to reliability. For example, compute test-retest reliability coefficients from available repeat measures. The second method is to use the original data-collection instrument on a sample that is representative of the population for which data are available. To illustrate, a test of knowledge was used for collecting data from public assistance clients, although there was no empirical evidence for reliability. The same test is administered to a representative sample of public assistance recipients, and reliability coefficients are computed (see Nunnally and Durham 1975 for computational procedures).

For purposes of program evaluation where data are gathered and presented simultaneously for many persons, it is particularly desirable to obtain empirical evidence of reliability. However, if the evaluator has confidence in the procedures employed for data collection and there is an estimate of reliability on a representative sample, he or she can use available data.

When the data pertain to one client, it is unlikely that empirical evidence of reliability was previously obtained. Hence, it is especially important that the evaluator examine the procedures used for gathering data and decide on their potential reliability. If the procedures for gathering data were systematic and nonbiasing, the evaluator can use the data for that particular client.

3. Validity. The validity of the data can be examined in two basic ways: contents and predictability. The contents of the data must be judged as appropriate and relevant to the evaluator's purposes. Relevancy can be checked by referring to the operational definitions for measuring key concepts. For example, "depression" might be the concept in which an evaluator is interested, but the operational definition used by previous investigators may or may not coincide with his or her use of the concept. An evaluator interested in ratings of perceived depression may find that previous investigators crudely defined depression in terms of number of hours slept, which is an inadequate index of depression.

Data are also valid to the extent there is evidence of predictability (e.g., statistically significant correlation coefficients) to other data. Data categorized as ratings of depression for clients are valid if they are highly correlated with ratings of significant others and with such observable symptoms of depression as crying and lack of affect.

If the data are accurately categorized and tabulated, and if they pertain to the contents of evaluative research, they should be used. Of course, empirical evidence of validity is desirable, but data that are reliable and have relevant contents are sufficient. When there are more than two indicators of the same concept, they should both be used in evaluative research. To the extent that similar results are produced with two or more indicators, validity is enhanced.

4. Accessibility. Data are accessible when the evaluator has permission to use them. Social agencies may not permit use of data unless consent is obtained from the clients and their workers. The evaluator locates those who are responsible for the data, attempting to secure their permission. She or he discusses whatever provisions of confidentiality were made with the respondents of data collection efforts. In this manner the evaluator determines whether the data are accessible, or whether additional steps are necessary such as securing permission from other organizations or clients. If the evaluator seeks permission to use data from the respondents, or their guardians, she or he takes into consideration their rights of privacy and confidentiality. As much as possible, the evaluator states the importance of the data and indicates how they will be used. Further, she or he indicates the extent to which her or his use of data preserves the rights to privacy and confidentiality of the original respondents.

Type II: Uncategorized Data

Type II includes quantitative data that have not been assembled and qualitative data in the form of narrative contents such as written documents, tape recordings, and films. Quantitative data may have been gathered, but not aggregated and categorized. These data are filed in agencies and organizations on agency face sheets, questionnaires, interview schedules, psychological tests, and so forth. Qualitative data are typically narrative, in the form of process and summary recordings, minutes, written policies, newspapers, tape-recorded interviews, and so forth.

POTENTIAL USES

1. Unassembled Quantitative Data. Data that are in quantitative form, such as responses to psychological tests, questionnaires, and interview schedules, are used for assessing and evaluating individual clients. They are excellent for use in program evaluation when they are assembled and totaled.

  a. *Assessment.* The eligibility of individuals for special benefits and treatment can be estimated from face-sheet information and other forms on which characteristics of clients appear. For example, a teen-ager may be eligible for an educational program geared to low-income, minority youth. Demographic information on ethnicity and family income from an agency face sheet indicate whether the teen-ager is, in fact, eligible.

  Social, psychological, and other needs can be estimated from psychological inventories and responses to questionnaires and interview schedules. A school social worker discovers that a referral, for example a sixth-grade child, is performing at a lower reading level than is appropriate for his or her ability. This discovery is facilitated by objective tests of performance in reading and arithmetic, as well as standardized intelligence tests that predict academic performance. As another example, the responses of a married couple to a marital inventory indicate disagreement about household roles and decisions on money management, and this information can serve as a diagnostic tool.

  b. *Evaluation.* Data for an individual might be avilable on basic variables that are pertinent to treatment objectives, and these data reflect that individual's status before and after social-work intervention. For example, the community mental health worker uses data about a client's history of hospitalizations; the probation officer, about a client's arrest record; and the school social worker, about a client's pattern of school attendance.

2. Unassembled Qualitative Data. Qualitative data that are not systematically categorized and collected can be used in three major ways: formulating hypotheses, describing, and testing for the existence of a phenomenon. (See Filstead 1978 for a detailed consideration of qualitative methodology.)

  a. *Formulating Hypotheses.* Hypotheses can be formulated about the effectiveness of program intervention or individual treatment, as well as unanticipated consequences or side effects. For example, recorded observations of social workers in the minutes of a meeting dealing with referral policies suggest that clients who are instructed to phone the referral worker after arriving at the referral destination are more likely to follow through on referrals than clients not so instructed.

  b. *Describing.* Narrative information provides a picture of the context in which treatment or intervention takes place. The historical context in which a social program is situated provides a frame of reference that lends perspective to the presentation of quantitative data, and it furnishes the consumers of evaluation with a description of the objects of intervention and the potential obstacles to the delivery of services. This information is available to evaluators in the form of treatment notes, process recordings, letters, and interviews. The news media as well as agency documents furnish additional information about the context of a social program.

c. *Testing.* Qualitative data can show that a phenomenon exists. For example, it might not be expected that discrimination against minorities exists in a social agency. However, minutes of meetings, documents pertaining to existing policy, and interview notes may indicate there is discrimination. It might be demonstrated that agency clients are aware of or are involved in a particular phenomenon, (e.g., drug or alcohol abuse) or that a special type of problem does or does not exist, (e.g., phobias).

3. Systematically Assembled Quantitative Data. Quantitative data can be aggregated, and qualitative data can be transformed into quantitative data by the use of procedures for systematic observation, construction of rating scales, and content analysis (Tripodi and Epstein 1980, chs. 4, 6, and 10). When the data are quantified, categorized, and assembled, they are transformed into Type I data. Hence, they have all the potential uses, as previously described, of Type I data, ranging from identification of eligible clients to knowledge of unanticipated consequences.

Criteria for use Type II data are potentially useful for evaluative research if they satisfy these criteria: content relevance, consistent availability, measurement potential, reliability and validity, and accessibility.

1. Content Relevance. The contents of the data should be directly relevant to the variables selected for evaluative research. Quantitative data that are directly relevant can be assembled and transformed into Type I data simply by totaling. Qualitative data may not be directly relevant, but they can be regarded as inputs for the construction of relevant variables. For example, the narrative information in case records or in tape-recorded interviews can be categorized into rating scales reflecting various degrees of improvement. Evaluators can form independent judgments of improvement, based on the qualitative contents of the case recordings. Since the original purpose of data collection may have been different from that of evaluation, the evaluator must judge how much information there is pertinent to the variable of interest. If client anxiety is being rated, there has to be information that bears on the client's symptoms of anxiety, perceived anxiety, and so on. Simply inferring that anxiety is not present because it is not mentioned often in case recordings is unwarranted. The social worker, for example, may only have recorded information pertinent to his or her immediate treatment objectives, and these may not include the management of anxiety symptoms.

2. Consistent Availability. Qualitative data should only be used as inputs for transformation to quantitative data when they are consistently available (Shyne 1960). The same procedures for recording data must be used from client to client if an evaluator is to sum up data across clients for purposes of program evaluation. What the evaluator should do is understand the procedures used for recording by asking persons responsible for or knowledgeable about the original data collection. She or he determines the extent to which the data collection procedures were systematically employed across workers, clients, and agencies. If the evaluator is interested in data for registering changes within clients, she or he must be satisfied that the same procedures for recording data are employed over time. Otherwise, the data will not be adequately representative.

3. Measurement Potential. This criterion is primarily used for the transformation of qualitative data to quantitative data. Qualitative data are transformed to the extent that they are categorized into nominal, ordinal, interval, or ratio-measurement scales. As an illustration, the contents of an interview can be categorized in several ways. A judgment is made as to whether or not there is evidence of anxiety; this forms a simple, two-category nominal scale. Or a rating is made on a 5-point scale ranging from "no anxiety" (1) to "severe anxiety" (5), which represents ordinal measurement. An interval measurement scale would consist of the number of words a client uses about himself or herself that are indicative of anxiety, or the amount of time a client speaks, or other similar items. The criterion of measurement potential is satisfied when there is a sufficient amount of information to which measurement scales can be applied.

4. Reliability and Validity. There may be available evidence about the reliability and validity of the instrument used to gather data. Data pertaining to reliability and validity are found in previous studies with the instrument or in a pretest by the data collector. In reviewing data collection procedures, the evaluator assesses whether they were employed systematically and whether the contents appear to be valid. If necessary, the evaluator also considers the possibility of obtaining estimates of reliability and validity in an independent but representative sample.

There must be checks for reliability and validity for qualitative data that are transformed to measurement scales. Moreover, the evaluator should carefully demonstrate that his or her procedures are not biased and are not far removed from the actual observations. The farther the data are from the actual source, the less valid they are likely to be. For example, data from tape-recorded interviews are more likely to depict client-worker interactions than are data from process recordings of completed interviews.

5. Accessibility. As with Type I data, these data cannot be used unless they are accessible to the evaluator. Accessibility is enhanced by cooperating with the administrative staff of a social agency in pursuing the goals of evaluative research, by employing procedures to safeguard the confidentiality of individual data, and by indicating the importance of the data for the evaluation to be conducted. In addition to permission to use the data, other practical matters are included in accessibility. The costs involved in abstracting and transforming qualitative data, as well as the clerical costs for collating quantitative data, are the most important. Furthermore, the data should be complete. A high proportion of incomplete data could lead to faulty conclusions based on biased selection (Campbell and Stanley 1966). This is especially significant for program evaluations based on totaled data.

The problems of accessibility are less difficult with an evaluation of an individual. In evaluations of practice with individual clients, the major problem of accessibility has to do with the lack of complete information systematically compiled over time; whereas the main obstacles in program evaluation are those of costs, informed consent (permission), and completeness.

Available Instruments

Instruments are devices by which reponses or observations are registered and recorded. They may be structured with specific sets of stimuli and response categories; unstructured with space for narrative statements, drawings, and so forth; or combinations of both. Thus, they appear in many forms: questionnaires, interview schedules, objective tests, projective techniques, observation forms, rating scales, personality inventories, aptitude tests, agency face sheets, sentence-completion tests, scales, thermometer charts, and more. Some instruments, such as the Rorschach test and the Thematic Apperception Tests, require a great deal of training to use appropriately, while others, such as questionnaires focused on client satisfaction, are relatively simple to administer and interpret.

Instruments are used to gather Type I and Type II data. Their specific structure and format is basic to the operationalization of variables that are measured in evaluation. Because much time and energy is involved in the construction and standardization of instruments for collecting reliable and valid data, it is efficient for evaluators to use instruments that are already available. Consequently, instruments can be considered a resource for data gathering. They can be used for evaluating programs and practices, but only when they satisfy such minimum standards as relevance, reliability, and validity.

POTENTIAL USES

1. Direct Uses. Instruments are used directly if they are administered in accordance with instructions from the person or persons who devised them. They are *not* modified or adapted to different circumstances confronting the evaluative research study. Their format is exactly the same as it was in previous data collection. For example, an evaluator who decides to use the Minnesota Multiphasic Personality Inventory for assessing personality change uses that test in exactly the same form in which it is copyrighted.

Instruments that are used directly can produce either quantitative or qualitative data; the type of data depends on the particular instrument employed. In general, data can have all of the uses previously discussed for Type I and Type II secondary data resources. More typically, instruments are sought that produce data that reflect either current status or changes in programs, groups, and individuals.

For some instruments, such as standardized reading tests, there are normative data. These data can be used in the assessment of individual clients; for example, to indicate whether a particular client is above or below his or her age group in reading performance. In addition, an individual can be evaluated with respect to whether or not the change in his or her reading performance due to a social-work intervention is sufficient to show that he or she is performing at age level.

Instruments that produce qualitative data, such as projective tests or open-ended questions in a questionnaire, are useful for the clues they provide for diagnostic assessment and for the development of ideas about individuals and social programs. For example, a client is asked to write down his or her problems, if any; the reason for seeking social-work help; and so forth. That information is used by the social worker to assess the client's problems. These data inform the evaluator of the basis for the practitioner's assessment of the individual, and they also can be analyzed to determine the extent of agreement between the problems as originally expressed by the client and finally worked on by the social worker.

2. Indirect Uses. Indirect uses of an instrument are the uses made of it after it has been modified or has served as a stimulus.

    a. *Modified Instruments.* An instrument may not be directly useful; but parts of it might be, or it can be changed to make it more adaptable. A questionnaire contains apparently useful items regarding mental health, but some of the items appear to be culturally biased, or they may be outdated due to differences in language and social structures over time. An evaluator can modify the questionnaire and adapt it to the evaluation, providing that permission is obtained from the person or organization that has copyrighted the instrument.

b. *Instruments as Stimuli.* Instruments are also used indirectly when they serve as stimuli for program staff, for evaluative researchers, or both. They should stimulate ideas related to specific purposes. In the case of a program worker, an instrument can be used to facilitate ideas and discussion in assessment interviews. For example, a client has filled out a questionnaire regarding child-rearing decisions. The worker uses that to probe client responses and to generate discussion. The program evaluator also uses an instrument for generating ideas about what areas and what type of questions to include in an original questionnaire that she or he is constructing.

Criteria for use These criteria are adapted from the work of Tripodi and Epstein (1980 ch. 3). They reflect major dimensions to be considered by an evaluator in his or her decision to use available instruments. These criteria are: purpose, bias, reliability and validity, availability of norms, direct or indirect use, and practical constraints.

1. Purpose. The evaluator should find out what the original purpose of the instrument was and then determine whether it is compatible with his or her plans for the evaluation. For example, if the instrument can provide quantitative data for measuring change and the evaluator desires to measure change, he or she should consider using the instrument. The more relevant the instrument is to the evaluator's purpose, the more likely it is that he or she will use it. Relevancy is easier to assess if the evaluator is as specific as possible about what he or she wants to measure. He or she must form tentative operational definitions and explain in detail all considerations about the type of instrument, that is, whether it should produce qualitative or quantitative data, whether it can be used repeatedly to provide data for time-series analysis and measurement of change, and so forth.

2. Bias. Instruments may contain built-in biases that can lead to improper inferences about certain groups of respondents. These biases typically occur in relation to social, demographic, and cultural characteristics of the populations that programs serve. Hence there may be aptitude test biases in favor of middle-class as opposed to lower-class groups, gender biases in relation to vocational inventories, and cultural biases in tests purporting to assess an individual's social functioning.

The evaluator can appraise the instrument by looking for contents that appear to be biasing, and, if norms are available, by judging the extent to which the groups for which the instrument was originally standardized represent the population to whom the evaluator now wishes to administer the instrument. The evaluator should also look for and read published critiques, noting any possible biases. Finally, she or he can administer the instrument to a small sample of representative persons, asking them to indicate the extent to which there is bias.

3. Reliability and Validity. Evidence for reliability and validity should be appraised. The specific type of reliability must suit the evaluator's intended use of the instrument. For example, test-retest reliability is necessary for repeated applications of an instrument. Moreover, there should be at least qualitative evidence bearing on the content validity of the instrument. If evidence for reliability and validity is not available, but the instrument appears relevant to the evaluator's needs, she or he might consider administering the instrument to a small representative sample to produce empirical data. A worker evaluating his or her own practice with a client, for example, may be interested in using a scale for rating the client's degree of participation in treatment. The worker and his or her supervisor use the scale to independently rate a client's participation on the basis of information obtained from several tape-recorded interviews. The extent of percentage agreement in the ratings of the supervisor and the worker is used to indicate inter-observer reliability.

4. Availability of Norms. Norms are average measures of a specific population on a particular instrument. There are average scores on reading and intelligence tests, interest preferences, self-reports of anxiety, and so forth. The population for which the norms or averages are calculated should be standardized and representative of the clients in which the evaluator is interested. Hence the evaluator must look for a description of the population on which the norms were based, paying special attention to such characteristics as age, gender and social class. An instrument that is developed for rural, lower-class youth, for example, is not pertinent for urban, middle-class youth, and the attitudes of a boy scout troop may be different from those of juvenile delinquents in jail.

5. Direct or Indirect Use. An instrument should be appraised in relation to its potential for direct or indirect use. If it is to be used directly, then the evaluator should consider whether the resulting knowledge is not only accurate but also quantitative or qualitative. For quantitative-descriptive knowledge, the instrument should produce reliable and valid data, but content validity is sufficient for an instrument devoted to producing qualitative, hypothetical knowledge.

The evaluator also considers whether there are other devices for obtaining information by indirect means and whether they might be used in conjunction with, or in place of, the instruments. For example, exploratory information is gathered by direct questioning of a respondent as well as by discussing his or her responses to a particular questionnaire, and the combination of devices may be more efficient than using either one separately.

6. Practical Constraints. Practical constraints refer to factors that block the efficient and effective use of instruments. They include such variables as costs, staff training, and respondent requirements. An instrument requires costs in terms of money for its actual implementation and time for its proper administration. The use of standardized instruments involves financial costs for their purchase. Moreover, if program or evaluation staff must administer the instrument directly, the costs for their time must be taken into account. There may also be costs for conducting reliability and validity tests.

Some instruments require a great deal of training for their proper use. The time devoted to such training can be excessive. A clinical social worker evaluating his or her own practice may have neither the time nor the inclination to learn how to administer the Rorschach but may be able to use some questionnaires with little background or training.

Respondents should be able to understand the stimuli to which they are to respond. When a questionnaire is used, for example, the language, syntax, and grammar should be understood by the respondent. This is why the evaluator must carefully appraise the instrument's "language," determining whether it matches that of the respondents.

Finally, the evaluator and the evaluation consumer have to balance practical considerations against the level of knowledge desired and the instrument's potential for producing adequate amounts of valid information. Although the evaluator strives to economize, she or he should not plan to do so unless sound, acceptable levels of knowledge can be obtained.

CHAPTER FIVE
DEVELOPING NEW INSTRUMENTS FOR GATHERING DATA

The following questions should be answered by an evaluator before she or he decides to collect primary data:

1. Are any data and instruments already available?
2. Are those secondary data sources reliable and valid?
3. Are those data sources pertinent to the evaluator's objectives?
4. Are there sufficient resources for developing instruments and for establishing their reliabilities and validities?
5. How much time is available for developing instruments and gathering primary data?

If the evaluator answers the first three questions negatively and has data, she or he is confronted with decisions about which instruments to develop. Since most evaluators use a combination of primary and secondary data collection procedures (Shortell and Richardson 1978, p. 91), they must decide whether or not to collect original data for each evaluation objective and its corresponding variables. For example, an evaluator uses existing school records to appraise the academic performance of a teen-ager and a newly devised questionnaire to describe that person's attitudes toward school. Both academic performance, as defined by school grades, and attitudes toward school can be used for evaluating the achievement of a school social worker's treatment objectives.

Developing New Instruments for Gathering Data

In view of the above considerations, the purpose of this chapter is to present some issues involved in developing and using instruments. As mentioned in chapter 4, instruments are devices for gathering original or primary data and include the following:

1. Electrical or mechanical apparatuses for recording physical and physiological changes such as heart rate, weight, temperature, and galvanic skin response
2. Forms for recording self-reported observations of clients, counting frequencies of behavior, or rating intensities of attitudes
3. Interest and aptitude tests
4. Projective and semi-projective techniques

The major kinds of instruments that researchers construct for evaluative studies are questionnaires, interview schedules, rating scales, and observational forms. These instruments are used to collect data for evaluating social-work programs and practices; however, they vary with respect to their relative costs and the amounts and types of information they can generate. Hence, the evaluative researcher should know their advantages and disadvantages prior to adopting them in any particular study.

QUESTIONNAIRES

Questionnaires contain a series of questions, statements, or other stimuli to which persons are asked to respond, either by writing short, narrative responses or by selecting among the structured alternatives presented. They may be brief, with only a few questions and their response alternatives, or very long, requiring from a few minutes up to an hour for their completion.

They are administered in a variety of ways: by mail, over the telephone, in face-to-face interviews, and by hand delivery. The mailed questionnaire is sent to a respondent who is instructed to mail it to a specified address after she or he has completed it. An envelope stamped with the appropriate return address is often included with the questionnaire, or a postcard with a brief questionnaire on one side is sent out. Questionnaires are also used as schedules for structured interviews in which the interviewer reads the questionnaire to the respondent and records his or her responses to each question. These interviews can be conducted over the telephone or in face-to-face interaction between the researcher and the respondent. Finally, questionnaires are personally handed to one or more individuals in convenient locations where they are also returned to the researchers. For example, a group of individuals waiting for appointments in a social service agency or a group of individuals in a settlement house are given questionnaires and asked to complete them.

Format

The basic format of a questionnaire includes an *introduction, instructions*, a *series of questions* or verbal stimuli and response alternatives, and a *closing statement*.

A typical introduction briefly describes the purpose of the questionnaire, explains who or what is behind the evaluation, describes what the data will be used for, and discusses to what extent the data are confidential. When informed consent to participate in the evaluation is desired, a cover letter attached to the questionnaire describes the purpose of the study in one or two paragraphs, stressing the importance of the study and soliciting the voluntary participation of respondents. This example of an introduction to a questionnaire given to adult clients of a mental health agency by a staff social worker was adapted from Epstein and Tripodi (1977, p. 16):

Dear Client:
    The staff at our agency are interested in evaluating the extent to which you need and have used our agency's child-care services. This information will be used to help us decide whether we should expand or reduce these services, or keep them as they are.
    Your participation in this study is voluntary; however, we hope you choose to participate since this information is vital for our planning. Your answers to this questionnaire will be kept confidential and they will not affect any decisions regarding the services you are currently receiving.
    Please complete this brief questionnaire and return it to your social worker.
    Thank you for your cooperation.

Instructions can be included in the introduction and the closing, as well as with the questions and responses. For example, an introduction instructs respondents to indicate the extent to which they agree or disagree with the enclosed statements by circling the appropriate response for each: *SA* (strongly agree), *A* (agree), *D* (disagree) or *SD* (strongly disagree). The closing statement includes two instructions: (1) Look over your answers to make sure you have answered all the questions. (2) After you've completed the questionnaire, deposit it in the red box on the table by the social worker's office.

Instructions are also included in the body of the questionnaire. For some questions, an instruction is "write in" or "please specify," indicating a narrative response. For others, instructions specify which kind of structured response to give: "circle one," "check as many as are applicable," and so on.

The body of the questionnaire includes a series of questions, their response alternatives, and specific instructions where needed. The questions are arranged in logical order, leading from simpler questions to those requesting more personal information. The structure of the questions is open-ended or closed-ended. Open-ended questions seek narrative responses; structured questions include response alternatives for the respondent to choose from. Examples of open-ended stimuli are:

How would you describe your feelings about your social worker? How long have you been unemployed (in weeks)? What services provided by this agency do you find useful?

There are different types of closed-ended responses. These range from relatively simple "yes-no" and identification responses to scalar types of responses (Jenkins 1975, pp. 134-37; Epstein and Tripodi 1977, pp. 9-19). This question is answered by a "yes-no" response:

> Did you use the day care center today? Yes ___ No ___ (check the appropriate response).

An identification response is an answer to a specific question chosen from a list of alternatives. For example, this is an identifying question:

> Which of the following social agencies provide marital counseling: A. Family Service Agency B. Child Guidance Clinic   C. Legal Services Agency?

Scalar responses can be "agree-disagree," frequency or intensity, or comparative. Agree-disagree responses are devised to secure information about respondents' attitudes toward particular items. They vary from a simple agree-disagree scale to scales indicating different intensities of agreement and disagreement (very strongly agree, agree, mildly agree, etc.), as well as an undecided response. Frequencies and intensities of response are registered by numbers, percentages, and adverb modifiers. An evaluator of therapy with a client who dreads leaving his or her home, might ask questions like these:

> How many times did you leave your home by yourself this week: 0 ___, 1 ___, 2 ___, 3 ___, 4 ___, 5 ___, 6 or more ___?

> What percentage of the time have you been away from your home this week: 0%-25% ___, 26%-50% ___, 51%-75% ___, 76%-100% ___?

> How often have you left your home by yourself this week: not at all ___, rarely ___, occasionally ___, frequently ___?

Comparative questions seek information about an object or event in relation to itself, at varying periods of time, or to other events. For example, this question might be included in a questionnaire to determine clients' perceived changes in anxiety.

> Compared to the way you felt when you came to the agency one month ago, how anxious do you feel now: more anxious ___, less anxious ___, about the same ___?

In general, scaled responses of intensity are used for assessing attitudes, while numerical scales and percentage scales are employed for responses to questions about behaviors. Yes-no responses are most appropriate for reports on actions of simple behaviors, but they can also be used for indications of positive or negative beliefs.

The closing statement of a questionnaire may include, as previously mentioned, additional instructions or reminders about where to place the completed questionnaires. Or it may simply thank the respondents for cooperating in the research. Sometimes the researcher also specifies on when and where to get information about the results of the study.

Construction and Administration Issues

The construction of questionnaires is discussed at length in standard textbooks on research (see, for example, Moser 1965, pp. 210-45; Goldstein 1963, pp. 135-42; Isaac 1971, pp. 92-99; Jenkins 1975, pp. 131-53; and Epstein and Tripodi 1977, pp. 9-19). Those texts indicate that questionnaires should contain questions appropriate to the education of the respondents, and the questions should progress logically from relatively general ones to more specific ones. Each question should contain one thought only, and it should be worded clearly and unambiguously. Moreover, questions and their response systems should be nonbiased.

When constructing questionnaires, evaluators are confronted with many decisions, ranging from the length of the questionnaire to when and where it should be administered. The following questions exemplify the types of decisions facing evaluators:

1. Should open-ended as well as closed-ended questions be used?
2. Should middle responses (undecided) be used in Likert-type scales?
3. How can the return rate of mailed questionnaires be increased?
4. What is involved in pretesting?

Open-ended questions are useful when an evaluator is seeking ideas and hypotheses, or when she or he is not sure what the appropriate response alternatives are. For example, questions are asked about a client's experiences with a program or practice and about his or her perception of changes. Narrative responses can lead to hypotheses about "unanticipated consequences."

It takes time to respond to open-ended questions, and sufficient space must be included in a mailed questionnaire for each response. An excessive number of open-ended questions is fatiguing for respondents and may lead to lower completion rates. In addition, responses to open-ended questions need to be categorized and coded if the evaluator is seeking quantitative-descriptive information. This requires more procedures in data analysis and a corresponding increase in time expended. Precoded responses are preferable for quantitative descriptions, for they provide a standard frame of reference to which clients can respond.

Many investigators believe that respondents have a full range of choices to open-ended questions but not to closed-ended questions. One device that can be used to increase respondents' choices and keep them within the framework of a closed-ended response system is to specify several response alternatives and then add an "other (please write in)" response. For example, a client is asked from which source or sources she or he learned about the social agency where she or he is receiving services: physician, police, friend, newspaper, radio, relative, and other (please specify).

An "undecided" response is useful when it refers to a middle position between "agree" and "disagree" on a Likert-type scale:

> My social worker is interested in me as a person. Indicate the extent to which you agree or disagree with the following statement by circling that response which comes closest to your belief: A (agree), U (undecided), D (disagree).

An undecided response can be misleading, especially if it is used as a catchall category to include noncommittal, "don't know," or inapplicable responses. The more ambiguous the category, the more unreliable the response. Several procedures can be used to avoid this difficulty. First, include DK (don't know) and NA (nonapplicable) response alternatives with the other response choices. Second, increase the range of agree and disagree alternatives and eliminate the middle item (e.g., agree, mildly agree, mildly disagree, disagree). Third, use a different response system. As an illustration:

> Rate the degree to which your worker is interested in you as a person by checking that one response which comes closest to your belief: not at all interested ___, somewhat interested ___, definitely interested ___.

Return rate is the proportion of persons completing and returning a questionnaire to the evaluator. Typically, the lowest return rates occur with mailed questionnaires, whereas the highest return rates are obtained with face-to-face encounters in which questionnaires are read or administered to respondents. The completion and return of a mailed questionnaire depends on several factors. To begin with, the respondents must actually receive the questionnaire. Second, they must feel motivated to answer the questions. Third, they must be literate and understand the questions. Fourth, they must know where the questionnaire is to be sent. And fifth, they must have the necessary resources to return the questionnaire (e.g., a self-addressed envelope with appropriate postage). Therefore, the evaluator is careful to use questionnaires with literate populations only, and she or he attempts to involve respondents by emphasizing the importance of the information requested. If the population is not large, a nominal fee can be paid to respondents, and all postage costs are paid by the evaluator. To the extent possible, anonymity of respondents and confidentiality is assured. A second mailing of questionnaires can be considered. The response rate of mailed questionnaires increases from 10% to 19% on a second mailing (Isaac 1971), and this is worth the extra cost when the return is below 50%. If the response rate is below 65% to 80%, and the evaluator wants accurate quantitative-descriptions, she or he can increase the return rate further by using such procedures as telephone surveys of those who didn't return questionnaires.

Prior to using a questionnaire for program evaluation, the evaluator should pretest it. Many of the issues in construction and administration can be resolved in a pretest, which is a trial run on a small representative sample of the population for whom it is intended. The evaluator uses a pretest to estimate the return rate by running it through the procedures planned for the actual administration. To the extent possible, respondents are interviewed about the questionnaire itself. They're asked whether they understand the questions and the purpose of the study, how the questionnaire could be improved, and so forth. The responses to the questionnaires serve as clues for improvement. Many similar responses to the same open-ended question lead to categories that can be used for closed-ended responses. Incomplete responses signify either lack of understanding or material that is regarded as private. Reasons for incomplete portions of a questionnaire are ascertained through an interview. Excessive use of middle items on DK and NA responses can indicate that the questions are inappropriate or that the respondents were fatigued.

If a questionnaire is to be used for evaluating the effectiveness of a worker's practice, the worker can review the meanings of questions and the response systems with the client. This process is particularly important if the questionnaire is to be used over different periods of time, for it serves to tailor responses to the client, thereby increasing the questionnaire's content validity.

After a pretest is conducted, the evaluator carefully goes over the information from the questionnaires and the respondents and makes appropriate changes. If the changes are minor, suggesting slight alterations in format and administration, the questionnaire is used in the actual evaluation. Major changes require a second pretest.

Advantages and Disadvantages

Questionnaires are relatively easy to construct. They are efficient when used with literate populations because they provide information at less cost than other data-collection instruments. Mailed questionnaires are less expensive than questionnaires that are read to respondents. Face-to-face encounters, when the evaluator travels to the homes of respondents, are more expensive than telephone interviews. On the other hand, face-to-face exchanges in one central location for a brief period of time can be relatively less expensive, for travel costs are considerably reduced.

Response rates to questionnaires are lower than those to interviews. The information is extensive, but it cannot be as intensive as that gained from interviewing. This is because "probing" questions cannot be asked to clarify responses on a questionnaire. Moreover, the actual conditions in which respondents complete questionnaires are unknown. The physical and mental states of respondents may differ, and they may fill out questionnaires in different orders than from beginning to end. Hence responses to mailed questionnaires are less valid than responses to questionnaires read to respondents.

Responses to precoded questionnaires are quickly processed and analyzed. They are especially useful for quantitative descriptions of facts and attitudes. Sensitive personal information may not be accurately registered, for the use of a questionnaire is impersonal and relatively mechanistic in comparison with interview procedures. However, to evaluate the effectiveness of practice with one client, a questionnaire can be supplemented and verified with additional information obtained during the course of social-work interviews.

Since responses to questionnaires are based on self-reports of respondents, they are subject to response errors. For example, questions about the past are sufficient for obtaining data about the respondents' perceptions. However, they may be inaccurate as facts, for there may be faulty memories as well as perceptual distortions.

A series of generalized, global questions can lead to errors in judgment such as *halo effects*, where responses to some questions are influenced by previous questions. For example, client ratings of the degree of trustworthiness and loyalty in social workers can influence their ratings of helpfulness and friendliness. This occurs because of the generality of the response dimensions, as well as the implicit component of social desirability within the system. A few specific questions focused on time and place, along with a counterbalancing of positive and negative responses, reduces the possibility of the halo effect; but these errors cannot be completely minimized without additional information from interviews.

INTERVIEWS

Interviews are two-way exchanges between an interviewer and a respondent. The interviewer seeks responses to questions or other verbal stimuli that she or he presents orally. The exchanges can be face-to-face, with the interviewer physically present in interaction with the respondent, or they can be by telephone. Unlike questionnaires that are completed by respondents, interviews are recorded by the interviewer. In addition, interviewers observe visual as well as auditory cues that may be emitted by respondents: gestures, tone of voice, facial features, appearance, and so forth. Interview schedules are forms in which responses to interviews are recorded. The forms are similar to questionnaires but differ in that instructions are written for the interviewer rather than for the respondent. Structured interviews consist of specific topics for which information is sought, primarily through closed-ended questions and their response alternatives. They are most often used as devices to gather quantitative-descriptive information, as in surveys and experiments. Questionnaires read by an interviewer are used in structured interviews; however, an interview schedule may also include space for recording such observations as credibility of responses, obvious physical characteristics, and extent of cooperation.

Semistructured interviews include specific topics, but there is a combination of open-ended and closed-ended questions. These interviews are also regarded as focused interviews (Jenkins 1975, p. 135-36). They are used, for example, to derive information about the subjective experiences of clients who have participated in social-work treatment programs and to find out how well treatment plans are understood and implemented. Unstructured interviews are relatively nonspecific in topics covered and include mostly open-ended questions. They are used for exploratory purposes. For example, they are used with social-work clients to gain clues about unexpected effects due to social-work intervention.

Format

The format of an interview schedule varies with the purpose of the interview, its desired structure, and the extent to which mechanical devices are employed. Unstructured interview formats may consist of a list of open-ended questions that introduce the interview. The exact content of the interview may change from respondent to respondent, where additional questions are formulated during the interview to follow interesting leads of the respondent. The information can be tape recorded, or the interviewer can take notes or write his or her impressions after the interview. He or she then analyzes those qualitative data content for clues to possible new themes that can be followed up.

Principles for constructing structured interview schedules are similar to those for developing questionnaires (Goldstein 1963, pp. 123-50; Jenkins 1975; Weiss 1975; Tripodi and Epstein 1980, pp. 17-34). The basic notions about questionnaire format discussed previously are applicable here. In addition, it is important for the evaluator to distinguish whether the interview is to be used by many interviewers with many clients, as in program evaluation, or simply by one interviewer with one client. The greater the accuracy desired, the more standardized the interview should be. To increase standardization, provisions must be made to reduce variability due to interviewer error and to increase the validity of responses. This can be achieved to a certain degree by specifying precise instructions for interviewers and by collecting pertinent observational data.

The format of structured interview schedules used in program evaluation should specify the order of content areas and questions and the extent to which the interviewer can deviate from the printed questions. Interviewers are usually instructed to read questions exactly as stated and to refrain from explaining in detail the meaning of the questions. Instructions should be included as to when to seek clarifying responses and when to probe for more information. The conditions of the interview, in other words, time, place, interview length, and so on, also need to be specified.

Standardization is less necessary in semistructured and unstructured interviews, where the primary purpose is to generate ideas rather than provide accurate quantitative descriptions. The interviewer makes observations regarding the degree of cooperation and the validity of the responses obtained. She or he notes the state of the respondent, his or her appearance, and any other pertinent information that might verify or invalidate the responses. Precoded categories are used to make judgments about the client's situation. For example, in an interview conducted in an aged client's home, the condition of the home, number of rooms, and so on, as well as access to shopping facilities, are observed and recorded.

Construction and Administration Issues

Interviewing should be conducted in an efficient, professional manner. It relies on good rapport between the interviewer and respondent. Perhaps the most important ingredients are the extent to which the interviewer conveys the importance of the interview, his or her honesty and sincerity, and his or her assurances of confidentiality. A complete description of the interview process is provided by Kadushin, who discusses a variety of strategies and procedures for conducting different types of interviews (1972). Weiss presents a comprehensive analysis of the use of interviews in program evaluation (1975). Among the key issues in the conduct of interviews are the following:

1. To what extent can interview error be minimized?
2. Should the social worker engage in treatment activities while obtaining evaluative information?
3. When should telephone interviews be used?

Interview error is the result of invalid, inaccurate responses. According to Weiss there are four basic sources of error: predispositions of the respondent, predispositions of the interviewer, interview format and procedures, and interactions between interviewers and respondents (1975, pp. 364-67). The respondent may try to please or displease social-work staff by exaggerating program success or failure; she or he may be suspicious, hostile, and unwilling to participate completely; she or he may pretend to understand the language of the interview when she or he doesn't; and so forth. The interviewer may not comprehend the culture of those being interviewed or may be uncomfortable during the interview. There might be biasing elements in the format of the interview or in the place where the interview is held. For example, long, complex interviews can lead to fatigue, which in turn can increase response errors. Extremely positive or negative reactions of interviewers and respondents can lead to inaccurate responses that overestimate or underestimate the impact of social-work intervention on the respondents' lives.

Response errors can be reduced by strategies such as these:

1. The evaluator constructs a format with clear questions and response alternatives. She or he makes it clear that the respondent's answers are confidential and will not affect the service he or she receives. The respondent must believe that he or she can honestly answer questions that put social-work programs or practices in either a good or bad light. The evaluator constructs the format to minimize possible response errors such as unbalanced scales and ambiguous categories (Epstein and Tripodi 1977, pp. 9-19, 20-28).
2. Prior to actual interviews, the evaluator makes sure that interviewers understand the purposes of the interview and the procedures to be followed. If several interviewers are used, they are trained to correctly use the procedures without letting their own biases affect their work. Simulated interviews are useful for locating systematic interviewer biases.

3. During the interviews, the interviewer maintains a neutral posture in which she or he conveys her or his interest in what the respondents say without attempting to influence them with her or his own opinions. To clarify ambiguous or nonspecific responses, the interviewer uses probes, that is, neutral questioning that draws out further information. Questions like these might be used: "In what way?" "What do you mean by that?" "Could you tell me more?" "Could you give an example?"
4. If more than one interviewer is employed, the evaluator arranges to spot-check completed interview forms, checking for completeness and possible inconsistencies. This is particularly important for structured interviews that are conducted to derive accurate quantitative data.
5. After the interview, the evaluator codes open-ended responses that are to be used for quantitative descriptions. She or he develops coding procedures and then determines the inter-rater reliability of two or more independent judges, following the same systematic procedures used in content analysis (Tripodi and Epstein 1980, pp. 103-20).
6. Interviewers pretest the forms and procedures with a representative sample of respondents. They check for length of time it takes to complete the interview, possible difficulty of respondents with understanding the questions, feasibility of enlisting respondents' cooperation, and so forth. Any obvious problems and distortions are modified.

The primary purpose of interviews in evaluative research is to seek information. The interviewer is seeking help from the respondent in that she or he relies on the respondent's participation in the interview process. This is different from the use of interviews as a mode of social-work intervention, where social workers use interviews as a dynamic of treatment and to gather pertinent diagnostic information. When interviews are used to provide data for evaluative purposes, the social-work evaluator should not attempt to provide treatment during the interview. That would tend to distort the data. After the interview, the client-respondent is referred to social-work or other helping agencies, if he or she should so request.

This problem of dual roles and purposes is most likely to occur where clients are interviewed in follow-up studies. The evaluator and her or his staff should decide on their procedures for possible referrals, and those methods should be standardized for all interviewers.

The situation of the practitioner-evaluator is somewhat different. When the social worker is evaluating the effectiveness of her or his interventions with one client, she or he is both a practitioner and an evaluator. Although she or he attempts to gather unbiased information and to keep the evaluative role distinct from the helping role, there are instances when it may not be possible. Nevertheless, the social worker attempts to keep an evaluation interview separate from treatment interviews. If it is impossible to do so, and an unbiased evaluative interview is desired, then, although more costly, it may be advisable to have another social worker conduct the interview.

The costs of interviewing in follow-up studies are considerably reduced by using telephone rather than face-to-face interviews (Dillman 1978). Telephone interviewing is particularly recommended when the respondents have telephones and live in different geographical areas, and the length of the interviews is relatively short, say less than one-half hour. Telephone interviewing is made easier by sending the interview schedule to the respondent in advance and arranging for an interviewing time. Complex questions involving the use of visual and graphic stimuli cannot be used in telephone interviewing. However, a great deal of useful information can be produced. Pretesting should be employed to determine the feasibility of telephone interviews for particular situations. As a device for gathering follow-up information from ex-clients of social agencies, telephone interviews are especially useful for formative program evaluation. Relatively accurate information can be fed back to social agencies at moderate costs.

Advantages and Disadvantages

Interviews provide more verifiable, in-depth data than self-administered questionnaires. Face-to-face interviews are more likely to yield high response rates than questionnaires and telephone interviews when sensitive, personal information is sought. However, face-to-face interviews are more costly.

Valid data are obtained from interviewing because the interviewer can make observations that verify the respondents' verbal statements. Moreover, the use of probes clarifies responses in interviews, whereas ambiguous responses to questionnaires cannot be verified.

The interview is a less valid means of gathering data when the social worker is also the evaluator, for the mixing of roles can lead to contaminated information and socially desirable responses.

The unstructured interview is expensive, but it, along with participant observation, is best employed for developing new ideas and insights and for formulating hypotheses about programs and practices. The interview is a desirable data-gathering device with respondents who are not very literate, are from different cultural and class backgrounds, and are suspicious of the evaluation process.

Telephone interviews are relatively inexpensive, but they should be used with caution. Sudden calls from a representative of a social agency to ex-clients may be embarrassing, leading to lower response rates. Or, respondents may have other business and may not be able to speak for a period of time, unless it is previously arranged. Hence interviews are often interrupted prior to their completion.

Data from questionnaires and interviews reflect opinions and perceptions of respondents who may be "significant others," such as key program personnel and family members, as well as clients of social programs. Respondents' opinions are subject to faulty memory and subjective biases, whereas data obtained from ratings and observations of respondents by significant others are independent of those particular biases.

RATING SCALES

Rating scales are used for self-ratings on questionnaires and interview schedules and for rating others. They are a continuous sequence on which people or objects are placed in categories. A client may be rated as to his or her degree of involvement in treatment, for example, from no involvement (0) to a moderate degree of involvement (3), to maximum involvement (5). Scales vary in their response systems (e.g., verbal or numeric) and in the number of categories or scale points used in a dimension. Scales for rating others are particularly useful when questionnaires and interviews are both too costly and subject to distortion by respondents. Hence they can be used by social workers to rate clients, clients to rate significant others in their lives, parents to rate children, supervisors to rate employees, and so forth. Goal attainment scaling has been used by social workers for evaluating their practice efforts with particular clients (Kiresuk and Sherman 1968; Sherman 1977). Ellsworth has developed scales for evaluating psychiatric patients (1975), and other investigators have developed rating scales for program evaluation (see, for example, Lyerly and Abbot 1966; Shaw and Wright 1967; and Lake, Miles, and Earle 1973).

Format

Rating scales are structured response systems, and they are often used as items on questionnaires and interview schedules. When rating scales are used to rate others, their formats are similar to those of structured questionnaires in that there are instructions, dimensions to be rated, and response systems. They differ in their details.

Raters are carefully instructed regarding the standardization of rating procedures. They are told what information should be considered or ignored and what time periods should be covered. They are often provided with examples of ratings. As an illustration, raters are instructed to base their ratings of a child's degree of participation only on observations made within a 10-minute segment of a class and to focus specifically on his or her verbal utterances.

In addition to scalar responses in questionnaire formats, such as Likert-type scales and intensity-of-response scales, evaluators use scales for judging the presence of traits, for summative rating, and for goal attainment scaling. Examples of presence-of-trait scales would rate, for instance, whether or not clients have cried (Yes = 1, No = 0) or whether housing conditions are sanitary (Yes = 1, No = 0). These simple two-part scales can be expanded into scales with more degrees of intensity, or they can be used to form summated scales.

A summated scale is comprised of responses to two or more presence-absence scales. To illustrate, depression is considered to consist of these symptoms: insomnia, loss of appetite, sadness, unexplainable crying, and reduced sex drive. With detailed explanations of these five symptoms, and instructions about what information to include, raters can judge each symptom as being present (1) or absent, (0). Responses to the symptoms are totaled, leading to a scale of depression ranging from no symptoms observed (0) to all symptoms observed (5). This type of scale ranging from 0 to 5, differs from an intensity scale of depression where one rating is made.

Anchoring illustrations are verbal descriptions of steps on a scale. For example, a client's involvement in a community organization is described as "no involvement" or "the maximum degree of involvement." These descriptions of involvement can range from a sentence to a case illustration. Anchoring illustrations are provided in much greater detail when scales are used for rating others than when scales are used as response systems for questionnaires and interviews. This allows for a greater degree of standardization among the raters.

Goal-attainment scales are based on the specification of client objectives. The format includes five levels of predicted goal achievement: "much less than the expected level of outcome," "somewhat less than the expected level of outcome," "expected level of outcome," "somewhat more than the expected level of outcome," and "much more than the expected level of outcome." A social worker and his or her client negotiate objectives, and the social worker operationally defines the points (i.e., provides more specific anchoring illustrations) on the scale. For example, it is decided that "an expected level of outcome" for an adolescent who has had unexcused absences from school four out of five days a week would be three days of attendance for each of three weeks. "Much less than the expected level of outcome" would be three weeks of no attendance, while "much more than the expected level of outcome" would be perfect attendance for the three-week period.

Construction and Administration Issues

Shaw and Wright (1967), Ellsworth (1975), and Marsh (1978) all discuss the issues involved in the use of scales and goal-attainment scaling for evaluative research. Several of the prominent issues involved in scale construction are:

1. How many points should be included on a scale?
2. How can inter-rater reliability be obtained and preserved?
3. How can potential rating errors be reduced?
4. To what extent can goal-attainment procedures be used for evaluating programs as well as individual clients?

The number of points on a scale should be sufficient to allow for sensitivity and variation in response, but there should not be so many points that discrimination among them is difficult to achieve. Goldstein asserts that only "expert judges, trained in the use of rating scales can reliably use scales of more than seven or eight points..." (1963, p. 105). Generally, it is more difficult to achieve reliability in the middle portions of a scale, and this is often used as a reason to reduce the number of scale points. Since the greatest amount of reliability is obtained with two-part scales, one solution to the production of reliable and sensitive rating scales is to construct summated rating scales. Another solution is to rigorously adhere to procedures for the achievement of inter-rater reliability.

The degree of inter-rater reliability can be assessed by correlating the judgments of raters who, given the same information, independently use the same rating scales for judging the same objects. The higher the degree of correlation or percentage agreement, the greater the degree of inter-rater reliability (Tripodi and Epstein 1980, pp. 64-67). Procedures for increasing the amount of reliability include the precise definition of dimensions to be rated with clear, operationally-specific anchoring illustrations; detailed instructions regarding the standardization of ratings; and pretesting of instruments under simulated conditions where raters can discern the reasons for their unreliability and make appropriate adjustments. Most important, investigators must continue to recognize that a "reliable" set of rating scales can be used unreliably. That is, for a particular evaluation, the rater or raters may not rigorously stick to rating procedures and their evaluations are then subject to response errors. This means that it is advisable for evaluators to build in a system of spot-checks for reliability, particularly when many ratings are made over many points in time in time-series or single-subject designs. Response errors are a result of response tendencies of the raters, as well as of biases that may occur in the scalar response systems. More specifically, they are due to such factors as unbalanced scales, acquiescent response sets, social desirability, central tendency, halo effects, fatigue, and carelessness.

In some forms of evaluation, clients' self-reported ratings are used. These ratings are particularly subject to error based on the clients' reactions to the use of the scales. Response errors are reduced by using fewer scales, balancing response systems, using anchoring illustrations to exemplify scalar points, obtaining stable responses with repeated measures, and giving specific instructions to raters. Unbalanced scales include responses that "are more heavily weighted in one direction or another" (Tripodi and Epstein 1980, p. 197). A scale with more scale points in favor of improvement than deterioration for clients who experience social-work intervention is an unbalanced scale (see, for example, the Hunt and Kogan movement scale, 1952). Equalizing the number of scale points for improvement and deterioration reduces the possibility of bias in favor of improvement.

Some raters tend to agree more than disagree when asked to use Likert-rating scales. This acquiescent response tendency can be reduced by including a balance of positively-worded and negatively-worded items or dimensions. For example, a positively-stated item is "my social worker is interested in me as a person"; a negatively stated item is "my social worker is rarely on time for appointments with me." This procedure also reduces halo effects, which, as mentioned before, are errors resulting from responses generalized from one scale to another. Halo effects are also reduced by having the raters judge specific dimensions rather than abstract, global ones that can be interpreted by respondents as socially desirable. The traits "reliable" and "helpful," as an illustration, are more susceptible to halo effects than "He consistently keeps his appointments on time" and "She gives useful advice when asked."

Errors resulting from the tendency to avoid extremes and to use central portions of scales are minimized by either avoiding the use of midpoints or increasing the number of scale points. A scale with the points of "always," "sometimes," and "never" is likely to lead to an excessive use of "sometimes." It can be changed to a scale that includes more scale points as well as more precise anchoring illustrations, for example, "always" (96% of the time or more), "almost always" (81% to 95%), "frequently" (51% to 80%), "infrequently" (21% to 50%), "almost never" (6% to 20%), and "never" (0% to 4%).

Errors are most likely to occur when the raters are tired, bored, or not interested in the task. These errors can be reduced by decreasing the number of ratings made during any one observation, by providing rest periods, and by performing reliability checks when a large number of ratings are made.

Goal-attainment scaling provides a format that can be made operationally specific for an individual client. A social worker can rate the extent to which she or he has achieved her or his goals (Marsh 1978). The use of goal-attainment scaling for program evaluation is somewhat controversial, however. Seaberg and Gillespie argue that the procedure has not been validated and recommend that it not be used (1977), while Kiresuk and Sherman assert that it can be used with caution (1977). So long as the workers and clients have the same objectives, goal-attainment scalings for clients can be continued. On the other hand, when client objectives are dissimilar, the results should not be totaled.

Advantages and Disadvantages

Rating scales are used to obtain measures for evaluating change from the perspectives of social workers, significant others, and clients. They are found in questionnaires, interview schedules, and systematic observation; and they are relatively efficient. The judgments they provide by significant others serve as data to validate the self-reports of social-work clients.

The primary advantage of rating scales is that they provide more sensitive measures for assessing opinions, attitudes, and traits than yes-no response systems. However, their basic disadvantage is that they are subject to response errors resulting from biases in the response systems and possible distortions by the raters. Rating scales are less accurate for rating clients' moods than are client self-reports, but they are excellent sources of observation data when there is evidence of reliability and validity.

OBSERVATIONS

Observations are data based on visual or auditory sensory impressions. The social worker observes his or her client by seeing what she or he does and by listening to what she or he says. Observational data are used for evaluating changes in individual clients, as well as observing changes in groups of clients who may be in closed settings, that is, residential treatment centers, settlement houses, recreational facilities, classrooms, and so forth. Rosen and Polansky discuss a number of different settings in which observational data are gathered (1975), and Howe indicates that clients themselves can participate in data-gathering efforts in clinical evaluations by observing themselves and significant others with whom they interact (1976).

Unstructured observations are not based on some precoded system of classification. The social worker observes his or her client, recording what he or she sees either during or after the observation. These recordings of worker-client and client-significant-other interactions are either narrative impressions written by the worker or written or spoken words of the client, the latter taped or filmed. In contrast, systematic observations or structured observations are those that are recorded on forms with rating scales, precoded categories, or both. An evaluator observes, for example, the degree of cooperation manifested by a client and records his or her observation on a rating scale of cooperation. Or, in a content analysis of a tape-recorded interview he or she counts the length of time spoken by the client, the number of self-deprecatory statements, and so forth.

Observers can be participating or nonparticipating with the objects of observation. The clinical social worker who attempts to effect changes with a client, as well as observe those changes, is a participant observer. Nonparticipant observation occurs when there is no interaction between the observer and the observee.

Format

There are three basic forms for recording observations: narrative accounts, scales, and categorical systems (Rosen and Polansky 1975, p. 160). Narrative accounts are written impressions of what is observed, and they serve primarily as a qualitative description and a source of ideas for hypotheses about client's needs and problems and social-work interventions. What is required for the research is a good supply of paper and pens or pencils, a tape recorder, and other mechanical devices. Principles and issues involved in constructing rating scales were discussed previously; they are also applicable to the use of rating scales for recording observations. The forms for constructing categorical systems include the definition of instructions, operational definitions of the categories, and space for recording (Tripodi and Epstein 1980, pp. 54-74). Instructions indicate when the observer should observe (e.g., between the hours of 9:00 A.M. and 10:00 A.M. on Mondays in a psychiatric ward), which item of information she or he should pay attention to, and how the observations should be recorded. Recordings are made on a tally sheet where space is provided for counting the number of times an observational event occurs, or on a checklist where the presence or absence of an event during a particular time period is indicated. For example, the group worker counts the number of times a client initiates conversation with other members of a group, or a school social worker observes whether or not a student leaves the classroom. As with other instruments, forms for systematic observation should be carefully constructed (Epstein and Tripodi 1977, pp. 42-53), and the observers should be trained to foster the gathering of reliable and valid data. Operational definitions are specified precisely, and observers are provided with examples of events to be observed.

Construction and Administration Issues

As previously indicated, observational data are subject to the same types of problems that confront rating scales. In addition, evaluators who use observational data should be aware of questions such as these:

1. What is an appropriate unit of analysis?
2. To what extent are data influenced by participant observers?
3. For what time period should observations be made?

For purposes of observing social interactions, the unit of analysis can be specified in terms of verbal, nonverbal, or paraverbal communication (Rosen and Polansky 1975). Within each type of communication the unit of analysis can represent different levels. For example, a worker analyzes the contents of an interview by observing linguistic features of language such as phonemes (Labov and Fanshel 1977), words (Kogan 1951), thought units and sentences (Marsden 1966), or the entire interview itself. The evaluator must specify what to use, because if various observers use different units, the results will be unreliable. The appropriate unit is the one which most clearly provides data pertinent to the variables for assessing effectiveness. Phonemes are too small if the evaluator is seeking a change in his or her client's expressions of hostility, but the entire interview is too long a unit to use. In thinking of an appropriate unit of analysis, the evaluator should look for a unit that is small enough to increase the sensitivity of observation but not so small that the costs of recording data are prohibitive.

Participant observers can influence the people they are observing. There can be direct influences that stem from the participant observer's social interactions with the observer or indirect influences that are products of the imaginations of observees in the presence of the observer. The potential distortions in observation cannot be completely eliminated, but they can be reduced by these procedures:

1. The observer refrains from making statements that directly influence the observations.
2. The observer doesn't record any observations until the observee is used to his or her presence and is more interested in the social interactions than in the process of observation.
3. The observer arranges to have samples of the observational interactions recorded, and estimates inter-observer reliability by comparing observations with an independent observer.

Sampling of observations is necessary since it is impossible to obtain constant data over all time periods. An adequate time sample is one that represents the domain of time to which one wishes to generalize. Time samples depend on the nature of observed data, practical constraints, and judgments regarding the length of time sufficient for generalization. For example, a time sample for observations of a student in a classroom that meets one hour a day, five days per week, consists of the following: observations are taken on Tuesday, Thursday, and Friday for thirty minutes. They are taken in three parts—the second, fourth, and fifth 10-minute segments within each hour. This time sample is intended to represent the domain of classroom activity for a given week. It could be drawn as a purposive sample or by use of random procedures (e.g., for selecting three out of five days, and one-half of the six 10-minute time intervals within a one hour period).

Advantages and Disadvantages

Observations are particularly useful when self-reports of respondents obtained through questionnaires or interviews are unreliable and the competency of the respondents is in question. For example, observational data are obtained for making assessments of infants, emotionally disturbed persons, and those regarded as mentally incompetent. When client behavior is the variable of interest, systematic observations are probably the most valid source of data collection. Systematic, nonparticipant observations provide a relatively nonbiased description of social interactions, and they can be easily assessed for reliability (see Howe 1976, and Ciminero, Calhoun, and Adams 1977). However, observations can't be used to describe directly the moods and attitudes of clients.

Participant observations provide a frame of reference based on experience, in which the evaluator develops ideas about the implementation of social-work interventions. They also provide vivid accounts of the phenomena that are the objects of evaluative research. In addition, observational data indicate possible side effects and problems with internal validity that aren't controlled in the evaluator's implementation of his or her research design. However, data from participant observation may reflect the biases of the observer with respect to his or her perceptions and influences on those he or she is observing (Mills 1970). Quantitative-descriptive data are especially subject to those biases.

Systematic observations are expensive. They require rigorous enforcement of procedures, constant checking of reliability, and training of observers. The smaller the unit of analysis and the larger the period of time covered, the greater the costs. However, the costs are reduced when standardized systems, such as Bales' interaction process analysis, are used (Bales 1970).

CHAPTER SIX
THE LOGIC OF EVALUATIVE RESEARCH DESIGN

Evaluative research designs include plans, structures, and strategies for obtaining information pertinent to the questions and hypotheses of evaluation. Their purpose is to provide a set of systematic procedures for producing quantitative and qualitative data for the development, modification, and expansion of knowledge about policies, programs, and practices. While chapters 7 and 8 contain a number of research designs for evaluating practices and programs, this chapter focuses on basic assumptions and procedures that enable the evaluator to devise these research designs. It presents a logic for choosing research designs for evaluating individuals (single-subject designs) or programs (group designs), discusses criteria for developing levels of knowledge and empirical generality, and reviews selected procedures for producing empirical generality.

THE PROCESS OF FORMULATING RESEARCH DESIGNS

When applied to evaluation, the formulation of research designs involves a process that includes a number of interrelated decisions (Tripodi 1981). These can be roughly outlined as follows:

1. The evaluator chooses the appropriate unit for evaluation, whether a particular client, a group of clients, or a combination of both. For example, a social worker interested in the effectiveness of his or her practice with one client appropriately uses single-subject designs (chapter 7). A worker interested in the effectiveness of an agency program employs group designs, where more than one subject is involved at one period of time (see chapter 8).
2. The evaluator specifies the evaluation objectives. These are delineated in relation to the practice or program objectives of the social worker (see chapters 2 and 3). The evaluator groups multiple objectives into similar and dissimilar objectives and ranks the dissimilar objectives in terms of importance for the consumer of evaluation. This is done because different research designs might be used to provide information for different objectives. Moreover, the evaluator may not have enough resources to adequately pursue all of the objectives, and ranking them helps to focus research designs on those considered most important.
3. The evaluator categorizes the evaluation objectives selected for study into levels of knowledge: level 1, hypothetical-developmental; level 2, quantitative-descriptive; level 3, correlational; and level 4, cause-effect (see chapter 1). Having selected knowledge levels, the evaluator decides on the kinds of evidence appropriate for producing the desired knowledge.
4. The evaluator specifies relevant criteria for the chosen knowledge levels: level 1, hypothesis researchability; level 2, measurement accuracy, reliability, and validity; level 3, empirical relationships; and level 4, time order and control of internal validity factors. These criteria are essential for choosing appropriate research designs.
5. The evaluator decides on the degree of desired generality. The scope of the research may be formative or summative. When the intent is summative, generality is necessary, and the evaluator must consider procedures and empirical evidence that are useful for making valid generalizations.
6. If the evaluator seeks generalizable knowledge, she or he specifies criteria for generality as well as procedures for satisfying them. She or he delineates criteria for each knowledge level and incorporates systematic procedures into the research designs.
7. The evaluator devises research designs geared to the desired knowledge levels and degrees of generality and modifies and implements them in relation to available resources, costs, and time.

CRITERIA FOR DEVELOPING KNOWLEDGE

Level 1: Hypothesis Researchability

Hypothetical-developmental knowledge is produced when the criterion of hypothesis researchability is met. Since the goal of level 1 knowledge is the production of hypotheses pertinent to programs and practice, it is most important that those hypotheses be applicable and operational. Hypotheses are applicable when they are relevant and when they can be implemented and tested in social-work practice. These criteria are used to assess the extent of hypothesis researchability, that is, the degree to which a hypothesis can be tested:

1. The concepts included in the hypothesis are operationally definable, and there are available techniques and procedures for measuring them. For example, in this hypothesis, "anxious clients who receive two casework contacts per week are more likely to exhibit reduced anxiety than those who receive one casework contact every two weeks," the concepts of casework contact (the independent variable) and anxiety (the dependent variable) can be operationalized so that measurements can be obtained. The concepts are precisely defined, with a specification of all the operations necessary for translating them into variables. And there are techniques, such as questionnaires and rating scales, that can be used for gathering and categorizing data related to anxiety.
2. The relationship between the concepts is clearly stated. It should be made clear whether or not the hypothesis posits a correlational or cause-effect relationship. To the extent possible, the magnitude and direction of the relationship are indicated. For example, "there is a strong inverse and statistically significant association between the number of casework contacts and the degree of client anxiety" specifies the relationship between independent and dependent variables, as well as indicating its strength and magnitude.
3. The concepts are distinct and not overlapping. In the hypothesis that an information and referral service (independent variable) can increase clients' knowledge of financial aid programs (dependent variable), the independent and dependent variables are conceptually and operationally distinct.
4. The hypothesized phenomenon occurs frequently, so it can be observed. This means that the phenomenon occurs often enough that the evaluator can study the extent to which it changes. It is impractical to study the effects of a program on changing the number of suicide attempts for a specific age group and subculture if there has been no previous evidence of suicide attempts for that particular group. For either program or practice evaluation, the independent variable is identified and observed. However, the dependent variable or variables may or may not be observable.

5. For evaluating groups of clients, hypotheses specify a particular population, time, and place. Specific hypotheses are more easily operationalized and tested by research procedures than vague, unclear hypotheses. Obviously, hypotheses pertaining to the effectiveness of a practice technique with one client cannot be specified by population characteristics, but they can be specified by time and place. For example, a social worker can hypothesize where his or her practice is more effective, in the client's home or the worker's office.

Level 2: Measurement Accuracy, Reliability, and Validity

Quantitative-descriptive knowledge is generated when there are clearly-specified variables and questions, as indicated for level 1, plus accurate measurement. Accurate, reliable, and valid measurement of change variables (dependent variables) is necessary for obtaining all levels of knowledge except level 1. This is true whether the knowledge is for formative or summative purposes, or whether it is for assessing the effectiveness of social-work practice with one or with more clients. Accuracy of measurement refers to the accuracy of processing data. As previously stated, reliable measures are relatively free from error, and they produce consistent results on repeated application of a measurement instrument. For evaluating groups of clients, as in program evaluation, test-retest reliability is necessary when the evaluator employs repeated measures of a dependent variable to assess change. Split-half reliability and inter-observer agreement are more appropriate when measurements are made at one point in time. Inter-observer reliability is employed for assessment of an individual, but split-half reliability and test-retest reliability procedures do not lead to interpretable correlations, since there is only one subject. In the absence of empirical data, the evaluator should provide evidence that the measurement procedures are clearly operationalized and standardized. Moreover, she or he should be able to demonstrate that the data-gathering procedures are nonbiasing.

Measurements should be valid in terms of their contents. When many clients are subjects for evaluative research designs, it is preferable to have some evidence of predictive validity such as statistically significant correlations with independent criterion variables. For example, self-reported knowledge of a reduction in alcoholic consumption should be highly correlated with the observations of significant others.

Level 3: Empirical Relationship

An empirical relationship between a program or practice component, an independent variable, and a dependent variable is obtained when the following types of evidence occur:

1. There is statistical significance between the average differences of the distributions of one variable with respect to another.

2. There is a correlation coefficient that is statistically significant.
3. There is a correlation of sufficient magnitude to result in a relatively high degree of predictability (Tripodi 1981).

For example, an evaluator shows that an experimental group receiving social casework has a statistically significant greater proportion of clients who increase their positive self-perception than a control group that doesn't receive any social-work intervention. The statistical significance of the association between the variables is tested by using a *chi square* statistic. A further illustration is that of a social worker evaluating his or her effectiveness with one client in terms of changes in anxiety. A statistically significant shift in the time-series of measurements of anxiety at baseline (i.e., when there is no intervention) compared with the time-series of measurements during intervention is demonstrated by a statistic such as the binomial (Kazdin 1978).

Cook and Campbell (1979) list a number of threats to statistical conclusion validity, which refers to the extent to which inferences about whether two variables covary are valid.* These threats relate to the adequacy of statistical hypothesis testing, characteristics of respondents, and the setting of research. They are as follows: low statistical power, violated assumptions of statistical texts, error rates in multiple comparisons, measurement reliability, reliability of treatment implementation, random irrelevancies in the experimental setting, and heterogeneity of respondents. These criteria are useful for determining the extent to which there is an empirical relationship for making causal inferences in experimentation. Other detailed discussions about inferring empirical relationships are presented in Blalock's *Causal Inference in Non-Experimental Research* (1967) and Susser's *Causal Thinking in the Health Sciences* (1973).

Correlations between variables are more likely to be used in program evaluations where there are usually many clients exposed to the social-work interventions. Statistical significance between groups is obtained with a small degree of correlation when there is a large number of subjects. Hence the evaluator should observe the strength of correlation as well as its statistical significance. The amount of evidence for an empirical relationship is proportional to its degree of predictability, which can be roughly estimated by squaring the correlation coefficient (r^2) and multiplying by 100. Correlations ranging from 0.3 to 0.5 can be regarded as indicative of some evidence for an empirical relationship; correlations of 0.7 or higher provide 49% predictability or higher, which is a strong degree of relationship.

Level 4: Time Order and Internal Validity

To achieve correlational knowledge, there must be evidence that the criteria for knowledge levels 1-3 have been met. Cause-effect knowledge is obtained when correlational knowledge is evident and the criteria of time order and internal validity are satisfied.

*This is intended for advanced students in evaluative research.

The criterion of time order refers to the relationship between interventions as independent variables and measures of effectiveness as dependent variables. The evaluator should show that changes in independent variables (e.g., from no program to a particular program) occur prior to changes in dependent variables. For example, an evaluator should document that changes in a client's knowledge about available social services occurred after the social-worker intervention, rather than before it.

Internal validity is a concept developed by Campbell and Stanley (1966). It refers to variables, other than the independent variables, that explain observed changes in the dependent variables. The degree of internal validity is proportional to the extent to which those other variables can be controlled. The fewer alternative explanations there are, the greater the likelihood that the independent variables are causally related to the dependent variables.

The evaluator should provide information about his or her research procedures and assumptions in addition to empirical evidence showing that potentially influential internal-validity factors are controlled. According to Campbell and Stanley (1966) there are eight sets of variables that constitute internal validity threats:

1. *History.* These variables affect, or occur between, measurements of the dependent variables. For example, a client's increased knowledge of drugs results from information she or he receives from her or his neighbors, rather than from the social-work intervention.
2. *Maturation.* These variables refer to physical changes that occur within research participants over time, such as developmental growth, fatigue, and so on. For example, a client reports differences in his or her behaviors and moods depending on the extent to which he or she is physically ill.
3. *Instrumentation.* These variables are indicative of the lack of standardized procedures in the evaluator's process of obtaining measures. For example, observations of clients' cooperation with staff in a residential treatment setting show changes over time due to different biases by different observers.
4. *Initial Measurement Effects.* This refers to the possibility that responses to repeated administrations of an instrument may be affected by responses to the first administration. Having responded to the items in a personality test, the client may think about those items and answer them differently the second time, not because she or he has changed, but because she or he has reconsidered their meaning.
5. *Statistical Regression.* This refers to the tendency of groups selected on the basis of extreme measurement scores to regress to more average scores. For example, clients whose average measures of aggression are extremely high show an average reduction in aggression in a second observation. This regression effect occurs whether or not an independent variable is present. A related phenomenon is that of a *statistical trend.* A client may show high anxiety on the first test, reduced anxiety on the second test, a still further reduction on the third test, and so on. This downward trend occurs for a particular client, irrespective of whether a social-work intervention has been delivered.
6. *Selection Biases.* These variables refer to selection differences between comparison groups. For example, a social program is designed to reduce the consumption of alcohol in clients. An experimental group receives

the program, while a comparison group doesn't. The groups are selectively different prior to program intervention, in that the experimental group contains more females who are more highly educated. These differences in gender and education may be responsible for differential changes in alcohol consumption.
7. *Experimental Mortality.* This refers to a differential loss of research participants in two or more comparison groups, which results in differences in variables that are potentially related to the dependent variable. For example, an experimental and a control group both have equivalent distributions of gender and age prior to an experiment. During the course of the experiment, differential dropout rates in the experimental and control groups result in the two groups not being equivalent in gender and age.
8. *Interactions.* This refers to the combined effects of any of the seven factors already discussed. For example, interactions between history, maturation, and selection biases occur when participants in comparison groups differentially take medication that combines with other selective factors to produce various degrees of fatigue. This, in turn, affects observations of dependent variables, such as measurements of anxiety and depression.

Cook and Campbell have added several other internal validity factors to this list (1979, pp. 53-55). These are:

1. "Ambiguity about the direction of causal inference" (there should be evidence regarding the time order of interventions followed by changes in the dependent variables)
2. "Diffusion or imitation of treatments" (subjects in control groups may receive treatment by talking with subjects in experimental groups)
3. "Compensatory equalization of treatments" (reluctance of program personnel and participants to tolerate perceived inequities when experimental groups receive desired services and control groups don't)
4. "Resentful demoralization of respondents receiving less desirable treatments" (control-group members do worse than experimental group members because they are demoralized and resentful that they are not receiving desired interventions)

Procedures for ruling out these internal validity threats are used in experimentation as well as in single-subject designs. They include the use of baselines and repeated measurements, client control and comparison groups, manipulation of social-work intervention variables, randomization, and so forth. Procedures for ruling out Campbell and Stanley's eight internal validity threats are discussed in subsequent chapters. Techniques for minimizing threats of additional internal validity factors are discussed in detail by Cook and Campbell in their treatise on *Quasi-Experimentation* (1979).

CRITERIA FOR GENERALITY*

Generality refers to the extent to which knowledge can be generalized from one program or practice to other programs or practices. Whereas generality is not essential

*Although this section can be read by beginning students, it is primarily intended for advanced students in evaluative research.

for formative evaluation, in which the results are intended only for a particular agency, program, worker, or client, it is paramount for summative evaluation. There are several types of generality that roughly form a continuum related to levels of knowledge: conceptual generality, representativeness, replications, and external validity control. For inferring generality of cause-effect knowledge (level 4), all of these types are pertinent. Representativeness, replications, and conceptual generality pertain to quantitative-descriptive knowledge (level 2) and correlational knowledge (level 3). Conceptual generality is relevant for hypothetical-developmental knowledge (level 1).

Level 1: Conceptual Generality

Conceptual generality is the extent to which concepts and hypotheses can be generalized for use in situations other than those in which the evaluation takes place (Tripodi 1974, p. 60). For hypotheses to be useful, they should be generalizable to other situations and other clients. A program based on a token economy is not bound to specific program contents. It is based on learning and reinforcement theory, concepts which can be generalized from residential treatment settings to classrooms, groups, and so forth.

Level 2: Representativeness

The criterion of representativeness refers to the extent to which the sample of participants in the evaluative research study is representative of a target population. A sample is representative if it is a replica of the population with respect to relevant characteristics (Labovitz and Hagedorn 1981, pp. 57-67). For example, a representative sample of a population of mental patients should show proportions equivalent to the population on variables such as diagnosis, length of hospital stay, number of previous hospital admissions, age, gender, social class, and race. If a sample is not representative on relevant variables, the degree of generality is restricted. That is, an evaluator who studies a nonrepresentative sample of clients and describes quantitatively the number of interviews they received, their average age, and so forth cannot generalize those descriptions.

Level 3: Replication

Correlational knowledge can be generalized by providing evidence of conceptual generality and representative sampling. The degree of generality can also be strengthened by replications, that is, repeated evaluative research studies that provide consistent results. Replications are obtained when the empirical correlations in a number of research samples result in approximately the same strength, direction, and level of statistical significance (Tripodi 1974, p. 67). For generalizing correlational knowledge based on the use of single-subject designs, Hersen and Barlow suggest that "...one successful experiment and three successful replications will usually be sufficient to generate systematic replication on topographically different behaviors in the same setting or the same behavior in different settings" (1976, p. 334).

Level 4: External Validity Control

Cause-effect knowledge is the most difficult level to generalize. In addition to satisfying criteria for the first three levels, it must meet the criterion of external validity control. Campbell and Stanley (1966) define external validity as the extent to which inferences can be made to larger populations, and they have determined four factors that should be controlled to increase external validity:

1. *Interaction between initial measurement and the independent variable.* There are combined effects of these variables that are specific to a given evaluation study and not generalizable to other populations.
2. *Interaction between selection biases and the independent variable.* The participants in the evaluation respond differently to the social-work interventions than other potential clients.
3. *Reactive effects of experimental arrangements.* This refers to the possibility that some clients may change due to their expectations and beliefs, positive or negative, about the social program or intervention they receive. This belief in authority, suggestibility, or faith is often regarded as a "placebo effect."*
4. *Multiple-treatment interference.* This refers to the possibility that clients may be receiving programs and interventions from sources other than the particular program or practice being evaluated. A social worker wishes to evaluate the effectiveness of his or her intervention on a particular client, but it is difficult to generalize the results when the intervention takes place in a setting where other interventions or treatments are also being applied. A patient in a psychiatric hospital may be receiving medication, group therapy, occupational therapy, and so forth.

PROCEDURES FOR INFERRING GENERALITY**

Level 1: Qualitative Judgment

The extent to which conceptual generality is achieved depends on qualitative judgment. This judgment involves a consideration of whether or not hypotheses can be generalized to other situations. Generalizations can be made to workers, clients, interventions, and their combinations. If hypotheses are researchable in contexts other than those in which they originated, they are conceptually generalizable. For example, a social worker may, in working with one client, hypothesize that assertiveness training for the client, whose spouse is abusive, leads to an increase in spouse abuse. A worker in a different agency can test that assertion if she or he believes it ethical to do so. The concept of assertiveness training can be operation-

---

*Cook and Campbell (1979) have extended the concept of external validity to include construct validity. Their discussion combines notions of representativeness and replication. It is not used here because it appears to be based on generalizing cause-effect knowledge only, and it doesn't distinguish generalizations based on different levels of knowledge.

**This section is primarily intended for advanced students in evaluative research.

alized, manipulated, and taught in a variety of different settings; while spouse abuse can be measured by systematic procedures and generalized. In determining the extent of generality, the social worker follows these steps:

1. Determine the extent to which the hypothesis is researchable.
2. Specify situations, (i.e., agencies, workers, etc.) to which one wishes to generalize.
3. Decide whether the hypothesis is researchable in those situations. The extent of conceptual generality is proportional to the number of situations in which the hypothesis is applicable.

Level 2: Sampling Procedures

There are three basic methods for producing evidence of representativeness. The first procedure is a simple census or enumeration of every element in the population to which one wishes to generalize. In this special case, the sample is the population and the issue of generality is irrelevant. With the second technique, an evaluator compares a sample, obtained by whatever means, to a finite population for which there is available knowledge of the statistical distributions of relevant variables. For example, social workers in a family service agency wish to generalize their results to social workers in other family service agencies. Relevant variables are age, gender, education and professional training, years of experience, expectancy of success, and case-load size. Distributions of those variables are compared between the family service agency workers and the larger population. If the distributions are not statistically different, the workers in the family service agency are representative of other workers. However, they are representative only on those known variables.

A third set of procedures is the use of sampling strategies for selecting representative samples. For a detailed consideration of sampling issues, refer to Cochran, Mosteller, and Tukey, who provide a lucid discussion of the basic elements of sampling theory (1970); Stephan and McCarthy, who discuss the statistical foundations of sampling theory in relation to surveying opinions and attitudes (1963); and Yeakel and Ganter, who illustrate the use of sampling techniques in social work research (1975). Here it is sufficient to indicate some of the basic strategies of sampling to obtain representative samples.

Sampling procedures are divided into probability and nonprobability sampling. In probability sampling, the degree of error in obtaining representative samples can be estimated, whereas this is not possible in nonprobability sampling. The three basic types of probability sampling are simple random sampling, stratified random sampling, and multistage or area sampling. The degree to which a sample is representative of a population depends on "the degree of precision to which the population is specified, the adequacy of the sample, and the heterogeneity of the population," (Labovitz and Hagedorn 1981, p. 59). Large samples from well-defined, homogeneous populations are more likely to be representative than very small samples from vaguely defined and heterogeneous populations. The chances of obtaining representative samples are increased when probability sampling is employed. In simple random sampling, the elements of a population are defined, and each element and each combination of elements has an equally likely chance of being included in the sample. A random process, such as random number tables or lottery, is used to draw the sample. The evaluator estimates by statistical-sampling theory the size of sample sufficient for obtaining a representative sample with a specified degree of error. For example, if he or she is choosing a sample to be representative of a known population proportion (P) of a given size (N) and a 0.05 probability level with a tolerable error of E, the following formula is used to estimate sample size, n (adapted from Walker and Lev 1953, p. 70):

$$n = \frac{4Z^2 NP(1-P)}{NZ^2 P(1-P) + (N-1)E^2} \quad \text{where } Z = 1.96.$$

A sample size for a population of 10,000, with $P = 0.5$ and E set at 0.10, is calculated as:

$$n = \frac{(4)(1.96^2)(10,000)(.5)(.5)}{(4)(1.96^2)(.5)(.5) + (10,000-1)(.10^2)} = 370.$$

Hence a simple random sample of 370 cases is sufficient for obtaining a representative sample with respect to the population proportion, P.

A stratified random sample is more precise than a simple random sample. It involves dividing a larger population into two or more levels, for example males and females; listing the subpopulations within each level; and randomly sampling within each level. With stratified random sampling, the evaluator builds representativeness of the variable being stratified into his or her sample. The subpopulations can be sampled either proportionately (i.e., the proportions of males and females in the sample are identical to their population proportions) or disproportionately. So long as the random process is used, the resulting samples are apt to be representative on all known variables at specified probability levels, such as 0.05, which was used above in the calculation of sample size.

Simple random sampling and stratified-random-sampling procedures depend on having accurate lists of all the elements in the population. This is possible when one is sampling agency clients and workers where there are up-to-date lists. However, lists may not be available for community surveys of large populations. Multistage or area sampling is used to overcome this problem. It is the least efficient of these probability sampling methods, but it is also the least costly. A population of areas is first specified and a random sample of areas is drawn. Within the sample of areas, smaller areal units are specified and random sampling is again applied. This is done until the areas are sufficiently manageable, such as blocks within a city. Within blocks, lists of residents are developed, and random sampling is conducted with those lists. Hence the area being sampled becomes smaller in successive stages until a population of people is specifiable.

Nonprobability procedures do not specify the chances that population elements have of being included in a sample, and the extent to which they are likely to be representative of unknown variables can't be estimated. However, they are useful for obtaining representative samples on known variables. Three types of nonprobability sampling strategies are systematic sampling, quota sampling, and purposive sampling.

Systematic sampling is useful in sampling from agency files. It involves specifying a sampling fraction, $\frac{1}{k}$, and then choosing every k^{th} case in order of appearance. For example, from a roster of clients whose names are alphabetized, every fourth one (the sampling fraction) is selected for inclusion. Or every new fourth client accepted as eligible for a social program is included in a 25% sample. The extent to which the sample is representative on known variables is determined by comparing the sampling distributions to those of the population, using such statistics as *chi square* (Epstein and Tripodi 1977, pp. 89-90).

Quota sampling is a procedure in which the sample is selected to be exactly representative of designated population characteristics. The sample is constructed, for example, of 50% males, 10% blacks, and 20% persons over the age of sixty-five. It should be emphasized that although the sample is representative of those designated variables, it can be nonrepresentative of other variables.

A purposive sample is a sample selected on the basis of previous evidence indicating its representativeness. For example, clients located in a particular district office of a state public-welfare organization were representative of all clients in the state on previous surveys related to client satisfaction. An evaluator chooses that district office as a purposive sample in a study of client satisfaction with a new program. Purposive samples can only be representative if there is representativeness over time. If the types of clients in various district offices change at different points in time, the purposive sample can be extremely biased, or nonrepresentative. Moreover, the purposive sample, as is possible with other nonprobability samples, can be nonrepresentative on other variables that are important but unknown or unavailable to the evaluator.

Level 3: Replication Procedures

Hersen and Barlow discuss the use of three replication strategies for generalizing experiments with single subjects: direct replication, clinical replication, and systematic replication (1976, ch. 9). Direct replication focuses on generalizing across clients when the same worker provides the same treatment in the same setting. Clinical replication is similar to direct replication and is defined "...as the administration of a treatment package containing two or more distinct treatment procedures by the same investigator or group of investigators" (Hersen and Barlow 1976, p. 336). The apparent difference between these two types of replication is that direct replication deals with a single behavioral or emotional problem which is treated by one intervention technique, whereas clinical replication deals with more complex behaviors and intervention packages. Systematic replication is a procedure that follows direct replication; it attempts to provide evidence for consistent results across different settings, workers, or client problems.

The following guidelines for direct replication are indicative of the strategies that Hersen and Barlow (1976, pp. 334-35) use in their discussion of generalization by means of replication:

> First, therapists and settings should remain constant across replications. Second, the behavior disorder in question should be topographically similar across clients, such as a specific phobia. Third, client background variables should be as closely matched as possible, although the goal of identical clients can never be attained in applied research. Fourth, the procedure employed (treatment) should be uniform across clients until failures ensure...

These procedures are pertinent to evaluating the effectiveness of a social worker's practice with one individual. They can also be generalized to replications of social programs. This is possible when clients have similar problems and needs, the programs have identical objectives, and the staffs use the same interventions. The more complex the program, the more difficult it would be to meet the conditions of similarity; hence estimations of generality across programs are less precise than those for a single intervention across clients.

Statistical procedures are used for assessing a sufficient number of replications. Assuming all the conditions of direct replication are satisfied, the evaluator estimates whether there is an expected, specifiable probability of replication that is plausible. For example, a social worker, in the absence of previous knowledge, assumes that it is likely for an intervention or program that is replicated to be successful. The probability of success would be 0.5. If each client or group of clients is seen as independent of every other client or group of clients, there is no problem of autocorrelation. A binomial statistic is applied in which the evaluator calculates the number of successes out of a given number of trials for achieving statistical significance, at a specified probability level (Tripodi 1980).

It is clear that the degree of generality is proportional to the number of replications having consistent results. What is more ambiguous is what makes up an adequate criterion of consistency. This can vary, depending on the consumers of evaluation and their expected degree of precision. For purposes of evaluative research, it is suggested that consistency should refer to variables directly related to the achievement of program or practice objectives. The criteria for consistency vary from practice to practice. However, to generalize the results of a particular intervention it is necessary to specify the criteria of generality beforehand and to obtain agreement between the evaluator and the evaluation consumer regarding the specific, qualitative nature of the criteria for consistency. It is also suggested that the criteria be quantitative, and that they include such notions as these:

1. Similarity, within one standard deviation, of the magnitude of correlation coefficients, or of mean differences between groups of clients

2. Sameness in the direction of association, for example, a positive correlation between program and effectiveness variables in replicated program evaluations
3. Statistically significant associations at conventional probability levels, 0.05, 0.01 or 0.001

Level 4: Experimental Procedures

External validity is enhanced by the use of procedures for establishing representativeness and producing replications. Interactions between selection biases and programs or practices can only be controlled by employing replication procedures. The independent variables of intervention are manipulated as they are presented to different individuals and subpopulations. To the extent there is a sufficient number of replications with consistent results, the evaluator can infer that the problem of interactions between selection biases and independent variables is minimized. On the other hand, inconsistent results are not easily interpretable, and it would not be possible on quantitative grounds for an evaluator to claim that this internal validity factor is controlled.

Multiple-treatment interference can be controlled by producing evidence of the amounts and types of relevant interventions, other than those being evaluated, that are received by clients in their exposure to social-work programs and practices. For example, in evaluating the effectiveness of a group work intervention on the extent to which clients decrease their amounts of alcohol consumption, an experimental design is used. One group of clients receives the group work intervention while, for purposes of comparison, another does not. Within the experimental group there are several subgroups comprised of different clients and group workers. The evaluator surveys the extent to which clients in the comparison groups have received other treatments. The effects of similar amounts of other interventions in both groups are subtracted when randomized experiments are used. A related procedure is to study participants who have not had prior treatment. In addition, replications of studies in which both procedures are involved increase one's inference that multiple treatments are under control. The specification of treatment program and intervention variables is necessary to control for the effects of other "treatments," since they cannot be identified as different from the program without clear operational definitions. Included in other treatments are a host of possibilities such as drugs and psychotherapies. The more familiar the evaluator is with the substance of the client problems and with alternative treatment modalities, the greater his or her chances to identify other treatments that need to be controlled.

The interaction between initial measurement and the independent variable is controlled by using experiments with comparison groups that do not have initial measurements prior to the introduction of the independent variable. For example, a randomized experiment with an experimental group that receives the independent variable and a control group that doesn't has measurements on the dependent (effectiveness) variables only after the intervention (independent variable) has been completely implemented and received by clients. The Solomon Four-Group Design also controls for this external validity threat (Stanley and Campbell 1966).

Placebo effects or other reactive effects to the experimental arrangements and procedures employed in the social-work program or practice are reduced by using comparison groups that receive the attention of persons dispensing the treatment but not the contents of treatment. Thus, in evaluating the effectiveness of psychotherapy, one can call untrained therapists a placebo group (Rosenthal and Frank 1956; Poser 1966).

In a randomized experiment, the effects due to the placebo group are subtracted from those in the experimental group, on the assumption that the placebo effects are additive across both groups. Placebo effects can be reduced when employing single-subject designs, by having the social worker refrain from intervention while making assessments. If no changes take place during those baseline periods and if the observations are reliable, it might be inferred that the placebo effect is not operative. The longer the period of baseline observations with no changes in client behaviors, the greater is this inference. However, due to the possibility of complicated interactions, such effects cannot be completely controlled with one client; hence comparison groups and replicated, consistent results are necessary.

SELECTING AN EVALUATIVE RESEARCH DESIGN

Devising evaluative research designs is a creative process that involves the specification of an ideal design modified by compromises due to practical and ethical constraints. Insofar as possible, compromises approximate those designs necessary to achieve the level of knowledge the consumer of evaluation desires. An example of selecting an evaluative research design on the basis of the concepts presented in this chapter follows.

Suppose an administrator of a state mental health department desires knowledge about the extent to which patients' needs are met by community mental health centers. In the state there are ten community mental health centers, one for each of ten catchment areas. Within each center, there are at least ten mental health professionals (psychiatrists, psychologists, social workers) serving an average of six hundred patients per month.

The unit of evaluation is the program as administered by the mental health professionals. The administrator is interested in the effectiveness of the program on all of the patients. Hence the evaluator turns his or her attention to designs for evaluating programs with the total number of clients, rather than to single-subject designs.

The basic objective of the program is to provide services that meet patients' mental needs. Since the program is in a relatively early stage of development, the contact stage, the evaluator must determine whether contacts are made between patients and mental health workers and whether those contacts are sufficient for accomplishing the program objective. The administrator also wants to provide uniform service delivery and is interested in whether or not there is variation of services among the mental health centers. After much discussion, it is decided that the most important objective at this stage in the program's development is to provide services that are perceived as satisfactory by patients. A variable directly related to this objective is client satisfaction, which is measurable by the Client Satisfaction Questionnaire, CSQ, (Larsen, and others 1979). The knowledge level that the administrator desires is quantitative-descriptive. Accurate, reliable, and valid information must be obtained to achieve that level. The evaluator observes that the CSQ is operationally defined. It includes eight questions that each patient-client rates on a four-step rating scale. A sample question is: "Have the services you received helped you to deal more effectively with your problems?" The rating scale includes: "Yes, they helped a great deal" (4), "Yes, they helped somewhat" (3), "No, they really didn't help" (2), "No, they seemed to make things worse" (1) (Larsen, and others 1979, p. 204). The CSQ has been used on patients in mental health settings with a *coefficient alpha* of 0.93, demonstrating a high degree of internal consistency. There is also some evidence of predictive validity. In one study, patients' ratings of improvement were significantly correlated with their ratings of satisfaction on the CSQ ($r = 0.53$, $p < 0.001$), and in another investigation there was a statistically significant correlation between therapists' ratings of client satisfaction and clients' ratings ($r = 0.56$, $p < 0.01$).

The evaluator is interested in obtaining information that represents all of the patients' perceptions of satisfaction. Moreover, he or she wants to provide information that is adequate for comparing client satisfaction among the 10 community mental health centers. Therefore, the evaluator decides to use a stratified random-sampling procedure. Lists of clients who are or have been provided with services are available within each of the 10 centers. Since the administrator wants to use the information to modify current practices, if necessary, the lists are restricted to those clients who have received services within a specified period of time, say the past 6 months. These lists are constructed. Suppose each list contains 1,000 names. With a 10% error of estimation and at the 0.05 level of statistical significance, a sample size of 278 is calculated as adequate within each level (community mental health center). A total sample size of 2,780 will be drawn, 278 from each center. However, in a pretest sample, it is determined that the response rate for completing the questionnaires is 70%; hence 397 $\left(\frac{278}{0.7}\right)$ names need to be drawn within each stratum to obtain the required number of 278, or a total number of 3,970 from all 10 strata.

The research design the evaluator selects is a cross-sectional survey design which involves obtaining a representative sample of a population and observations from each person in the sample once, at a specified time period. Satisfaction scores ranging from eight to thirty-two are tabulated, and the distributions of scores within centers are calculated and compared. If there are variations among centers, the evaluator suggests that the administrator or his or her proxy visit the centers to determine possible reasons for the discrepancies. Similar distributions among the agencies would indicate the degree of satisfaction perceived consistently across community mental health centers. If the degree of satisfaction is high, goal attainment is achieved. On the other hand, if the degree of satisfaction is low, further inquiry is necessary.

CHAPTER SEVEN
RESEARCH DESIGNS FOR EVALUATING SINGLE-CASE INTERVENTIONS

Research designs for evaluating individuals are single-subject designs. They are appropriate when a social worker is interested in obtaining information about the actual or potential effectiveness of his or her practice with client units—individuals, couples, or families.

The purpose of this chapter is to present research designs that can provide evidence to satisfy criteria of knowledge for appropriate knowledge levels. This is an operationalization of the notion presented in chapter 6: There are different levels of knowledge, and different research designs are used for developing different knowledge levels. Table 7-1 summarizes the relationship between knowledge levels, criteria for knowledge, and selected research designs. For example, the case-study designs provide logical arrangements for producing evidence of researchable hypotheses for knowledge level 1. Although the eleven research designs presented in this chapter are not exhaustive, they exemplify how different strategies are used for evaluating single-case interventions.

LEVEL 1: HYPOTHETICAL-DEVELOPMENTAL DESIGNS

These designs are predominately qualitative case studies. Their major purpose is to produce insights and ideas that can be applied in subsequent practice efforts. They

TABLE 7-1 Evaluating Single-Case Interventions

KNOWLEDGE LEVEL	CRITERIA FOR KNOWLEDGE	RESEARCH DESIGNS
1. Hypothetical-Developmental	1. Researchable hypotheses	1. Cross-sectional case study Longitudinal case study
2. Quantitative-Descriptive	2. Measurement accuracy, reliability and validity	2. After-Intervention Measurement Design Longitudinal Quantitative-Descriptive Design
3. Correlational	3. Empirical relationship	3. One Case Before/After Design Interrupted Time-Series Design Interrupted Time-Series Design with follow-up Replicated Time-Series Design
4. Cause-effect	4. Time order, control of internal validity factors	4. Withdrawal/Reversal Design Graduated-Intensity Design Multiple-Baseline Design

provide hypotheses for practice and its evaluation. When the hypotheses are developed by a practitioner working with an individual client, the knowledge is formative. In contrast, hypotheses developed after the client has terminated sessions with the worker are used as summative knowledge when there is conceptual generalization.

1. **Cross-Sectional Case Study, $\overset{O}{X}$, XO**

The cross-sectional case study is symbolized as $\overset{O}{X}$ or XO, where X refers to a set of one or more independent variables of practice and O represents a set of one or more dependent variables. The placement of O above the X indicates that observations or measurements occur while practice is taking place, whereas X followed by O signifies that the observations are made immediately after the intervention has occurred. The observations are taken at one point in time. Such information is obtained by participant observation of the worker with his or her client; by review of existing reports of clients' progress, if available; and through unstructured or semistructured interviewing of the client, significant others, or both. The evaluator forms impressions about whether the client is changing her or his attitudes, behaviors, knowledge, skills, or situations. He or she discovers whether there are any specific components of intervention, worker or client characteristics, and so on that might be associated with change or lack of change. The worker can also be interviewed by an independent evaluator, who might provide another perspective on what has happened with the client. Because the knowledge is conceptual, information need not be precisely measured. The strategy is to obtain as broad a view as possible, although this doesn't prevent the social worker from using available quantitative measures. The evaluator attempts to synthesize information, conceptualize possible interrelationships among variables, and formulate researchable hypotheses.

As an illustration, suppose a woman client has completed five interviews with a family-service worker. Ostensibly, the woman was seeking to increase the positive aspects of her relationship with her husband. The client expresses her belief that the intervention was not successful; her husband won't cooperate with her, and she wants to discontinue treatment. The worker inquires as to whether she could interview the husband, but the client indicates that he would not participate. The worker observes that the client doesn't appear to be involved in treatment and shows little affect when discussing her husband. In an intensive interview the client indicates the worker was nice, but too "nosy." As the worker confronts the client and probes for her apparent lack of interest in treatment, the client indicates that she found another lover and doesn't care about her husband. It is apparent the treatment objectives of increasing positive aspects of the marital relationship can not be accomplished under the present set of circumstances.

From information such as this, the worker hypothesizes that change in treatment is a function of the client's motivation to be engaged in treatment and be willing to change. Moreover, in terms of formative information, it is clear that the objectives for the client were not realistically based on the client's situation. If further work with the client should occur, a reassessment would be necessary, with a resulting reformulation of treatment objectives. For example, the worker might assess the extent to which the client is willing to pursue new goals, as well as consider the reasons why the client sought counseling in the first place.

The information produced from this type of design is speculative. It can lead to good ideas, but they need further evaluation. Internal validity factors, with the exception of selection biases and experimental mortality, are not controlled, and no evidence of empirical associations can be produced. Since the evaluation takes place as part of the intervention process, no extra costs are involved when the worker is the evaluator. If an independent evaluator is used, such as the worker's supervisor, more costs are involved, but the expenses can be reduced if the evaluation occurs during supervision. For example, the worker tape-records his or her interviews. The supervisor and the worker listen to the interviews, speculate about the case, and develop hypotheses about further practice.

2. Longitudinal Case Study, $\overset{OOO}{X}$

The longitudinal case study, which takes place as treatment unfolds, involves a set of repeated observations. It is symbolized as $\overset{OOO}{X}$, where X refers to the independent variables and OOO above the X refers to three or more multiple observations that occur while treatment is taking place. It is possible to secure multiple observations after treatment. However, this is costly, impractical, and difficult to justify in a case study where specified measures are not indicated at various follow-up periods, and the purpose of the follow-up visits is basically for the worker's benefit, that is, to develop hypotheses.

The evaluator seeks to observe the qualitative relationship between variables over time. He or she notes whether there are any significant changes in the client's life and attempts to discern whether there are manipulable variables related to those changes. For example, if it is observed that a client gets headaches after she or he is involved in family arguments, it can be hypothesized that the frequency of headaches will decrease in relation to the reduction in family arguments. The social worker's intervention is concentrated on the objective of reducing family arguments.

There are several data-gathering strategies that can help in the production of hypotheses with this design. In addition to interviewing and participant observation, the worker uses content analysis, client logs, and graphing. Content analyses are done on process or summary recordings, as well as with tape-recorded interviews (Tripodi and Epstein 1980, pp. 103-120). The evaluator discerns the themes of interviews and observes the occurrence of particular events associated with manipulable variables. For example, in reviewing the contents of process recordings, the evaluator notices that every time the social worker perceives the client is angry, she or he refrains from focusing in interviews. This lack of focusing is hypothesized as being related to the client's feelings of frustration. If so, it can be rectified by the social worker, who can consciously attempt to stay on the topic after she or he perceives that the client is angry. In addition, the social worker can deal directly with the client's anger during the intervention.

Gottman and Leiblum indicate that the annotated record and the study of concomitant variation of two or more graphed variables are useful for producing hypotheses about intervention (1974, pp. 130-37). The annotated record is a log that the client keeps about significant events over time, and this record is used in conjunction with a graph of a quantitative change variable. For example, a client is receiving social-work intervention to increase the amount of time he spends with his family. He is asked to keep a record each day for two weeks of the number of hours he spends with them, the activities in which he is involved, and how he feels about his involvement. The number of hours can be graphed in the vertical axis; the days of the week, on the horizontal axis. The graph in figure 7-1 illustrates this example.

On eleven out of fourteen days the client spends one hour a day with his family. On three other days he spends five hours each day. This information, along with the client's log, indicates that the client felt good on the days in which he was more involved with his family, and he felt good because he slept for eight hours each previous night. On nights in which he had less sleep, he became cranky and argumentative. The logs are used to explain deviations in the pattern of the graph.

When two or more variables are graphed, the evaluator can study concomitant variation. The strategy is to observe the dependent variable (change variable) and discern whether other associated variables are correlated with the change. If the pattern of the associated variable can be changed, then it is hypothesized that the

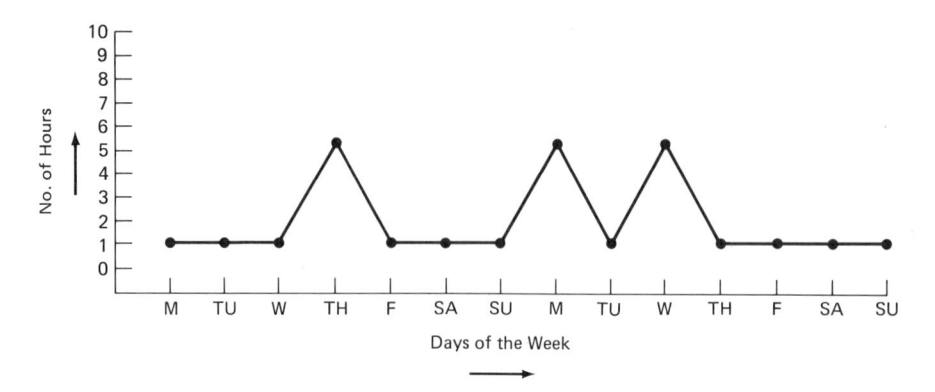

FIGURE 7-1

dependent variable or variables would show a corresponding change. For example, a client desires to decrease his or her caloric intake for the objective of reducing weight. The social worker plots the client's daily caloric intake as well as a few other possibly related variables. These variables were obtained from the client's speculations during an interview: degree of anxiety, number of hours of sleep the previous night, and the client's relationship with his or her son. All of these variables are assessed by the client's self-report. A high degree of anxiety might be related to increased amounts of caloric intake. Systematic desensitization, tranquilizing drugs for the reduction of anxiety, or both can be hypothesized as treatments that might lead to decreased caloric intake.

The longitudinal case study has the same degree of control for internal validity factors that design 1 has. Because there are multiple observation points, it can provide some quantitative-descriptive information. Although the reliability and validity of the quantitative descriptions are unknown, they are not at issue so long as the data are used for developing hypotheses which require further testing for their implementation and evaluation. Since the resulting knowledge is specific to a particular client, it is intended to be more directly formative than summative.

LEVEL 2: QUANTITATIVE-DESCRIPTIVE DESIGNS

These designs are used to produce descriptive information about specified variables that indicate change in dependent variables; that is, they produce information about the extent to which the treatment objectives for a particular client have been achieved. They cannot be used to provide evidence of the association between independent and dependent variables, nor to control for internal validity factors. The extent to which they produce useful quantitative-descriptive information depends on the accuracy, reliability, and validity of the variables that are measured. Therefore, insofar as it is possible, the evaluator uses previously validated procedures or measurement devices that can be validated while the evaluation takes place.

Quantitative-descriptive designs are symbolically the same as the hypothetical-developmental designs previously discussed. They differ in the purposes of the research and the measurements used. Quantitative-descriptive designs produce accurate quantitative-descriptive knowledge, that is, simple facts; whereas hypothetical-developmental designs develop researchable hypotheses. Hence for the most part, the questions for research in quantitative-descriptive designs are operationalized prior to the research; in contrast, questions and hypotheses are developed as a result of procedures used within the framework of hypothetical-developmental designs (see the preceding section).

1. After-Intervention Measurement Design, XO

In this design, measurements are taken at one point in time—immediately after intervention or treatment is completed. Measurements are obtained by telephone interview, questionnaire, rating scales, tests, and so forth. They are operationalized during intervention and refined so they can be used at the end of intervention.

Three basic strategies are used to obtain quantitative descriptions about the client's perceptions of treatment: the formulation of questions related to treatment, goal attainment scaling (Kiresuk and Sherman 1968), and "Then" ratings and "Post ratings" (Howard 1980, p. 100). The first strategy involves the use of questionnaires or structured interviews. Questions are posed in which the client is asked to describe his or her perception of the extent of association between intervention and change. Questions of this general form might be asked:

> To what extent have your symptoms (e.g., feelings of anxiety) changed since you have received treatment: decreased ____, no change ____, increased ____?

> If your symptoms have changed, to what extent do you believe this is due to the interventions you received from this agency: not at all ____, slightly ____, considerably ____, a great deal ____?

> What were the objectives you had for treatment at this agency ____; were those objectives accomplished ____?

> To what degree was your social worker helpful: very helpful ____, helpful ____, not helpful ____, not at all helpful ____?

> Please explain in your own words what you mean by "helpful."

The goal-attainment strategy requires that the worker, client, or both do the following things:

1. Specify what the treatment goals are
2. Operationalize the levels of goal attainment for each goal with respect to these levels: "much less than the expected level of outcome," "somewhat less than the expected level of outcome," "expected level of outcome," "somewhat more than the expected level of outcome," and "much more than the expected level of outcome" (Kiresuk and Sherman, 1968)
3. Observe at the termination of treatment the level of goal attainment that is achieved.

Howard suggests that retrospective ratings be made at the end of treatment (1980). The evaluator instructs the client to rate himself or herself on a rating scale relevant to the treatment objectives, that is, a postrating. Then the evaluator asks the client to recall on the same rating scale what he or she was like at the beginning of treatment, that is, a Then rating. The difference between the Postrating and the Then rating is the client's perception of change. This perception is followed by a direct question about whether or not the perceived change, if any, is due to the treatment or other factors. If there is change and the client indicates it is due to treatment, there is then descriptive information of a perceived association between treatment and client change. For example, a treatment objective for a client is to reduce his or her degree of loneliness. A scale of loneliness ranging from extremely lonely (1) to not lonely at all (10) can be used. A rating of 8 at the end of treatment compared with 1 at the beginning of treatment reflects change in the desired direction; whereas ratings of 8 at both the beginning and end of treatment indicate no change.

The advantage of this design is that it provides quantitative-descriptive information that indicates whether or not there is any perceived effectiveness. It refers to one client, but the evaluator can draw inferences that are summative if she or he replicates the same treatment with other clients who have similar characteristics and problems. The design is relatively inexpensive and can be easily incorporated into social-work practice.

The primary disadvantage in the design is that it does not indicate whether the observed changes will persist over time. Inferences about the stability of change can only be derived from follow-up data.

2. **Longitudinal Quantitative-Descriptive Design,** X^{OOO} , XOOO

Whereas the longitudinal case study develops hypotheses by examining suggestive relationships, the Longitudinal Quantitative-Descriptive Design provides accurate measurements of dependent variables that are indicative of effectiveness. Variables that can be validly measured are selected, and multiple measurements are taken over time. These measurements, OOO, can be obtained while the intervention (treatment) is operative, X^{OOO} , after completion of the intervention, XOOO, or both.

The basic function of the design while intervention is in effect, $X\overset{OOO}{}$, is to provide quantitative descriptions of change variables, so the social worker can use the information to make an assessment of the extent to which progress is achieved and maintained. Data are collected by interview, rating scales, observations, and so forth. The measures should be repeatable, reliable, and relevant to the worker's treatment objectives. The number of measurements is a function of the time intervals chosen. For example, a social worker interested in measuring change in a client's self-ratings of various moods or frequencies of specific behaviors obtains measurements at each counseling session; the number of measurements equals the number of counseling sessions. The choice of time intervals should be realistically geared to the possibility of change. Thus, smoking and drinking behavior should be observed daily, rather than hourly or monthly. The social worker gives a client forms on which she or he is to make self-reports of moods and behaviors on a daily basis. She or he subsequently brings the forms to her or his appointments with the social worker, or the social worker telephones the client to obtain the observations. When the client gathers the basic data, it is necessary that she or he be thoroughly instructed in the use of forms, rating scales, and so forth. The measurements are graphed, and they serve as indicators of the extent to which change is occurring. This information has a formative function and may indicate that the social worker needs to change the independent variable, that is, the component of practice he or she is using. For example, a client's behavior may not change after ten sessions, and this may lead the social worker to conclude that no progress is evident. One of his or her alternatives is to change the intensity of treatment, another is to employ a different treatment strategy, and so on.

Often observed change is reflected in a design such as the After Intervention Measurement Design, XO; then the treatment is terminated, and it is assumed the changes will persist. The follow-up design with repeated measurements at designated periods after treatment has ended is also a Longitudinal Quantitative-Descriptive Design. It is symbolized as XOOO. Follow-up information is obtained by telephone interview, mailed questionnaires, or face-to-face interviews. Time intervals are arranged in advance by the worker and client at termination; for example, immediately after treatment has ended and at intervals of three months. Similar results are those for which there are no significant differences among measures.

Although this design (XOOO) can be costly when the social worker engages in follow-up interviewing at the clients' homes, it produces important information about what is happening in their lives subsequent to social-work intervention. It provides information related to the effectiveness of social-work practice; for the data it produces bear on policies regarding the necessity to contact clients after they have received social-work services. While Longitudinal Quantitative-Descriptive Designs produce evidence of the perception of the association between client change and social-work interventions, they are not constructed to provide empirical evidence of such an association.

LEVEL 3: CORRELATIONAL DESIGNS

Correlational designs provide the structural arrangements for producing evidence from which an association between intervention and change can be inferred. In addition, they can provide some evidence necessary for causal inference: independent variables precede the possible occurrence of change in the dependent variables, and, with time-series designs, a few internal validity factors can be controlled. Moreover, since correlations between interventions and outcomes are regarded as necessary (but not sufficient) conditions for inferring causal relations, the lack of correlation between interventions and outcomes can also be interpreted as evidence that a causal relationship is not in effect. That is, it is unlikely there is a causal relationship between intervention and outcome if they are not correlated.

Correlational designs also provide quantitative-descriptive information about intervention and change variables. As with quantitative-descriptive designs, they require measurements that are accurate, reliable, and valid.

1. **One Case Before/After Design,**
   $X_O \; O_1 \; X \; O_2$

The One Case Before/After Design includes measurement of a set of one or more dependent variables at two points in time: O_1 before intervention X and after X_O, no intervention; and O_2 at the end of intervention X (Campbell and Stanley 1966). Evidence must also be obtained (e.g., from interviews with the client or significant others, records, and other documents) to show that the client has not received or is not currently receiving the intervention. If the client has received a previous intervention, the design is more appropriately indicated as $X_A \; O_1 \; X_{A+B} \; O_2$, where X_A refers to the previous intervention and X_{A+B} refers to the joint effects of intervention A and the intervention that the social worker wishes to test (B). Differences between O_2 and O_1 reflect an association with the intervention, either $X - X_O$ or $X_{A+B} - X_A$. Since there are only two measurement points and one client, the change in $O_2 - O_1$ cannot be assessed by statistical analysis. The change is inferred by noting whether it is consistent with the objective for change, or by making a judgment that the change is of sufficient magnitude to be regarded as practically significant. For example, a client's self-rating of confidence increases from 1 to 4 on a 5-point scale ranging from extremely confident (5) to not confident at all (1). The change of magnitude is considered significant. If the objective was to increase the self-rating by two or more steps, there is evidence of change.

This design does not control for the internal validity factors of history, maturation, instrumentation, initial measurement effects, statistical regression, and their interactions. The factors of selection biases and experimental mortality are not relevant, since comparisons are not made with other clients. The evaluator infers that maturation and history are apparently not influential by a supplementary inquiry (Carter 1972). The client is interviewed with respect to any other changes and influences that might have occurred between O_1 and O_2. Although not controlled, it is plausible that history and maturation are not operative if no additional changes and influences on the client's life are discerned. Nevertheless, at best the design provides only a first approximation of correlation, and it is a poor design for inferring causal relations.

An example of this design is as follows. A mother and her daughter request treatment from a mental health clinic. The basic problem is that they argue frequently, and they wish to diminish the number and intensity of the arguments. The social worker, as the mental health professional assigned to their case, interviews them both in order to make an assessment and formulate a treatment plan. Mother and daughter agree that they argued 3 times a day the previous week, for approximately ½ hour each time. Hence, there were 21 arguments per week, consuming approximately 10½ hours; this is O_1. It was also determined that the clients had not received any previous treatment, X_O, and that no one else was living with them. The arguments focused on the daughter's cleaning of her room and on their respective dating patterns. Behavioral therapy was the intervention chosen, and it was estimated that it would range from 2 to 3 months, with treatment scheduled once weekly for mother and daughter simultaneously. At the end of treatment, 3 months later, mother and daughter were asked to indicate the number of arguments and the duration of those arguments for the preceding week. They agreed that they had had 2 arguments for a total of 10 minutes, O_2. The difference, $O_1 - O_2$, is 21 arguments minus 2, or a reduction of 19 arguments per week and 10½ hours minus ⅙, or 10 hours and 20 minutes less time spent arguing. This constitutes evidence of a correlation between the particular type of behavioral therapy the worker employed for the mother-daughter couple and the indicators of change.

2. **Interrupted Time-Series Design,**

$$X_O OOO \quad \overset{OOO}{X}$$

In this design, a set of measurements or observations is taken over 3 or more points in time prior to the introduction of the intervention, X, and after there is evidence that the intervention was not previously administered or received by the client from other sources, X_O. During the intervention, $\overset{OOO}{X}$, measurements are taken at 3 or more points in time. The intervals between measurements before intervention are typically equidistant and identical to the intervals between measurements during treatment (Gottman and Leiblum 1974, pp. 138-41; Hersen and Barlow 1976, ch. 3). As indicated for design 1 above, when there is previous treatment it is symbolized as X_A and the intervention of the worker as X_{A+B}. The difference between X_{A+B} and X_A is construed as X_B, where B is the intervention the worker is testing.

Before introduction of the intervention, there should be stability, or little variation among the repeated measures, OOO (Kazdin 1978). Some investigators suggest that the number of measurements be repeated until there is stability in measurement (Tripodi and Epstein 1980, ch. 11). These measurements taken before intervention are referred to as baseline measurements and are shown in figure 7-2.

When the baseline measurements are horizontal to the X axis or perpendicular to the Y axis, there is stability and consistency among the measures. Stable measurements of this type control for the effects of previous measurement, instrumentation, and statistical regression. The choice of time intervals depends on the clinical problem being worked on, the variables that are measured, and the extent to which stability can be achieved. Variables such as tardiness and attendance can be measured daily; ratings of moods can be obtained either daily or weekly; and variables of wages, grades in school, and so on can be gathered monthly. Gottman and Leiblum suggest procedures to be used for stabilizing baseline measurements (1974). For example, unstable measurements for specified time intervals can be averaged to represent longer time intervals; and an exponential pattern of measures can be transformed to a linear pattern by a logarithmic transformation.

After there are stable baseline patterns, the intervention is abruptly introduced, so that it is clear at what point there is and is not intervention. After the onset of intervention, measurements of the dependent variables are systematically recorded over time. There are three procedures for discovering whether there are changes in the series of measurements at baseline, OOO, compared with the series of measurements after intervention is introduced, $\begin{smallmatrix}OOO\\X\end{smallmatrix}$. The first method is to specify an objective of desired change before the introduction of treatment. If the objective is achieved, there is perceived evidence of an association. The second is to graph the measures and visually examine the data (Jayaratne and Levy 1979, p. 110). This "eyeballing" technique depends on the evaluator's judgment that a change has actually occurred.

Third, employ statistical methods when there are a sufficient number of observations. For example, with five observations during baseline and five during treatment, an evaluator can employ the binomial test to determine whether there is a statistically significant shift in the time-series (Kazdin, 1978). The median

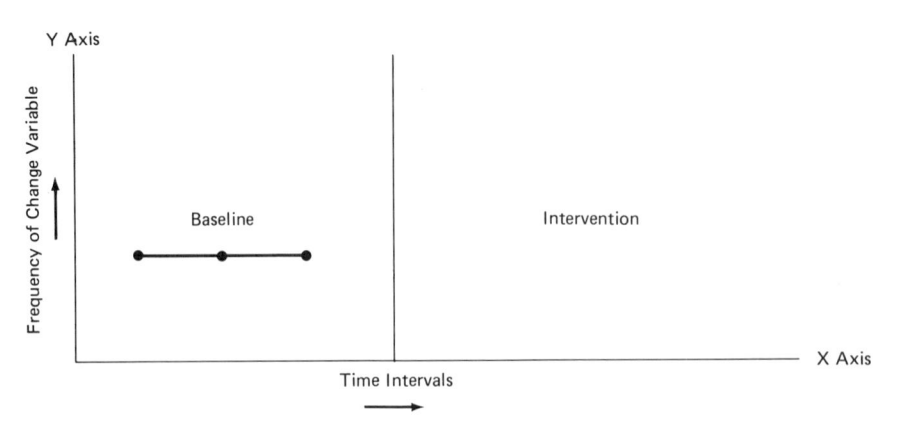

FIGURE 7-2

measurement at baseline is calculated, and measurements during treatment are judged as to whether they are above or below the median. If all five measurements are consistently above or below the median, there is statistical significance at the 0.05 level of probability. Gottman and Leiblum suggest the use of Shewart control charts (1974, pp. 142-51). Calculate the arithmetic mean and standard deviation for baseline measurements; construct confidence limits by adding to and subtracting from the mean two standard deviations. If the limits are exceeded during intervention, there are statistically significant results at the 0.05 level of probability. To illustrate, a social worker assesses the extent to which there is an association between his or her intervention and a significant other's ratings of the client's assertiveness. If on a rating scale ranging from not at all assertive (1) to extremely assertive (10), the mean rating at baseline is 2.1 and the standard deviation is 0.5, the confidence limits are 3.1 and 1.1. Ratings of assertiveness that are 4 or higher indicate increased assertiveness.

The internal validity factors of selection biases and experimental mortality are not pertinent to this design. The factors of history and maturation are not controllable; however, as with the One Case Before/After Design, it is possible to obtain supplementary information. To the extent it is plausible that historical and maturational factors are not responsible for any observed changes, cause-effect knowledge can be approximated.

This design depends heavily on the type of measurements obtained. There must be independent measurements in repeated observations. The chief difficulty is the procurement of repeated measurements at baseline before intervention. In many social-work settings this is not feasible. However, there are several alternative procedures that can approximate this design: reconstruction, lengthy assessment, and differential treatment focus. In reconstruction, the evaluator interviews the client, uses available sources of data to reconstruct baseline data, or both. For example, clients in institutional settings such as schools and hospitals have previous data recorded on relevant variables. The social worker reconstructs baseline data from an initial client interview for extreme client behaviors. The heavy smoker, drinker, drug user, or whatever can specify fairly exact degrees of drinking, smoking, and drug abuse for a period of time before intervention. The procedure of lengthy assessment simply refers to the fact that treatment can be delayed while baseline measures are gathered during assessment. For example, a client is asked to provide daily measurements (e.g., on self-rating scales) from one weekly appointment to another. Seven measures are sufficient for the establishment of a stable baseline. Differential treatment focus calls for this design variation, X_A OOO OOO X_{A+B}. While treatment takes place at X_A, measurements are obtained on a variable which is not the focus of treatment. For example, X_A may be devoted to the strengthening of interpersonal relationships but not to the client's weight reduction. The client's weight can be measured, OOO, and subsequently, treatment could focus on the weight reduction as well as on the strengthening of interpersonal relationships, $\overset{OOO}{X_{A+B}}$.

3. Interrupted Time-Series Design
   with Follow-up, $X_O \; OOO \; \overset{OOO}{X} \; OOO$

The Interrupted Time-Series Design with Follow-up allows the social worker to determine the degree of maintenance and stability once a change has occurred. This information is not sufficient for generalization, but it provides an instance in which an intervention may be effective. Knowing that an intervention produces desired changes within one client unit, the social worker proceeds to use it again with slightly more confidence. In terms of utilization, however, the chief advantage of correlational designs 2 and 3 is that they provide formative information while intervention takes place. If no changes or deterioration occur after a specified period of time, the social worker can change, modify, or scrap the intervention. Repeated observations during intervention provide data useful for practice decisions.

There are three different observation periods for this design: baseline, during intervention, and after intervention has been terminated. The same dependent variables are measured during each observation and for each observation period. Prior to the first set of observations before intervention, the evaluator establishes the extent to which the client has had previous interventions, X_O or X_A. After a stable series of baseline measures have been established, the intervention, X or X_{A+B}, is introduced, and the dependent variables are measured at intervals similar to those at baseline. Following the termination of intervention, measurements are again taken of the dependent variables. The design is shown in figure 7-3.

Comparisons are made between observations at intervention and at baseline to determine whether the series at intervention is significantly different statistically from the series at baseline. These data establish whether or not there is an association with the change from X_O to X, or from X_A to X_{A+B} when the evaluator is comparing the addition of a new intervention (B) to the one the client received before (A).

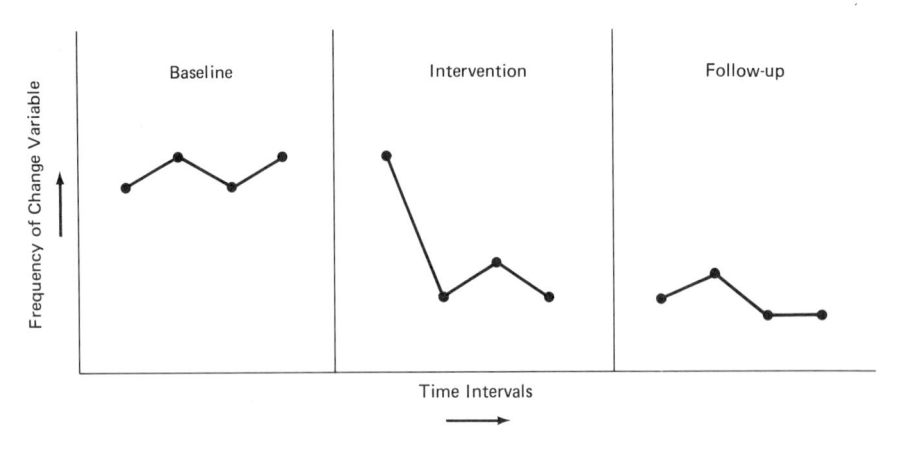

FIGURE 7-3

Data are also analyzed to determine whether or not there is persistence in the change (Tripodi and Epstein 1980, pp. 224-25). Two comparisons can be made: follow-up versus intervention and follow-up versus baseline. In the first, the series of observations at intervention are tested as if they constitute a new baseline; the observations at follow-up are compared against that "new baseline." If the comparisons result in a statistically significant shift in the time-series, there is no evidence for persistence or maintenance of changes that occurred at baseline; in contrast, a nonstatistically significant change indicates that the changes are being maintained. The second comparison provides evidence about the client's net change. The evaluator determines whether a change observed during treatment is still in effect. It is possible for statistical shifts to occur between baseline and intervention, intervention and follow-up, and baseline and follow-up. The advantage of making the comparison between intervention and follow-up is that it enables the evaluator to observe a reversal in the trend of progress, that is, deterioration that might not be apparent in the comparison of follow-up to baseline.

For example, in figure 7-4 there is a statistically significant shift from baseline to intervention, which is desirable if the objective of intervention is to reduce the frequency of some variable, say drug abuse. Follow-up data compared to baseline data also show a statistically significant shift, but of a lower magnitude. Evidence of a deterioration or a trend reverting to the original baseline is observed by comparing follow-up to intervention, which is also statistically significant, but in a direction opposite to that noted in the other comparisons.

This design controls for the same internal validity factors as the second correlational design, Interrupted Time-Series Design. Its basic disadvantage is that it requires follow-up information from a client. It depends, therefore, on the accessibility of the client, his or her willingness to participate in data collection, and the extra costs involved to secure the data. Time-saving data-collection devices like telephone interviewing and questionnaires can be utilized (Dillman 1978). As part of the intervention process, the social worker can enlist the services of the client or a significant other to gather data on the change variable or variables during the

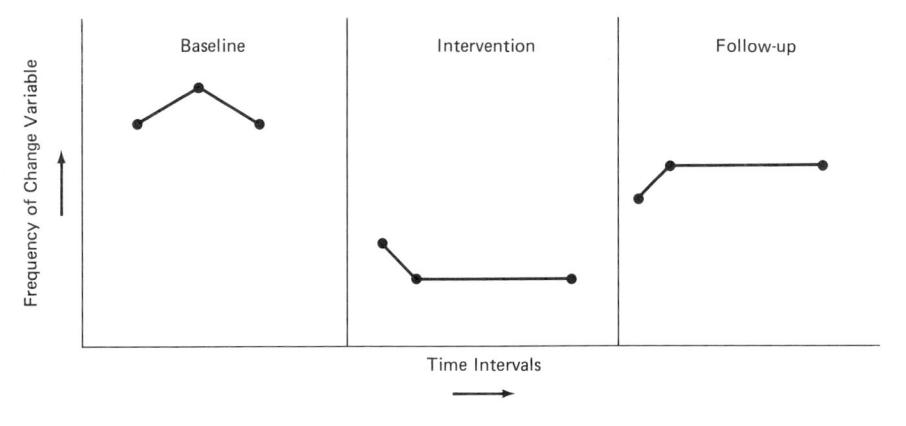

FIGURE 7-4

follow-up period. Arrangements for data collection can be discussed with the termination. This makes gathering the data easier.

Supplementary information is obtained at follow-up as well as during the intervention period. These data indicate what has happened to the client. Have there been major influences on his or her behaviors, moods and attitudes? Are there new problems with which he or she must cope? Data resulting from questions like these assist the worker in deciding whether or not historical and maturational factors are influential.

4. **Replicated Time-Series Design,**

$$\begin{array}{c} OOO \\ OOO \quad X \quad \quad OOO \\ \quad \quad \quad OOO \quad X_1 \quad \quad OOO \\ \quad \quad \quad \quad \quad \quad OOO \quad X_2 \end{array}$$

This design involves the use of two or more replications of a time-series design. The first replication is represented by $OOO \; \begin{smallmatrix} OOO \\ X_1 \end{smallmatrix}$ and the second by $OOO \; \begin{smallmatrix} OOO \\ X_2 \end{smallmatrix}$. After one time-series design, $OOO \; \begin{smallmatrix} OOO \\ X \end{smallmatrix}$, has been completed with one client and there is evidence of a statistically significant shift in the time series, the first replication is conducted. As indicated in chapter 6, the worker attempts to replicate with another client who has a similar problem and for whom there are similar objectives. To the extent possible, as in direct replication (Hersen and Barlow 1976, p. 318), clients should be similar in important characteristics such as gender, age, and ethnicity. The same intervention procedures are used in the first replication, the second replication, and subsequent replications.

Generalization becomes more possible with each successful replication. Success is defined as consistency in results, that is, statistically significant shifts of observations from baseline to intervention. Time-series designs with follow-up are also replicated to determine whether the same patterns of time-series take place across clients.

Correlational knowledge is generalized as consistent results are repeated from client to client. To produce generalizations, it is vital that the social worker specify the intervention procedures used. This is done in two ways. First, she or he indicates the basic limits and contractual agreements of the intervention, such as the ingredients of the basic techniques employed. Second, the worker writes notes or keeps a log of what she or he actually did during intervention sessions. She or he tape-records interviews and, after the intervention is completed, performs a content analysis to specify more precisely what was done (Tripodi 1980, ch. 5).

LEVEL 4: CAUSE-EFFECT DESIGNS

Cause-effect designs provide additional control over internal validity factors; in particular, they are devised to control for the potential effects of history and maturation. Unlike group designs (chapter 8), which control for these validity threats *a priori* (i.e., before the data are gathered), single-subject designs only control for these factors *a posteriori* (i.e., after data collection).

1. Withdrawal/Reversal Design,
$$X_0 \; OOO \; \overset{OOO}{X} \; OOO \; \overset{OOO}{X} \; *$$

The Withdrawal/Reversal Design (Hersen and Barlow 1976, pp. 92-100) symbolically adds one more phase, $\overset{OOO}{X}$, to the Interrupted Time-Series Design with Follow-up. However, the designs are different in that it is assumed in the withdrawal/reversal design that client change is not permanent, and that when intervention is withdrawn there will be a reversal to baseline. In contrast, the basic assumption in the use of the follow-up design is that change is permanent. Obviously, the assumption of stability at follow-up can be empirically invalidated. The investigator can switch to a reversal/withdrawal design when there is an empirically-obtained reversal pattern, in an ethical desire to reinstate the intervention. (Note that the name Withdrawal/Reversal refers to withdrawal of intervention with an empirically-obtained reversal pattern, regardless of whether or not that is the intent of the evaluator. It is not to be confused with a reversal design, where the intervention is applied to the changed behavior in the opposite direction in order to experimentally produce a reversal in a baseline pattern.)

The Withdrawal/Reversal Design can only be implemented if the data follow a pattern similar to the ideal one shown in figure 7-5. Baseline observations are

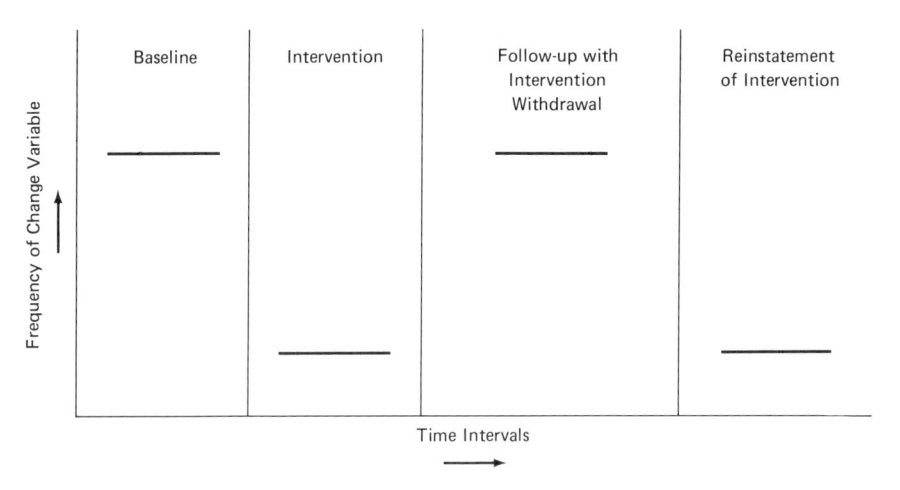

FIGURE 7-5

*Xs and Os are used in a manner derived from Campbell and Stanley's notations for group designs (1966) rather than the more conventional notations employed in the single-subject-design literature, such as ABAB for reversal design. The reason for this is to illustrate in this chapter and the next that the basic logic is similar for individual and group designs—to provide structural arrangements for producing evidence to infer different levels of knowledge.

obtained until they are stable and horizontal to the X-axis; then intervention is abruptly introduced. Observations at intervention are compared to those at baseline. If there are significant shifts in the time-series, the intervention is withdrawn. Observations are made during the withdrawal/follow-up phase. The data show either persistence in change or another significant shift in the time-series when follow-up data are compared to those at intervention. With no change, the design reverts to the Interrupted Time-Series Design with Follow-up. However, if there are significant shifts that show a reversal in the data pattern back to the baseline frequencies of observation, intervention is reinstated. Observations during the reinstatement of intervention are compared with those from the preceding phase at follow-up. If the resulting data pattern shows a significant shift in the time-series similar in magnitude to the observations at intervention, then a second reversal occurs.

Historical and maturational factors cannot be controlled with complete certainty. However, their control can be approximated by invoking the principle of unlikely successive coincidences (Carter 1972; Jayaratne and Levy 1979). One reversal in the data pattern may be coincidental, two reversals are less likely, three are even less probable, and so forth. The greater the number of reversals, the more likely it is that historical and maturation factors are controlled.

This design has the primary advantage of providing potentially more control over internal validity factors than correlational designs. However, the control is at best approximate, and it depends on the following factors:

1. A reversal in the data pattern to baseline at withdrawal/follow-up
2. The extent to which it is possible to reinstate the intervention after it has been withdrawn
3. A second reversal in the data pattern from withdrawal/follow-up to a significant shift during the period of reinstated intervention

Jayaratne and Levy imply that it may be difficult for many behaviors and attitudes to revert to baseline conditions at withdrawal, from a successful intervention (1979, p. 141). Moreover, the reinstated intervention may be dissimilar to the original intervention. The logic of the design calls for the reinstated intervention to be identical to the original intervention. The more dissimilar the intervention, the less control there is.

The use of this design is relatively expensive in that it requires additional time and effort to procure follow-up data and reinstate interventions. It can be regarded as unethical if the intervention is withdrawn prematurely or against the practitioner's best clinical judgment. Procedures for extinguishing a desirable change to obtain a reversal pattern (Hersen and Barlow 1976) are clearly unethical and their use is not advocated here.

An example of the design is as follows. An adult client who is married and lives apart from his mother is excessively dependent on her. An objective of treatment is to reduce his dependency as indicated by the number of times he calls his mother. The purpose of reducing the number of calls is to decrease the friction it has apparently caused between the client and his wife. Within the context of other treatment objectives that the worker and client have contracted, the worker decides to use direct advice. The baseline observations are stable at ten calls a day. The worker instructs the client not to phone his mother more than once a day. Following five sessions in which the worker gives direct advice, the number of calls goes down to an average of one a day. Although the worker sees the client for other objectives centering around marital difficulties, the worker ceases giving direct advice. The worker enlists the client's mother to gather data on the client's telephone calls. She is supportive of the treatment objectives because she too believes the number of calls has been excessive. Three weeks after the intervention of direct advice ceases, the client reverts to nine calls a day. The worker reinstates direct advice and there is another reversal to one call a day.

Information from this design is used to inform the practitioner as intervention progresses. To the extent that it consistently produces data that show client behavior depends on the social worker's interventions, it also provides data for summative evaluation.

Graduated-Intensity Design,
$$X_0 \; ooo \quad \begin{matrix} ooo \; ooo \\ X_1 \quad X_2 \end{matrix}$$

The Graduated-Intensity Design is used for demonstrating the impact of increasing or decreasing amounts of intervention. Changes in the amounts of intervention are symbolized by X_1 and X_2. They are of the following types: addition or subtraction of interventions (X_A to X_{A+B}); changes in duration and frequency of intervention, that is, an increased number of intervention sessions per week; changes in the social worker's level of activity, that is, from passive reflection to an increased number of statements that confront the client.

After establishing a stable baseline, the worker introduces initial intervention, $\begin{matrix} ooo \\ X_1 \end{matrix}$. A significant shift in the time-series from baseline to intervention, X_1, is followed by a change in the intensity of intervention, X_2. Subsequently, the time-series in X_2 is compared with data in X_1. Significant shifts from X_1 to X_2 are two unlikely successive coincidences, and they provide an approximation to the control of history and maturation (Carter 1972).

There are three basic limitations to implementation of this design: ceiling or basement effect, conceptualization of intervention intensity, and occurrence of ideal data patterns. Suppose data are based on a rating scale that ranges from 1 to 10; then the "basement" is 1 and the "ceiling" is 10. If the ceiling or basement has been obtained after X_1, there can be no further changes when X_2 is implemented. Hence changes in an intervention can only be implemented when intervention is partially, rather than completely, successful. Moreover, it is vital that the changing levels of intensity be conceptualized so that it is clear that they are additions or subtractions to the same type of treatment. Otherwise, the principle of unlikely successive coincidences cannot be used to control for history and maturation (Carter 1972). Finally, there must be evidence of significant shifts from the data at baseline to X_1 and from X_1 to X_2. Therefore, the graduated intensity design is also one that can only be implemented *a posteriori*.

On the other hand, this design is extremely useful in clinical situations where progress has occurred but the treatment objective has not been realized. It provides immediate feedback to the social worker, and she or he can vary the intensity as a function of further client progress. It is probably no more costly than an interrupted time-series design, since the intervention could still take place even if the objective were not achieved, the only difference being change in the intervention, X_2, as opposed to continuation of X_1.

Multiple-Baseline Design,

```
           OOO
A:  OOO   X
           OOO OOO
B:  OOO   X₀   X
```

Multiple-Baseline Designs are employed for controlling the internal validity factors of history and maturation, as well as for providing some empirical evidence of generalizability. They can be focused on evaluating the effectiveness of intervention on two or more behaviors or situations with the same client, or on two or more clients with the same behavior.

Multiple-Baseline Designs which are focused on behaviors can be drawn as in figure 7-6. Data are obtained simultaneously on variables A and B for the same client until a stable baseline is established for each variable. For example, A refers to cigarette smoking and B to rated dependency by significant others. The intervention is first focused on A, but not on B. There is a significant shift from baseline observations of variable A to the intervention period. In contrast, there is no significant shift in observations of B. The intervention is then focused on B, and there is a significant shift in the time-series for B.

To implement this design the following assumptions must be met: A and B are not significantly correlated, that is, they are independent; the intervention is substantially the same for A and B; data patterns that show the necessary significant shifts in the time-series are obtained. Otherwise, the evaluator has two Interrupted Time-Series Designs, one for each variable (Hersen and Barlow 1976, ch. 7; Jayaratne and Levy 1979, p. 179).

Multiple-Baseline Designs focused on situations follow the same schematic pattern as those for behaviors; however, A and B refer to the same variable in two situations instead of two different variables. For example, a social worker has the objective of increasing a client's expression of anger. Situation A is during intervention with the worker, and situation B is in the client's home. The situations should be independent; ideal data patterns should be obtained; and it must be demonstrated that the intervention can be focused on only one situation at a time.

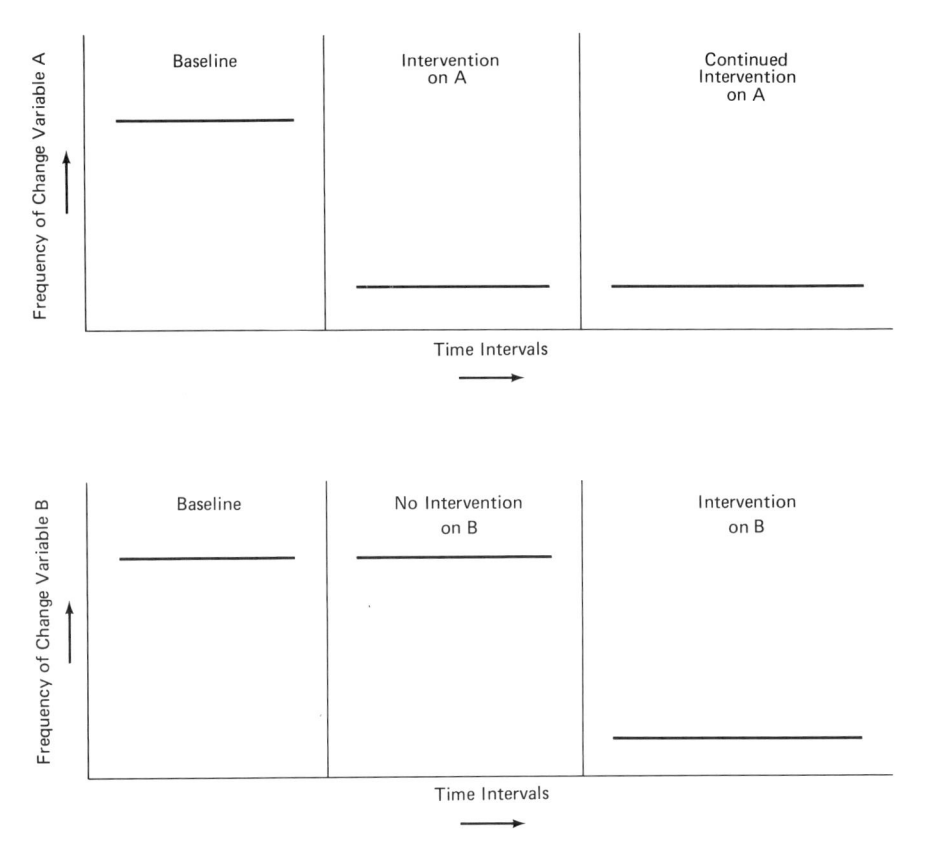

FIGURE 7-6

The most difficult problem for the social worker is trying to focus intervention on one situation but not on the other.

When the conditions for Multiple-Baseline Designs with behaviors or situations are realized, the principle of unlikely successive coincidences is invoked. Moreover, one replication across behaviors or situations is provided. With more replications, empirical generality increases, but only for data pertaining to the same client.

Multiple-Baseline Designs focused on two or more clients increase generality across clients, as well as control for internal validity factors. Since more than one client is used, this Multiple-Baseline Design is not technically a single-subject design. It bridges the gap between single-subject and group designs. It has also been called a Time-Lagged Control Design (Gottman and Leiblum 1974, pp. 139-40). Refer again to figure 7-6. This time A and B represent the same change variable for two different clients. There should be similar objectives for both clients (e.g., to decrease the frequency of drinking alcoholic beverages) and the interventions should be identical. Baseline observations are taken until there are stable baselines. The intervention is administered to one client, A, but not the other. After significant shifts in the time-series from baseline to intervention are observed for client A, the intervention is provided for client B. Significant shifts in a favorable direction for both clients provide evidence of two unlikely successive coincidences for the control of history and maturation, as well as evidence for one replication.

The basic difference between the fourth correlational design, Replicated Time-Series, and the Multiple-Baseline Design focused on two or more clients is the time at which observations are recorded. The Multiple-Baseline Design requires that baselines be simultaneously established, so that observations for the second client, B, serve as a control for the client who initially receives the intervention, A. Replicated Time-Series Designs, in contrast, do not require the simultaneous establishment of baselines.

Although intervention is not denied the client, in some instances it may be impractical for the social worker to delay it. It is most easily implemented when there are waiting lists. Its primary advantage is that the social worker gains formative information about the first client with whom she or he is working. Moreover, it provides summative data that can be generalized for use with the second client. If the procedures work well and are effective with the first client, the social worker can be more confident in using the same intervention with a second client. On the contrary, a failure with the first client causes the social worker to think carefully about whether she or he would use the same intervention with a second client.

CHAPTER EIGHT
RESEARCH DESIGNS FOR EVALUATING PROGRAMS

This chapter follows the same approach as the two previous chapters. It presents research designs as structures for gathering evidence in relation to different levels of knowledge. The logic for selecting designs is identical to that for devising research designs for evaluating single-case interventions. Accordingly, the same symbolic notation employed in chapter 7 is used here. The basic difference between research designs for evaluating single-case interventions and for evaluating programs is the unit of analysis. Whereas single-subject designs focus on single units (i.e., one subject, case, or organization), group designs involve more than one unit.

The variables in group designs reflect collectivities of individuals or properties of groups, organizations, and so forth. Individuals grouped together are represented by numbers, proportions, and measures of central tendency. Organizational variables reflect agency or organizational characteristics such as monies allocated to various departments within an organization, number of referrals made by a program to other social agencies, rate of staff turnover, and number of sponsored research projects in a school of social work.

Table 8-1 summarizes the relationship between levels of knowledge, criteria for achieving those levels, and the thirteen group research designs discussed in this chapter. As in chapter 7, the designs are illustrative but not inclusive. A variety of other research designs are available in *Quasi-Experimentation* (Cook and Campbell 1979) and *Evaluation* (Rossi, Freeman, and Wright 1979). Those sources offer

TABLE 8-1 Evaluating Programs

KNOWLEDGE LEVEL	CRITERIA FOR KNOWLEDGE	RESEARCH DESIGNS
1. Hypothetical-Developmental	1. Researchable hypotheses	1. Cross-sectional group study Longitudinal group study
2. Quantitative-Descriptive	2. Measurement, accuracy reliability and validity	2. Cross-sectional survey Replicated cross-sectional surveys
3. Correlational	3. Empirical relationship	3. One group before/after design Group comparative design Interrupted time-series designs Nonequivalent control group design
4. Cause-effect	4. Time order, control of internal validity factors	4. Controlled time-series design Randomized before/after control group design Randomized after only control group design Solomon four-group design Crossover design

additional examples of evaluation with a number of different social programs and organizations. After reading this chapter, refer back to the designs in chapter 7 to study the similarities between devising single-case and group designs. These similarities become more apparent when tables 7-1 and 8-1 are compared; these charts reinforce the concepts discussed in chapter 6 and previous chapters.

LEVEL 1: HYPOTHETICAL-DEVELOPMENTAL DESIGNS

Cross-Sectional Group Study, $\overset{O}{X}$, XO

The basic difference between this design and the cross-sectional case study for evaluating individuals is the observations, O. The observations refer to qualitative or quantitative measurements on a group of two or more subjects, and to a set of one or more variables measured at one period of time, $\overset{O}{X}$, or after the intervention or program has occurred, XO. Data are procured through participant or nonparticipant observation, interviews, questionnaires, documents, agency records, newspapers, and so forth. A vast array of information is collected to represent divergent and contrasting experiences, leading to an historical perspective. The strategy is to thoroughly describe what has occurred with program participants at a particular point in time. Then hypotheses about program implementation and its effectiveness are developed. The sampling procedure is purposive rather than representative. The objective of the design is to develop ideas that can be conceptually generalized. Evidence of empirical generality is not necessary. Program participants who represent extreme and varying experiences (e.g., deviant cases) provide a context for the development of researchable hypotheses. For example, clients who drop out are compared with those who complete a social program, and their reasons for program completion or drop-out are solicited and studied.

This design is used for assessing whether a program should be evaluated by more rigorous designs. Weiss indicates that programs should be evaluated when there are sets of clear, uniform, and consistent objectives in an agency or program (1972). This "pre-evaluative" information is especially important in the initiation and contact stages of program development, when the program staff and administration are locating resources and developing ideas for program implementation. The evaluator observes and asks staff what their basic functions are and inquires as to their purposes and objectives. In this way, any lack of awareness in the staff and inconsistencies in the program objectives are identified.

Staffs of experimental community development programs often formulate their objectives in the context of client-worker interactions and within the ethic of client self-determination. A cross-sectional group study might specify the issues that clients choose as important, those who participate and what will happen to the participants. This approach depends on a skillful gathering of historical information. It relies on documents, staff and participants' memories, and information recorded in logs or diaries. From this historical perspective, the evaluator determines staff strategies to use in attempting to deliver program technologies to specified target populations (Harris and others 1978).

One illustration of a cross-sectional group study is a project in social medicine in Giugliano, Italy, sponsored by the European Economic Commission (Carrino 1977; Tripodi 1980). The project focused on low-income women, children, and the elderly, who came to a medical center for help. The staff planned to study their clients' social needs and to organize clients with similar problems to seek services from appropriate authorities. For example, elderly ex-mental-patients sought recreational facilities, mothers of crippled children demanded that their children be integrated into normal classrooms, and so forth. The staff of the project kept logs and recorded such information as the following: the reasons why the patients sought help, the extent to which the patients' problems were appropriately medical, the number and type of groups formed by clients with similar needs, the number and type of proposals developed by the groups, and actions that followed on group proposals. Evaluators interviewed staff and patients, observed meetings and assemblies of patients pressing for social actions, and reviewed logs and case records.

An analysis of the information clearly indicated that a large number of patients were ignorant of medical services and that many requests for medical services were inappropriate. For example, the elderly were seeking companionship and freedom from isolation, rather than a specific form of medical treatment. In contrast, there were persons in the community who did not understand the nature of physical and mental handicaps, drug dependency, and physical problems related to pregnancy. It was hypothesized that appropriate medical referrals would increase as a function of information distributed by the program staff via radio, newspapers, and leaflets. Moreover, it was postulated that participation in group activities for social change would increase in relation to demonstrated success. This hypothesis derived from the fact that participation increased in groups centered on recreational activities, apparently as a result of a confrontation of mothers of handicapped children with local government officials. Approximately fifty to one hundred persons argued that transportation to and from the ocean should be provided for handicapped children and their mothers. That social need was met by the local officials.

The cross-sectional group study focuses primarily on qualitative data; quantitative data are gathered when available, but they are not usually collected on the same variable over time, as with the longitudinal group study. No internal validity factors are controlled. Although qualitative descriptions of a program are made, procedures are not employed to produce accurate, reliable, and valid data. Hypotheses are articulated for the purpose of providing ideas about program development. They are focused on collections of program participants, rather than on single clients, and are supposed to be probabilistic rather than deterministic. For example, "community residents who have been exposed to knowledge of venereal disease are more likely (a statistically significant, greater proportion) to comply with medical regimens for that disease than those who have not been exposed."

Longitudinal Group Study, X^{OOO}, XOOO

The longitudinal group study involves repeated measurements on one or more dependent variables over time — either during the implementation of the program, X^{OOO}, or during and after the program has been completed for a group of participants, XOOO. The use of the word "group" refers to a collection or aggregate of units such as individuals, as opposed to a single unit. This design is called by other names as well: longitudinal case study, panel, cohort, developmental, and dynamic case study (Tripodi 1981; Riley 1963).

The basic strategy is to describe a number of program participants over extended periods of time. The evaluator focuses on a set of dependent variables and observes their normative patterns of growth or maturation. In addition, she or he observes relationships of potentially independent variables and dependent variables. If changes in the dependent variables occur with the onset of independent variables, the evaluator uses that information for developing hypotheses. For example, the evaluator observes over a two-week period of a reading program administered to low-income children that there are sudden spurts in reading, as measured on performance tests of speed and comprehension. The evaluator observes no apparent changes in the administration of the program, the community environment, or the media. However, by interviewing participants and asking them whether any changes occurred in those two weeks that could have led to their increased performance, the evaluator discovers that the children's parents became interested and helped them learn to read. Hence it is hypothesized that tutorials with parental involvement are more likely to lead to change than tutorials without parental involvement.

When participants are followed up after receiving a social-work intervention, XOOO, it is possible to describe the patterns of change and discover whether there are other variables affecting those changes. For example, a group of clients complete a medical social-work program aimed at having them take medication. The clients are interviewed at weekly intervals for four weeks of follow-up. The worker observes changes in medical routines and asks the clients such questions as why they quit taking pills. It might turn out that their families discourage their use. Thus, it is hypothesized that the results of such a medical program should be directed toward clients *and* their families. Otherwise, changes might persist only when there is consistent monitoring by social workers at follow-up.

Hypotheses are generated by studying contrasting groups. Program dropouts and clients who complete a program provide a set of contrasting experiences. Workers can ask clients the reasons for their progress or lack of progress and their opinions of why the program is or is not successful. Another contrasting set of experiences can be devised by measuring the extent to which clients are satisfied with the program. An evaluator obtains information from extremely satisfied and extremely dissatisfied clients and relates it to dependent variables of change. By selecting deviant cases (i.e., extreme cases), the evaluator provides a context in which hypotheses can emerge.

This design is also used for developing measurements and for testing their test-retest reliability on a group of program participants. Measurements are taken repeatedly on variables of interest, and the experiences of the participants are described. These experiences (obtained by interviewing, nonparticipant observation, and other data-gathering devices) suggest factors that influence the degree of reliability for the change variables. For example, it is hypothesized that clients' responses about program satisfaction are proportional to their satisfaction with significant areas of their lives such as school, jobs, and interpersonal relationships. Hence instability of measures of program satisfaction may be related to clients' moods rather than to successful program implementation.

Since administrators of social agencies use selection processes when they specify criteria for eligibility to their program, the evaluator should develop variables related to program eligibility. Then he or she can use this design to look at the potential relationship between those variables and the designated variables of change. Eligibility variables are ethnic status, minority group status, national origin, gender, age, physical health, mental health, education, income, social class, and so forth. For example, an information and referral service is set up in a particular community. For two months an evaluator observes the number of referrals made to other social agencies, the number of appointments the clients keep, and the relationship of eligibility variables to referral patterns. In addition, he or she gathers information on the process of referrals as observed in interviews of workers with prospective clients. The evaluator hypothesizes that referrals to social agencies differ depending on whether the ethnic backgrounds of workers are similar or dissimilar to those of their clients. Information from interviews suggests that poor clients are less likely to follow through on referrals if they have to pay transportation costs.

The longitudinal group study does not control for internal validity factors. It provides a basis for the development of valid, reliable measurement, but it does not provide accurate quantitative descriptions. It requires a sensitive, prepared observer, who is able to collate and conceptually process large amounts of qualitative information in the search for independent variables related to sets of specified dependent variables. The observer can articulate hypotheses that contribute to program development, generate ideas about factors that help or hinder change, and pretest instruments for collecting data.

LEVEL 2: QUANTITATIVE-DESCRIPTIVE DESIGNS

Cross-Sectional Survey, RXO

The purpose of the cross-sectional survey is to provide accurate quantitative descriptions that are generalizable to a designated target population. The R in RXO refers to a random sample drawn from a specific target population, X designates an exposure of the sample to the social work program or intervention, and O indicates a set of one or more observations. When the entire population is studied, the design calls for an enumeration or census of all units or population elements.

The cross-sectional survey depends on accurate, reliable, and valid measures, which are developed and pretested before their use. Measures are obtained by any data-collection device, usually questionnaires and structured interviews (Tripodi, Fellin, and Epstein 1978; Austin and Crowell 1981). Facts and opinions are obtained from social-work clientele and their significant others regarding actions, attitudes, perceptions of services, degrees of satisfaction, expectations of intervention, and so forth. These data are gathered either at a point in time while social-work clients are receiving services or at follow-up.

There are several interrelated steps involved in conducting a survey (for more detail, refer to Moser 1965; Sudman 1967; Babbie 1970; Austin and Crowell 1981):

1. Develop evaluation questions and hypotheses before the survey to give direction to and focus the evaluation.
2. Operationally define the variables and locate or construct instruments for their measurement. Instruments such as these can be used: goal attainment rating scales (Kiresuk and Sherman 1968), satisfaction questionnaires, rating scales that reflect the psychosocial functioning of

clients (e.g., Walter Hudson's "Clinical Measurement Package for Social Workers" 1981), systematic observation schedules (Epstein and Tripodi 1977), and structured interview forms.

3. Define a population with respect to a specific time period, geographic area, and demographic and other characteristics related to eligibility for social-work services (e.g., reading achievement for children from low-income families). Compile lists of population elements (e.g., names of clients who receive social work services). The evaluator and the evaluation consumer decide whether there will be a census or a representative survey based on random-sampling procedures. The decision depends on desired accuracy, time, and available resources of staff, money, and so forth. Within a specified range of error, (e.g., several percentage points) a representative survey provides accurate information at a cheaper cost than a census. However, employ a census when it is important to identify every individual and to satisfy program sponsors that a precise "head count" has been made.

4. Develop sampling procedures and obtain permission from persons or representatives of organizations to participate in the survey.

5. Pretest sampling procedures and data-collection instruments for their estimated costs and response rates, as well as their accuracy, reliability, and validity. Dillman (1978) and Sudman (1967) suggest a variety of procedures, such as telephone interviewing combined with mailed questionnaires, to increase response rates and reduce survey costs.

6. Conduct the survey. Contact the participants. Collect, code, tabulate, and analyze the data (Austin and Crowell 1981).

The cross-sectional survey employs the same strategies for obtaining quantitative descriptions of clients' perceptions of social-work effectiveness as were discussed in relation to the After Intervention Measurement Design in chapter 7: formulating questions about social-work services, goal attainment scaling, and use of "Then and Now" ratings. In survey design, which is geared to obtaining measurements from more than one client, it is important to establish that the questions are reliable and valid. Goal attainment scaling and Then and Now ratings should only be used when it makes sense to combine the ratings for individual clients. This is possible when clients have identical program objectives, are measured on the same variables, and are exposed to identical social-work services. Average changes and their dispersions are shown for the aggregate of clients who participate in the survey. For example, a survey may indicate that clients' perceptions of their changes using Then and Now ratings show an average positive change of 2.0 points on a 10-point rating scale of progress having a standard deviation of 0.5.

An illustration of a cross-sectional survey design is as follows. The administration of a public welfare agency is interested in evaluating the extent to which clients have access to their workers and whether they have to wait for long periods of time before they receive social-work assistance. There are 1,000 clients currently listed as receiving services. Since there are 700 females and 300 males, and since the administration desires information for each gender, it is decided to obtain a nonproportionate stratified random sample. A random sample of 100 is drawn from the list of 700 females, and another 100 is selected from the list of 300 males. A structured interview is used as the primary data-gathering device. It includes questions pertaining to clients' contacts with their workers, opinions of workers and their services, types of services received, and the extent to which they met clients' needs, and so on. The interview schedule is pretested for 5 males and 5 females. Estimates are made of clients' cooperation, comprehension of questions, possible fatigue, and so on. The instrument is modified until it appears to be reliable and valid. Clients are contacted by letter and later interviewed by telephone if they have access to phones or in face-to-face contacts.

The cross-sectional survey provides descriptive information usable for formative purposes if the survey is conducted while clients are receiving services. For example, in the survey of public-welfare clients, it is discerned that males wait longer to receive service than females do. This information may lead to the development of policies and procedures to equate the waiting time for males and females, especially when they are requesting the same services. The data from surveys is also used as summative information about program contacts, indicating, for example, typical characteristics of clients seeking social-work services. Cross-sectional surveys do not provide the intensive, in-depth data obtainable from cross-sectional group studies. Moreover, they do not provide empirical correlations between social programs and change variables, and they provide no control over internal validity factors.

Replicated Cross-Sectional Surveys, R X^{OOO}, RXOOO

The Replicated Cross-Sectional Survey Design consists of repeated surveys of a designated population over selected periods of time. A different random sample of respondents is selected for each time period. The respondents for one set of observations are not necessarily the same ones selected for subsequent observations; hence net changes for aggregates of individuals can be described, but individual changes cannot. When the design is focused on net changes while the social-work program or intervention is taking place R X^{OOO}, it provides data for modifying the intervention as it occurs if necessary. Replicated follow-up surveys, RXOOO, provide data about changes after clients have terminated the social-work program. Such information is relatively expensive to obtain when respondents are interviewed face-to-face. It is obtained more cheaply by questionnaires and telephone interviews (Dillman 1978).

This design is similar to the longitudinal group study in that repeated measurements are obtained at different time intervals. However, it is different in these ways:

1. Repeated observations are not obtained for the same group of respondents.

2. Variables are operationally defined, with estimates of reliability and validity secured before conduct of the surveys. This is because the purpose is to provide accurate quantitative descriptions of change.

3. Measurements are obtained on the same set of variables for each survey.

4. Representative sampling is necessary to provide generalizable, descriptive knowledge. The extent to which the sample is representative of the population is tested against known distributions of population parameters such as gender, age, and ethnicity.

The length of time between surveys and the number of replications is arbitrary. The replications should, however, be related to program objectives or points in time for which changes are expected. For example, it is hypothesized that clients in a weight-reduction program will lose 5% of their weight after two weeks in the program; 10% in one month; and 15% in three months. Accordingly, surveys of weight loss can be taken at those times. Changes described in replicated cross-sectional surveys cannot easily be explained or attributed to independent variables or program intervention or services. This is due to the fact that no evidence is provided that can show an empirical relationship to changes in independent and dependent variables. In addition, internal validity factors are not controlled.

An example of a replicated cross-sectional survey follows. Probation officers are interested in accurately describing changes of young delinquents with respect to their attitudes toward school, school attendance, time spent studying, and so forth. Variables related to school are measures of effectiveness of a program in which friendly adults meet twice weekly with the youths for the purpose of increasing their school performance. Rather than seek correlational knowledge, the probation officers observe whether or not changes are taking place. If no changes occur, it is inferred that the additional services provided by friendly adults do not appear to effect any change. On the other hand, noticeable changes are due to many other uncontrolled influences. Approximately five hundred boys participate in the program. Repeated random samples of fifty boys are obtained at monthly intervals for three months. Opinions and attitudes about school are obtained for each boy. Data on grades and school attendance are also secured from the schools to validate the youths' estimates of their attendance, tardiness, and grades. Net changes for representative groups of boys are described; however, individual changes cannot be shown because the same group of boys was not used in each sample. If the evaluator is interested in individual changes, she or he studies the same sample of boys over different points in time.

LEVEL 3: CORRELATIONAL DESIGNS

One Group Before/After Design
$X_O \ O_1 \ XO_2$

The One Group Before/After Design is also referred to as the One Group Pretest-Posttest Design (Tripodi 1981, Campbell and Stanley 1966). It involves measurements of one or more variables, O_1, after it has been shown that participants have not been previously exposed to the social-work intervention, X_O, and before participants receive the intervention, X. After receiving the intervention, the participants are measured again on the same set of dependent variables, O_2. Differences between O_2 and O_1 are associated with the change in intervention status, $X - X_O$. Statistically significant differences constitute empirical evidence of a correlation between X and O. They are tested by using statistical methods such as the matched pairs t test and McNemar's *chi square* test of change (Siegel 1956), which reflect differences in the distributions of measures at X_O and X. The One Group Before/After Design is based on the same logic as the One Case Before/After Design. They both provide evidence of a temporal relationship between the independent and dependent variables. However, the group design contains measures for an aggregate of individuals at two time periods, which makes it possible for statistical procedures to be employed. In addition, data for any individual within the group constitute a One Case Before/After Design. Hence individual cases as well as the aggregate of individuals can be assessed.

If the participants for a planned intervention, X_B, have had a previous intervention X_A, the addition of B to A, X_{A+B}, can be evaluated and compared to X_A. As discussed in chapter 7 for the One Case Before/After Design, this incremental design is symbolized as $X_A \ O_1 \ X_{A+B} \ O_2$. Statistically significant differences between O_2 and O_1 associated with the change from X_A to X_{A+B} indicate evidence of an association between B and O. This design is especially useful for determining whether there is a correlation between change and new interventions being offered in addition to services already being administered to clients. Referring to the earlier example of a replicated cross-sectional survey, it is known that probation officers are providing services to delinquent youth, X_A. The addition of services provided by friendly adults is symbolized by X_{A+B}. Observation on the dependent variables of school performance can be taken for the same group of youth, say one hundred, before and after the provision of new services. This results in empirical evidence of a correlation between the addition of services offered by friendly adults and school performance, as measured by less truancy, better grades, and so forth. The evaluator is careful to note the extent to which X_{A+B} is different from X_A by observing whether or not the new services were offered in the two different time periods. If the services are identical for both periods of time, the design cannot be implemented.

Whereas the replicated cross-sectional survey provides an estimate of net change, this design provides evidence of an empirical correlation, and within that, actual changes of individual cases at two time periods can be described.

The One Group Before/After Design, $X_O\ O_1\ X\ O_2$, is frequently used in program evaluation (Rossi and Williams 1972; Rossi, Freeman, and Wright 1979). It doesn't control for internal validity factors, except biased selection and experimental mortality, which are not relevant since comparison groups are not employed. It does provide a first approximation of cause-effect knowledge, in that evidence of correlation is a necessary condition for causality. If a correlation is obtained, it indicates that it would be worthwhile to employ other procedures, such as experiments, to control for internal validity factors. The evaluator must provide evidence that there is a change of intervention status between X_O and X. This is monitored by asking the participants a series of questions pertaining to how long they have participated in interventions similar to the one offered by the social-work program. In addition, the evaluator should ascertain whether the program participants are receiving interventions from other agencies at the same time as the intervention being evaluated, X.

Group Comparative Designs,

$$\frac{X\ O_2}{X_O\ O_1},\ \frac{X_2\ O_2}{X_1\ O_1}$$

The strategy of Group Comparative Designs is to provide contrasting states of the intervention or program variable and to determine whether there are associated changes in the dependent variables. There are two basic variations of this design:

1. The Static Group Comparison or Correlational Design (Campbell and Stanley 1966; Labovitz and Hagedorn 1981), $\frac{X\ O_2}{X_O\ O_1}$

2. The Comparative Intensity Design (Tripodi 1981), $\frac{X_2\ O_2}{X_1\ O_1}$

In the Static Group Comparison, one group of subjects is exposed to the program, X, and the other group is not, X_O. Subsequent to program exposure, X, measurements are obtained on the dependent variables for both groups, O_2 and O_1. The dotted line indicates that the two groups are not obtained by random assignment. Hence selection biases related to O_1 and O_2 can occur. Statistically significant differences between O_2 and O_1 provide evidence of an empirical association between X and O. The *chi square* statistic and t tests between independent samples can be used to test for statistical differences of distributions for the variables O_1 and O_2. This design controls for the effects of initial measurement and statistical regression, since there are no measurements taken before program exposure. The effects of instrumentation are also controlled when there is previous evidence of reliable and valid measurements. Experimental mortality, maturation, biased selection, and interaction effects are not controlled. The influence of history is controllable if the evaluator can provide evidence that both groups have had similar experiences. To the extent it is possible, the evaluator gathers information about the distributions of both groups on relevant variables and tests for their equivalence. For example, data is available on previous social-work contacts, education, and so forth. If the distributions, that is, means and variances, are not statistically different, there is evidence of equivalence, and for those variables, biased selection is not operative.

The major problem in using the design is in selecting a comparison group. Ideally, the comparison group should be identical in all relevant variables to the group that received the program. One strategy for obtaining comparison groups is to seek persons who are eligible for the program but have not participated in it. Another plan is to locate persons who are on the waiting lists for social-work services and who have not received other services.

An example of this design follows. Suppose a program aims at job counseling for high school dropouts. The objective is to provide them with knowledge about filling out job applications and interviewing for jobs. All of the participants who completed the job-counseling program are tested on their knowledge of job applications. A comparison group is composed of high school dropouts who did not receive the program but who are eligible for it. Or it can be comprised of high school dropouts who were signed up for the program but didn't attend the job-counseling sessions. Special efforts have to be made to contact the members of both groups, for differential participation could lead to further biased selection. Both groups are tested and compared for differences. In addition, distributions of age, education, previous employment, gender, ethnicity, and reading comprehension are compared. If there are no statistically significant differences between groups on all comparisons but the knowledge test, there is evidence of an empirical correlation between job counseling and knowledge of job applications.

The Comparative Intensity Design, $\frac{X_2\ O_2}{X_1\ O_1}$, includes a comparison of two or more groups exposed to different levels of social-work intervention, $X_1\ X_2\ \ldots X_n$. Each group is measured after exposure to social-work intervention; that is, O_2 after X_2, O_1 after X_1, and so on. Statistically significant differences between groups provide evidence of an empirical association, so long as it can be demonstrated that the levels of X are different; for example, X_2 refers to twice as much intervention as X_1 within a specified time period. The design has the same degree of control over internal validity factors as the static group comparison. It is particularly useful when it is difficult to locate a comparable group that has not received social-work interventions, X_O. Different groups of subjects may have received varying portions or amounts of social-work intervention, and those groups can be compared with each other. However, the evaluator should continually be aware of the possibility of biased selection, and she or he should attempt to specify the degree of bias. For example, clients in a social-work agency have different numbers of interviews. Biased selective factors may explain why. The number of interviews may be related to the nature of the clients' problems, the degree to which the social worker likes or dislikes the clients, and so forth. The design is more interpretable when clients have similar problems and needs and when the same program objectives are operative for both groups.

A Comparative Intensity Design is illustrated as follows. Suppose the director of a family-service agency is interested in discerning whether there is a relationship between the number of hours of training for paraprofessionals and their clients' ratings of helpfulness. Paraprofessionals are employed to assist elderly clients with their household chores, transportation, and other areas of living. They are volunteer workers willing to work for ten hours a week for up to six months. A training program is developed for two groups of volunteers, 20 in each group. One group of volunteers receives two hours of training; the other, four. After training, each volunteer works with five to ten clients a week. Subsequent to each client contact, a social-work supervisor obtains client ratings of perceived helpfulness. Measures for both groups are averaged, and their distributions are tested for statistically significant differences. In addition, distributions of relevant variables are compiled and compared between groups, to provide some evidence of comparability. If ratings of helpfulness are similar for both groups, and if there are no apparent differences due to biased selection, there is no evidence of an empirical correlation. The director, noting that the shorter training period is as effective as the longer one, decides to routinely implement a two-hour training program for new volunteers. In this way he or she reduces the costs from the training program but achieves the same degree of effectiveness.

Interrupted Time-Series Designs,
$$X_O \; OOO \quad X^{OOO} \quad OOO$$

Interrupted Time-Series Designs for evaluating programs are symbolically identical to interrupted time-series designs for evaluating individuals. First it is established that there is no intervention, X_O. This is followed by three or more baseline measurements, OOO, until there is a stable data pattern. Next, the intervention or program is introduced, X, and measurements are taken while the program is operative, X^{OOO}. Follow-up measurements are taken after the program ends, X^{OOO} OOO. When used for evaluating groups or programs, the interrupted time-series design focuses on organizational variables or those that represent aggregates of individuals. Hence measurements in a set of observations, O, are typically comprised of numbers, averages, and proportions; for example, the number of referrals made by an agency, the average weight of clients in a weight-watcher program, and the proportion of clients who are employed. If average measures are obtained by aggregating measurements of clients, it is possible to evaluate individuals and programs simultaneously, but the following requirements must be met:

1. All clients must have the same objectives, with correspondingly relevant measures.
2. Each client must receive the same program.

To illustrate, clients have volunteered for a program designed to increase their assertive behaviors. A measurement of assertiveness for each client is based on self-reports in the form of a ten-point rating scale, ranging from low assertiveness

(1) to high assertiveness (10). There are one hundred program participants and each provides a rating of assertiveness every day for ten days before program intervention. An average rating of assertiveness is constructed for each day; this measure is based on the ratings of one hundred participants. Baseline patterns are then observed for any client, or for the aggregate of clients. For example, the average assertiveness rating for the group of respondents is 3 for the 10-day period, with average ratings ranging from 3 to 4, a relatively low degree of variability. After the program is operative, daily ratings are taken for a 20-day period, with the average ratings stabilizing at 8 after 10 days of intervention. This reflects change for the aggregate of clients; however, a particular individual may not show any change as indicated in baseline ratings of 3, and average ratings of 3, after 20 days of intervention.

Changes in baseline patterns as a function of the program are evaluated by statistical significance tests such as the single-mood test, Walker-Lev tests, Shewart Chart Analyses (Caporaso 1973; Gottman and Leiblum 1974), and other procedures for evaluating individuals discussed in the preceding chapter. Patterns of baseline and follow-up measurements vary from individual to individual, but this can be discerned by analyzing the range and variability around each average measure.

The aggregation and disaggregation of measures is also used as an exploratory device to develop hypotheses. Changes in measurements are analyzed in relation to selected subsets; for example, clients and social workers grouped by characteristics such as race, gender, and age. Such information is useful as feedback about program and practice development. Measurements during the program, $\overset{OOO}{X}$, are compared with baseline measures. It might be found, for example, that there are average changes for clients exposed to a social program, but that those changes are more pronounced for clients with certain characteristics (e.g., young females) than those with others (e.g., old males).

Average measures for clients and organizational variables provide indices of program effectiveness. Follow-up measures after the program has stopped indicate the persistence of change, and replications of the time-series designs with different workers, clients, and settings provide evidence of program generalizability. This is important information for judging the effectiveness of program implementation and for considering the extent to which similar programs should be instituted in other places.

This design controls for most internal validity factors; however, it cannot rule out factors of contemporary history that change simultaneously with program exposure (Mahoney 1978). Therefore, an evaluator should obtain information from program participants, significant others, or both regarding potential historical influences (Epstein and Tripodi 1977). Data can be obtained by questionnaire or interview after participants have completed their programs. Although the potential effects of contemporary history cannot be completely ruled out, data may suggest that their influences are relatively minimal. When there is an extensive baseline period, the influence of historical events can be regarded as not very plausible. For example, chronic, autistic schizophrenics who have not spoken for years may talk after the introduction of a therapeutic program. If there have been a large number of therapeutic programs instituted over the years with no changes observed, and if there are no other contemporary events other than the new therapeutic program observable to the patients' significant others, then it is reasonable that the changes are due to the therapeutic program.

As indicated in chapter 7, internal validity factors are only controllable with good data patterns. To the extent internal validity factors are controlled, the design provides a context for making inferences about cause-effect knowledge by approximating experimental design. Thus, the Interrupted Time-Series Design is regarded as a quasi-experiment (Campbell and Stanley 1966). Ideally, baseline data should be stable, with little variation between successive measures over time. Baselines are stabilized by averaging measures touching each other, that is, by "moving averages." However, this also reduces the number of data points, and the evaluator must be careful to use the same time intervals when comparisons are made between the time-series during and after the program with baseline data.

Time-series rely on accurate, reliable, and valid data. These data are obtained from agencies and programs that have good record-keeping and data-processing systems. Many agencies such as schools, jails, and hospitals routinely collect data that can be used to form time-series. When those data are not available, the evaluator should consider whether the costs of collecting repeated measures over time are justifiable in relation to the evaluation objectives and the budget at hand.

There are many applications of time-series analysis and the student can find a variety of other examples in these references: *Research Techniques for Program Planning, Monitoring, and Evaluation* (Epstein and Tripodi 1977), *Quasi-Experimentation* (Cook and Campbell 1979), *Quasi-Experimental Approaches* (Caporaso and Roos 1973), and "Applying Time-Series Strategies: An Underutilized Solution" (Knapp 1979).

As with other designs, it may be difficult to establish that there was no program or intervention to which the clients were exposed, X_O, before the introduction of the program, X. In that event, the evaluator considers the use of incremental control (X_A vs. X_{A+B}) where A is previous program exposure and B is the program whose effectiveness is being evaluated. This may be difficult to implement when evaluating programs based on aggregates of clients. It should be demonstrated that A can be specified, and that the previous interventions received by clients are similar.

The X_A OOO X_{A+B} OOO design is used in situations where clients are already receiving treatment or social-work interventions. In that event, the evaluator has less difficulty in constructing baseline measures; for data are easily gathered while intervention is taking place, X_A. When the new intervention, B, is instituted, it is in addition to the A intervention. Significant shifts in time-series from X_A to X_{A+B} provide evidence of the relationship of X_B to change in the dependent variables.

Nonequivalent Control Group Design, $\dfrac{O_1 \ X \ O_2}{O_3 \ X_O \ O_4}$

The Nonequivalent Control Group Design is a quasi-experiment that provides correlational knowledge as well as an approximation of experimentation (Campbell and Stanley 1966; Tripodi 1981). It is not a true experiment because randomization of experimental and control groups is not used. Two groups of subjects are selected. One group receives the program, and measurements are obtained before and after program exposure—O_1 X O_2. A comparison group is measured on the dependent variables before, O_3, and after, O_4, the experimental group receives the program, X. It receives no intervention and is symbolized as X_O. The measurements at O_1 and O_3 are taken at the same period of time before the program is administered; and the measurements at O_2 and O_4 are also obtained simultaneously, but after the program is completed. The differences between O_3 and O_4 are those due to the effects of previous measurement, instability of measurement, and historical and maturational factors. The differences between O_1 and O_2 reflect those same internal validity factors, as well as the influence of the program. Hence $(O_2 - O_1) - (O_4 - O_3)$ registers differences due to the independent variables or programs. Posavac and Carey assert that "The correct statistical tool to analyze data from such a design is the two groups by two time periods analysis of variance with repeated measures over time period..." (1980, pp. 205-06).

This design does not control for experimental mortality, regression effects, selective biases, interactions between selective biases and history, and maturation and measurement effects. Experimental mortality or differential dropout rates between groups can be monitored, which is easier for programs of limited time duration. The greater the length of time for the program to be completed, the greater the likelihood of program dropouts. Regression effects are possible with extreme scores on the dependent variables at O_1 and O_3. Their influence is reduced, of course, when extreme scores are not used; however, this limits the sample of participants that can be studied. The most serious problem is that of biased selection, which indicates that the two groups are not comparable on relevant variables.

There are three basic strategies that evaluators use to approximate control of selection biases: control by definition, control by individual matching, and control by aggregate matching (Rossi, Freeman, and Wright 1979, pp. 194-205; Tripodi 1981). Before the evaluator uses these strategies she or he should specify which variables are most important to control. Relevant variables are those that are either theoretically or empirically related to the dependent variables. As Rossi, Freeman, and Wright state, the selection of control variables depends on prior knowledge and a good theoretical understanding of the phenomena being studied (1979, pp. 196-97). They advocate that evaluators use a small number of variables for control, due to their belief that variables specified as control variables are usually highly correlated.

Control by definition is a simple procedure that simultaneously increases the homogeneity of comparison groups and reduces the extent to which the results can be generalized. The evaluator selects a control variable and specifies that aspect or level of the variable that is included in the evaluation. Social class, for example, with levels of low, middle, and upper, can be selected as a control variable. By definition, one level, say lower social class, is included in the sample; the other levels of class are defined out of the study. Therefore the comparison groups are equated with respect to social class, since only those from the lower social classes are studied.

Aggregate matching is a process in which the distributions of the control variables are equated for the comparison groups. Suppose fifty persons are designated as lower-class and seventy-five as middle-class for the experimental group, X. The evaluator then seeks to construct a control group with the same proportion of lower- and middle-class subjects. The extent to which the groups are equivalent is tested by statistics such as *chi square* (Epstein and Tripodi 1977). Whereas aggregate matching focuses on average distributions for the comparison groups, individual matching is a procedure by which pairs of individuals are identified with respect to the control variables, and each individual is arbitrarily assigned to one of the two groups. For example, a pair of individuals is identified as lower-class; each is assigned to a different comparison group. Another pair is identified as middle-class, and again each is assigned, and so on. The procedure is repeated until the desired number for each group is obtained.

Rossi, Freeman, and Wright suggest guidelines for choosing variables for constructing control groups (1979, p. 205). They assume there are characteristics at four different levels: individual, family, organizational, and community. Thus age, gender, marital status, ethnicity, and so on are regarded as individual variables; number of children, number of family members, and so on, as family variables; size, budget, number of subunits, and so on, as organizational variables; and population size, growth rate, population density, and so on, as community variables. Although the evaluator approximates control groups by selecting them to be similar to experimental groups on selected, relevant variables, it is impossible to achieve complete control since unknown variables may be relevant for any particular evaluation.

The basic advantage of this design is that it can approximate an experiment in which randomization procedures are employed (see cause-effect design 2). In some instances, where randomization is not permitted due to organizational constraints based on ethical principles or practical considerations, this design can be the most powerful of the available evaluation designs. Nevertheless, the problem of biased selection or lack of comparability between groups is a liability. Subjects that make up comparison groups may be difficult to locate, and those that are located may contain their own peculiar problems of selective bias. Subjects are found on program waiting lists, or they live in the same economic conditions as the program participants, or they are eligible for a program and are not receiving their services.

To the extent the evaluator can provide evidence that the comparison groups are equally motivated and desirous of program services and are equivalent on relevant variables, she or he can infer causal relationships between the program and changes in the dependent variables. Data from this design cannot be analyzed for one individual. The data represent average effects for a group of individuals exposed to a program or an intervention. Hence the intent of the design is to produce summative knowledge. Because data are collected after program completion, there is no opportunity for feedback to program staff while the program is taking place.

An example of this design is as follows. A social worker wishes to study the effectiveness of a film on birth control devices with teen-age, lower-class girls who live in a particular geographic area. Those girls come to a community center on Mondays and Tuesdays every week. Typically, the same girls do not come on both Mondays and Tuesdays. Approximately fifty to one hundred girls participate in the center's activities.

Volunteers are solicited for the film on a particular Monday night, and twenty-five participate. Before the film they are measured for knowledge of birth control devices and their effects. The film, which lasts for one and one-half hours, is shown, and the twenty-five girls are tested one week later. A control group is constructed from girls who go to the community center on Tuesday nights. They are asked if they would be willing to participate in an experiment designed to measure their knowledge of birth control. Twenty-three girls agree to participate. Measurements are taken one day after those taken for the experimental group, on Tuesday of two successive weeks. The evaluator believes the one-day separation in measurements is close enough in time to regard them as simultaneous. Moreover, measurements on two different days tends to avoid possible transmission of knowledge from experimental to comparison-group subjects. The 50-item test is objective; the higher the score, the greater the knowledge of birth control. Relevant variables are regarded as gender, social class, age, grade-point average in school, and family size. Gender, social class, and age are controlled by definition. Information on grades in school and family size is obtained for each girl participating in the study. Distributions for grade-point average and family size are not statistically significantly different for the comparison groups, which indicates they are equivalent with respect to those variables. In addition, average scores on the knowledge tests are virtually equivalent for both groups. The experimental group has an average score of 40%; the control group, 41%. On subsequent testing, the experimental group attains an average score of 75%, while the control group's average score is 43%. The changes for the experimental group are statistically different from those for the control group, and the evaluator concludes there is some empirical evidence that the film is effective in terms of increasing knowledge. To prove this result further, the evaluator also asks each subject by questionnaire whether she received or was exposed to any other knowledge about birth control before or after presentation of the film. Equal amounts of alternative "programs" (e.g., 10% of each group had a class on sex education; 20% of each group saw a program on television devoted to birth control) are regarded as X_A; the addition of the film for the experimental group is construed as X_{A+B}, where B represents exposure to the

film. Changes for X_{A+B} are greater than changes for X_A, and the program, B, is effective, as judged by this variation of the nonequivalent control group design,
$$\frac{O_1\ X_{A+B}\ O_2}{O_3\ X_A\ O_4}.$$

LEVEL 4: CAUSE-EFFECT DESIGNS

Controlled Time-Series Design,
$$\frac{OOO\ X\ OOO}{OOO\ X_O\ OOO}$$

The Controlled Time-Series Design is a combination of the Interrupted Time-Series and the Nonequivalent Control Group Designs (Posavac and Carey 1980, p. 209). With ideal data patterns, all internal validity factors can be controlled. The group exposed to the program is repeatedly measured on the dependent variables until stability occurs at baseline and after the intervention is completed, OOO X OOO. This part of the design is an interrupted time-series design, and it can control for all internal validity factors except history. The addition of the comparison group, X_O, provides a control for history and maturation, as well as for the effects of instrumentation, previous measurements, and statistical regression. An ideal data pattern is observed when there is stability in the time-series at baseline for both X and X_O, there are statistically significant shifts in the time-series for X, and there are not statistically significant shifts in the time-series for X_O. Figure 8-1 is a graphic portrayal of this data pattern. The evaluator uses the same strategies for, and encounters the same difficulties with, choosing comparison groups and control variables as those discussed in the section on the Nonequivalent Control Group Design. Analyses of variance are used so long as the time-series

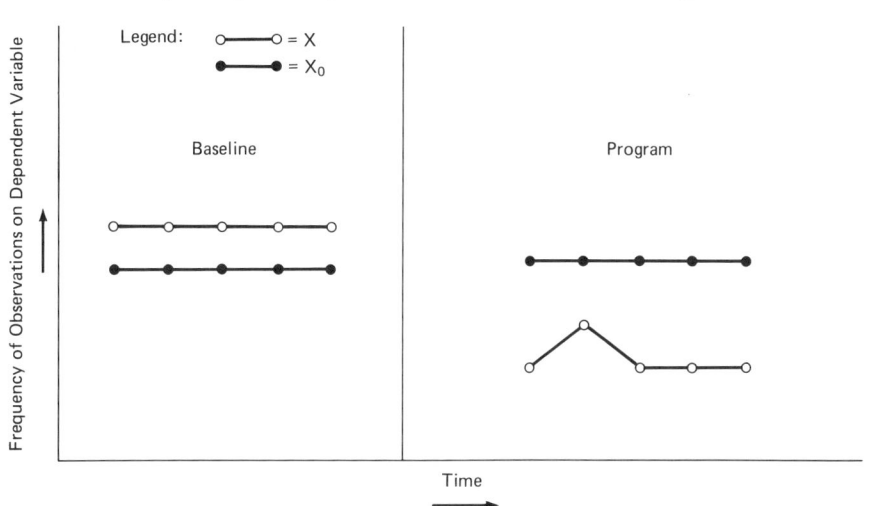

FIGURE 8-1

measures are independent of each other. In these between-group comparisons of time-series for X and X_O, selection biases are not completely controlled; whereas they are controlled in the within-group time-series analyses for X and X_O separately.

The Controlled Time-Series Design is expensive to conduct since it involves repeated measurements for two separate groups. It provides a good basis for inferring causality between a social-work intervention and effectiveness variables, without employing the randomization of true experiments. It is easier to implement this design in institutional settings than in open, community settings, where it is usually difficult to obtain repeated measures on comparison groups. A procedure often employed to cut down on reduction in the control groups is to pay the subjects a certain amount of money for participation. If that strategy is used, it is recommended that experimental subjects also be paid the same rate as control-group participants. This equalizes the potential effects of money, which can be called an intervention.

An example of this design is as follows. Suppose there is a training school for delinquent boys in which there is a problem of boys running away. The administration doesn't want to enforce maximum security procedures because the boys are there for relatively minor offenses and are not regarded as dangerous to themselves or others. The institution is composed of ten cottages, with approximately twenty boys in each cottage. An intervention is devised which consists primarily of increased privileges: two additional movies a week, later curfew hours, and job possibilities for one hour's pay each evening. Since this is additional to the privileges the boys already have, the design takes this form, $\frac{OOO \; X_{A+B} \; OOO}{OOO \; X_A \; OOO}$, where B refers to the increased privileges and A to the intervention already taking place. Two cottages are arbitrarily selected to receive the increased intervention, B; and two control cottages are selected that match the experimental cottages with respect to the boys' ages, previous offenses, length of time at the training school, and number of disciplinary infractions. Data on all of the cottages are available for the dependent variables of number and proportions of boys who ran away. Baseline data are analyzed. If they are relatively stable, the intervention is introduced in the experimental cottages. Data are tabulated and analyzed weekly, and comparisons are made after one, two, and three months. Since the boys in each of the cottages do not interact with boys from other cottages, the possibility of the occurrence of negative side effects is reduced.

Randomized Before/After Control Group Design, R O_1 X O_2
R O_3 X_O O_4

This is the classical experimental design, which is considered a true experiment. It is also known as the Pretest-posttest Control Group Design (Labovitz and

Hagedorn 1981; Campbell and Stanley 1966; Tripodi 1981). The Randomized Before/After Control Group Design is identical to the Nonequivalent Control Group Design except that subjects are randomly assigned to either the experimental group, X, or the control group, X_O. The process of randomization controls for biased selection on known as well as unknown variables; each subject has an equal chance of being included in the experimental or the control group. This procedure also enables the evaluator to handle the program variable or variables so that it or they occur before possible changes occur in the dependent variables.

Since randomization doesn't guarantee equivalence between groups, especially with small numbers of subjects (e.g., less than twenty-five), it is necessary for the evaluator to check the comparability of experimental and control groups on relevant variables. Variables that are not comparable are used as covariates in an analysis of covariance for observing the statistical significance of changes between the experimental and control groups.

When there are variables which the evaluator desires to represent, she or he can employ a stratified random-allocation procedure. For example, if equal representation is desired for males and females, the pool of available subjects is stratified by gender. Then subjects within each gender are randomly assigned to experimental and control groups. Riecken and others provide a detailed discussion of the use of random allocation procedures, with a number of examples of the experimental method used for evaluating social programs (1974).

The combination of randomization and a comparison group controls for statistical regression, effects of previous measures, measurement instability, history, and maturation. However, experimental mortality cannot be controlled, particularly in open settings where clients may drop out of experimental programs and control group members may seek social-program interventions elsewhere. Hence the evaluator carefully monitors the dropout rates, checking to see whether the randomization procedure is altered. If the groups are no longer equivalent on relevant variables, randomization is no longer in effect; and the design shifts to a Nonequivalent Control Group Design.

As with other comparative designs, the evaluator carefully determines that the control group, X_O, actually receives no program. If the control group is exposed to an intervention, X_A, then the evaluator provides evidence that the experimental group contains the intervention, A, as well as the intervention being tested, B. When it is impossible to assert that there is a group which has received no program, the evaluator employs this design variation: $R\ O_1\ X_A\ O_2$. Changes between O_3
$O\ O_3\ X_{A+B}\ O_4$
and O_4 reflect changes due to X_{A+B}; changes between O_1 and O_2 reflect changes due to X_A; and $(O_4 - O_3) - (O_2 - O_1)$ indicates changes due to the program or intervention being tested, B.

Experimentation is intended to produce cause-effect knowledge. It is especially likely to do so when there is a low dropout rate and when there are no extensive periods of time between preprogram and postprogram measures.

Randomized After Only Control Group Design, R X O$_1$
R X$_O$ O$_2$

The Randomized After Only Control Group Design is also referred to as the Posttest-Only Control Group Design (Campbell and Stanley 1966, pp. 25-27; Shortell and Richardson 1978, p. 53). This design is identical to the Randomized Before/After Control Group Design, except that there are no measurements of the dependent variables before clients are exposed to the social program. There is random assignment to either an experimental group, X, or control group, X$_O$. The experimental group receives the program, while the control group doesn't; and both groups are measured after the program is completed. If O$_1$ is greater than O$_2$, and the difference is statistically significant, there is an empirical association between the program and the dependent variables. All internal validity factors except experimental mortality are controlled, so long as the randomization procedures are effective. Experimental and control groups are checked for equivalence of their average distributions on relevant variables. Because there are no previous measurements, the external validity factor of the interaction of initial measurements and the program is controlled. Hence there is a greater degree of generality with this design than with the Randomized Before/After Control Group Design.

An example of this design is as follows. Suppose pre-delinquent youth are identified as those junior high school students who have been truant and have been suspended from school at least once in the preceding year. It is believed that a high proportion of these teen-agers will become involved in delinquent careers. The school social worker hypothesizes that "guided group interaction" with these youth will result in fewer court appearances for violations of the juvenile code. Pre-delinquent teen-agers are stratified by grade (seventh, eighth, and ninth) and by gender (male and female), forming six levels: seventh-grade males, seventh-grade females, and so on. Teen-agers within each level are randomly assigned to either the experimental group, in which they receive ten weeks of guided group interaction, or the control group. Equivalence between the experimental and control groups is tested on these variables: achievement-test scores, grade-point average, number of disciplinary infractions at school, social class, and family composition. The proportion of court appearances for the experimental and the control groups is measured after ten weeks of the program. The *chi square test* for independent samples is used to determine the extent to which there are statistically significant differences between the experimental and control groups.

It should be noted that this example also illustrates the Randomized Before/After Control Group Design. The procedures are identical, except that measurements on the dependent variable are taken for both experimental and control groups before introducing guided group interaction. Hence the evaluator obtains before and after measurements of school attendance, juvenile code violations, and number and type of school disciplinary problems. When the Randomized Before/

After Control Group Design is used, differences in mean changes between experimental and control groups are assessed by analyses of variance.

Solomon Four-Group Design,
R O_1 X O_2
R O_3 X_O O_4
R   X O_5
R X_O O_6

Shortell and Richardson state that the Solomon Four-Group Design (Solomon 1949) can be used for program evaluation (1978). It combines the Randomized Before/After Control Group Design with the Randomized After Only Control Group Design. It increases the external validity of the Randomized Before/After Design by building in one experimental replication. Random allocation is employed to assign subjects to four different groups, whose distributions on relevant variables must be equivalent. If $(O_2 - O_1) - (O_4 - O_3)$ and $O_5 - O_6$ are statistically significant, with both changes occurring in the same consistent direction, there is one replication. Although this added feature is costly, because it requires two experimental and two control groups, it does make empirical generalizability more possible. Therefore it is the most rigorous design the evaluator can use when attempting to provide cause-effect knowledge for summative purposes. Its basic disadvantages are:

1. It is costly to implement.
2. There must be sufficient numbers of subjects so that equivalence can be demonstrated in all four groups.
3. The dropout rates may be uneven in the different groups; hence the evaluator must very carefully monitor for experimental mortality.
4. The use of randomization for allocating subjects to experimental or control groups may be regarded as ethically unsuitable by program or evaluation personnel.

An example of the Solomon Four-Group Design is as follows. Suppose an administrator is interested in determining whether or not a training program of 2 hours' duration will increase social workers' interest in using tape-recorded interviews. The agency in which the social workers practice is a protective services agency which employs two hundred workers in a particular geographic area. The workers are randomly assigned to one of four groups, with approximately fifty in each group: two experimental groups and two control groups. Both experimental groups receive the training program, but only one receives before measurements; correspondingly, one of the two control groups receives before measurements on the dependent variables of rated interest in using tape-recorded interviews. The control groups do not receive the training program. Approximately one month after the training program, all four groups are measured on the dependent variables. If the experimental groups show consistent increases in their interest in and use of tape-recorded interviews compared with the control groups, the training program is effective.

Crossover Design, R O_1 X O_2
R O_3 X_O O_4 X O_5

The Crossover Design is an experimental design that uses a time-lagged control group which receives the social program after the experimental group has completed it (Epstein and Tripodi 1977). Subjects are randomly assigned to either an experimental or a control group, X or X_O. Measurements on the dependent variables are obtained before the program (O_1 and O_3) and after the program (O_2 and O_4). After the control group is measured on O_4, it receives the program. When the program is completed, measurements are again obtained. Differences between O_2 and O_1 and O_4 and O_3 are compared for statistical significance by analysis of variance. In addition, O_5 - O_4 is tested for statistical significance by use of a statistic such as a t test for matched pairs. If both results are consistent, there is one successful experiment with one replication. Referring to the example given for the Solomon Four-Group Design, an evaluator could use one experimental group and one control group to evaluate the effectiveness of the training program. Both groups are measured on the dependent variables of rated interest in using tape-recorded interviews and the number of tape-recorded interviews. The experimental group receives the two-hour training program, and the control group doesn't. One month later both groups are measured on the dependent variables. If there are statistically significant differences in favor of the experimental group, the control group then receives the training program. One month later the control group is measured again to determine whether desirable changes occurred after it, too, had received the training program.

There are two major advantages to this design: (1) it employs randomization, but no subjects are denied the opportunity of participating in the program and (2) it increases empirical generalizability, due to built-in program replication.

The Crossover Design controls for the same internal validity factors as other true experiments. It doesn't control for experimental mortality. Although it provides a built-in replication, it doesn't control for the external validity factor of the interaction between initial measurements and the program, as does the Solomon Four-Group Design.

The design is most useful for programs of short, specified time periods: educational and training programs, short-term interventions, and so forth. Moreover, it is defensible ethically when there are many more persons eligible for a program than there are resources, that is, when there are waiting lists. Assuming equivalent degrees of program need, those who are serviced first are chosen by randomization, a nonbiased mechanism.

CHAPTER NINE
INTERPRETING AND REPORTING RESULTS

RESEARCH AND STATISTICAL PROCEDURES

The evaluator determines appropriate research and statistical procedures for the production of sound knowledge. This is made easier by locating the evaluation within the context of these interrelated factors: type of evaluation, level of knowledge desired, discovery of unanticipated consequences, control and degree of generality. The type of evaluation refers to whether the evaluation is focused on programs or practices with one individual or with groups or aggregates of individuals. Locating the desired level of knowledge helps the evaluator specify the evidence necessary to attain his or her knowledge objective. Hence as illustrated in chapter 6, the researchability of hypotheses is necessary evidence for hypothetical-developmental knowledge; reliable, valid measures, for quantitative-descriptive knowledge; empirical associations as well as reliable, valid measures, for correlational knowledge; and control of internal validity factors, empirical associations, and reliable, valid measures, for cause-effect knowledge.

Regardless of the type of knowledge level the evaluator hopes to attain, he or she should be prepared in any research study to discover the unexpected, that is, to ascertain whether any unforeseen results of social-work programs or practices occur. Moreover, since it can be assumed that many evaluation consumers hope to understand the extent to which changes are due to the social worker's program or practice, it is worthwhile for the evaluator to consider the degree of control he or she has achieved. This control may have been accomplished experimentally through use of randomization and control groups, statistically through such techniques as partial and multiple correlational analysis and analysis of covariance, or he or she may have achieved no control at all.

The degree of generalizability is a function of replications and representative-sampling procedures. It should be assessed for every evaluative study. It enables the consumer to consider whether the results of the research are unique and whether they can be used for summative as well as formative evaluation.

Once the evaluator has identified factors relevant to the evaluation, he or she attends to the use of research and statistical procedures for analyzing and interpreting the results. As shown in the chapters on research design, the analysis of results depends on: the types of data—qualitative, quantitative, or both; the research design; the representative sampling procedures; and the number of replications. In addition, the analysis of data requires the evaluator to be skilled in quantitative methodology and to make reasonable judgments in drawing inferences from the data.

It is not the intent of this chapter to provide a detailed treatise on data analysis. However, it should be emphasized that there are courses on data analysis and data interpretation in social statistics, biostatistics, survey methodology, experimentation, epidemiology, qualitative analysis, and so forth. These courses are given in university college departments of statistics, sociology, political science, public health, social work, psychology, and others.

Program evaluators should be acquainted with these topics: descriptive statistics; statistical tests such as t, *chi square*, and F; regression, multiple, and partial correlational techniques for discrete and continuous variables; analysis of variance and covariance models; multi-causal models and cross-tabulations in survey analysis; and information systems and the use of computers for processing information. Among the many textbooks available for analyzing and interpreting data, the following are exemplary:

H. M. Blalock, *Causal Inference in Non-Experimental Research*, University of North Carolina Press, 1967.

D. T. Campbell and J. C. Stanley, *Experimental and Quasi-Experimental Designs for Research*, Rand McNally, Chicago, 1966.

J. Cohen, *Statistical Power Analysis for the Behavioral Sciences*, Academic Press, New York, 1969.

J. Cohen and P. Cohen, *Applied Multiple Regression/Correlation Analysis for the Behavioral Sciences*, Lawrence Erlbaum, New York, 1975.

T. D. Cook and D. T. Campbell, *Quasi-Experimentation: Design and Analysis Issues for Field Settings*, Rand McNally, Chicago, 1979.

T. D. Cook and C. S. Reichert, eds., *Qualitative and Quantitative Methods in Evaluation Research*, Sage, Beverly Hills, 1979.

B. Glasser and A. Strauss, *The Discovery of Grounded Theory*, Aldine, Chicago, 1967.

J. M. Gottman and S. R. Leiblum, *How to Do Psychotherapy and How to Evaluate It*, Holt, Rinehart and Winston, New York, 1974.

R. M. Grinnell, Jr., ed., *Social Work Research and Evaluation*, F. E. Peacock, Itasca, Illinois, 1981.

M. Hersen and D. H. Barlow, *Single Case Experimental Designs*, Pergamon Press, New York, 1976.

T. Hirschi and H. C. Selvin, *Delinquency Research: An Appraisal of Analytic Methods*, Free Press, New York, 1967.

A. E. Kazdin, *Behavior Modification in Applied Settings*, Dorsey Press, Homewood, Illinois, 1975.

Q. McNemar, *Psychological Statistics*, 4th Ed., Wiley, New York, 1969.

S. Siegel, *Nonparametric Statistics for the Behavioral Sciences*, McGraw-Hill, New York, 1956.

M. Susser, *Causal Thinking in the Health Sciences*, Oxford University Press, New York, 1973.

B. J. Winer, *Statistical Principles in Experimental Design*, 2nd Ed., McGraw-Hill, New York, 1971

General Considerations in Presenting and Analyzing Data

Due to the importance of data analysis, evaluators use statistical consultants in both the planning and analytic phases of evaluative research. If statistical consultants are employed, they are most useful in the planning of evaluation. They indicate the extent to which research designs and data collection procedures are appropriate for different types of statistical analysis. Of course the evaluator must realize that statistical analysis depends on accurate, reliable data and adequate research design. No statistician can rescue a badly-conceived evaluation with invalid data. Statisticians can, however, suggest procedures for data analysis of which the evaluator may not be aware. Thus it is recommended that evaluators develop plans for statistical analysis and review them with a statistical consultant. This is done to verify the adequacy of the planned analysis and to seek alternative methods if they are available.

Shortell and Richardson indicate that there are necessary analyses to be performed for program evaluations in the health field (1978). Their advice is sound and can be generalized to social-work evaluations. First, the evaluator provides complete distributions of all important variables, in particular, descriptions of what happened to all individuals exposed to the social-work program or practice. These descriptions are quantitative-descriptive, and they should adequately summarize the distributions on all change variables; average measures, measures of dispersion, and kurtosis (showing peakedness or flatness) are used to depict the shapes of distributions. Variables pertaining to program staff and client population are also presented. This is especially significant when program objectives are geared to populations with specific characteristics such as race, income level, and education.

Second, there should be a description of the social-work program or practice. There should be qualitative information about the referral and intake processes, and how clients are chosen to participate in the program. The interventions must be described in sufficient detail to clarify what was done and when. Supplementary quantitative data should be presented to indicate the frequency and duration of program contact, (e.g., number of interviews and number of class sessions). Detailed narrative descriptions are useful when the evaluator attempts to develop hypotheses about what particular program tasks are related to unanticipated outcomes.

Third, for correlational designs, simple correlations are presented to show the relationship between program or practice variables and measures of effectiveness. In addition to correlations, the evaluator presents the numbers of cases used in the analyses, the amount of variation explained (e.g., $r^2 \times 100$ as the percentage of variation), and, where appropriate, the degree of statistical significance. Even for correlational designs, the evaluator attempts to provide some statistical control of relevant variables by using either cross-tabulations (Hirschi and Selvin 1967) or multiple and partial correlational analysis (J. Cohen and P. Cohen 1975). Relevant control variables are developed by referring to staff characteristics, client characteristics, and intervening program variables such as staff turnover.

Fourth, analyses are performed for relevant subsets of the client population. For example, it may be important for administrators to know whether or not there are differences in program effectiveness as a function of such client characteristics as gender, race, age, religion, and national origin.

To the above, add the following points:

1. The evaluator very carefully describes the response rates of clients. For example, in a given evaluation there is a 90% response rate to an interview schedule, but only a 40% response rate to a questionnaire. Response rates for particular populations help the evaluator to form judgments of representativeness. Moreover, the response rates can be examined by subsets of the intended population. There may be differentials in response based on client characteristics. The study of such phenomena can lead to the identification of unanticipated program consequences.

2. The evaluator obtains qualitative information pertaining to unplanned consequences. Clients are routinely queried at the termination of a social-work program, and social workers are requested to describe positive or negative changes in clients.

3. The worker presents any historical information on the program or practice and on the clients, to provide a context for evaluation. This provides a framework within which a particular evaluation can be appraised. Some programs may have been evaluated several times, showing consistencies in results as well as problems in analysis. A particular client may have received a large number of social-work programs from a number of different social workers, and no changes may have occurred; this provides a lower degree of expected change for that client than for another with a similar problem who has had no previous intervention.

4. When experimental designs are employed, evaluators indicate which internal validity factors are controlled. Moreover, they qualitatively describe the extent to which experimental procedures such as random allocation are actually implemented.

STATISTICAL VERSUS PRACTICAL SIGNIFICANCE IN MEASURING CHANGE

Statistical significance is a change in data patterns or observations that is not expected on a chance basis. Traditionally, levels of statistical significance are at the 0.05, 0.01 and 0.005 levels of probability. A 300-pound person who is a client of a medical social worker and must lose weight because of a heart condition and high blood pressure may lose five pounds, and that weight loss is statistically significant. But is it practically significant? Obviously it is not if the client needs to lose 100 pounds due to a variety of complicated health problems. Practical significance may or may not correspond to statistical significance. Practical significance is based on judgments made within the context of social values, while statistical significance is based on probability theory and the likelihood of rare occurrences.

In the chapters on research design, three criteria of change were used: change by *a priori* objectives, change by visual inspection of graphic data patterns, and change by statistically significant shifts in measurement. Change by achieving an *a priori* objective is equated with practical significance. It always involves assigning a value to the achievement of an objective. For example, program directors, evaluators, and program participants believe that an objective of 20% employment for those who complete a job-training program is realistic. Achievement of that objective is regarded as a practical significance. Depending on the particular subpopulation to which a program is directed, a quantitative statement of an objective may be appropriate or too ambitious, or trivial. Since judgments of appropriateness vary from person to person and group to group, it is evident that practical significance can be represented by different numerical values. In evaluative research, judgments of practical significance are most appropriate when they are made by evaluation consumers—clients, workers, administration, and program sponsors. This is why it is recommended that evaluators obtain desired change objectives from evaluation consumers in the planning stages of evaluative research.

The second criterion of change is visual inspection of graphic patterns in time-series analysis. This eyeballing technique involves observations of changes in size as well as slope. Since there can be individual differences in perception, it is reasonable that there can be different appraisals of whether or not change occurs. Differences in perception may arise as a function of the physical units of the coordinates of a graph, the complexity of the data pattern, the slope of time-series, the change in magnitude, the particular behavior observed, and so forth. Social workers using this change criterion make two basic judgments. First, they decide whether or not a change occurred. Second, if one has occurred, they make a judgment about the practical significance of that change. What does the change mean and what does it imply in terms of client progress? Since these judgments are made *a posteriori* (after the occurrence), it is recommended that the evaluative researcher assess the inter-observer reliability of the judges, that is, the extent to which different evaluation consumers independently agree on observed changes and their practical significance. This process of validation by consensus is more objective than one in which only the evaluator makes an appraisal of change.

The third criterion of change is statistical-significance testing. To use statistical tests appropriately, the evaluator should be aware of the assumptions involved in the statistical tests she or he employs. The achievement of statistically significant changes may be a more or a less narrow criterion than the criterion of practical significance. It may be practically significant for a client to register a one-step change on a rating scale of depression, but the change may not be statistically significant with respect to the client's pattern of previous ratings. On the other hand, there may be a statistically significant change, as in the example of the 300-pound person losing five pounds, and that change may not be practically significant. However, the criterion of statistical significance is used as a sign of progress, so long as the observed changes are in the direction that indicates practical significance. Hence, it is recommended that the criterion of statistical significance be routinely employed along with either of the other two criteria. Moreover, it is recommended that criteria for practical significance be defined *a priori* rather than *a posteriori*; for decisions made afterwards are more subject to biases of the evaluator and evaluation consumers.

USES OF DATA FOR PROGRAM EVALUATION

Both quantitative and qualitative data are employed in research that aims to formulate researchable hypotheses. Data are used for the evaluator's purpose of providing in-depth descriptions of social programs and the social interactions among staff, clientele, and significant community organizations. Control factors and evidence of empirical generality are not crucial in the development of this level of knowledge. This is due to the emphasis on obtaining contrasting, but not necessarily representative, experiences by purposive sampling. The evaluator describes distributions of variables and their quantitative relationships, looking for relationships that could serve as hypotheses for more rigorous research. The criterion of statistical significance is used to locate possible relationships of practical program significance.

Qualitative data could consist of accounts in the public media, for example, radio and newspapers, historical and program documents, case records, logs, and worker diaries. These data are assembled into a description of the program, its function and purpose, how it is perceived by community residents and program participants, and so on. In particular, the evaluator looks for unusual experiences and perceptions of extreme positive or negative changes. From this information, hypotheses are derived about unanticipated program consequences. Qualitative data from interviews with program staff and participants are used to locate consistencies and inconsistencies in program objectives and practices. And information is gathered about the viability of research designs for producing higher levels of knowledge.

There are three basic uses of quantitative data in research devoted to the production of quantitative-descriptive knowledge. First, there is the presentation of the data. Distributions are described by measures of central tendency and dispersion for all program participants and for other relevant populations such as program staff and community residents who are eligible for the program. Distributions are also described for various population subsets. For example, the number of program contacts is described for all program participants; then the distributions of that variable are described for subgroups of clients that vary by different age groups. Second, reliability and validity tests of the key variables are presented. Since quantitative-descriptive knowledge depends on accurate, reliable, and valid data, evaluators include reliability and validity tests within the evaluative research. Hence empirical data regarding inter-observer agreement, *coefficient alpha*, and other indices of reliability attest to the objectivity of the measurements employed in the research. Correlation coefficients, numbers of cases, and degree of statistical significance should be reported. Third, comparisons of the sample used in the research to relevant populations are made on relevant variables. Statistical-significance testing is used to indicate the extent to which the sample is similar to or different from the populations of interest.

Survey methodology is the primary strategy for analyzing data in cross-sectional and replicated cross-sectional surveys. Conventional procedures are followed for the tabular presentation of data and for their analyses (Hirschi and Selvin 1967). The evaluator is especially aware of possible distortions, so she or he presents data in the form of numbers and percentages, noting where there are missing cases in the analysis.

Qualitative data are also important in quantitative-descriptive research. They are used in three ways: to describe narratively the social program and its sociopolitical and geographic context, to suggest potential unanticipated consequences, and to provide data that bear on the content validity of variables used in the evaluation.

Data used for developing quantitative-descriptive knowledge are pertinent to the development of correlational knowledge. The evaluator uses quantitative and qualitative data in the manner described previously. In addition, she or he uses quantitative and qualitative data in these ways:

1. Use statistical procedures to indicate the direction, amount, and probability of occurrence of empirical associations. Employ bivariate analyses to show the existence of empirical correlations (Schuerman 1981; Gorsuch 1981) between intervention and outcome variables for research designs involving comparison groups; employ time-series analyses to show statistically significant shifts in the dependent variables in time-series designs (Caporaso 1973). Show the relative contributions of sets of independent variables to sets of dependent variables with multiple regression techniques (J. Cohen and P. Cohen 1975).

2. Detect potentially spurious relationships between intervention and outcome variables with cross-tabulation procedures and partial correlational techniques (Susser 1973; Cohen and Cohen 1975).

3. Demonstrate the equivalence of comparison groups by using statistical testing for independent samples. When there is nonequivalence, use covariance analyses to adjust for initial measurement differences on dependent variables between the comparison groups (Campbell and Stanley 1966; Shortell and Richardson 1978).
4. Obtain qualitative data to suggest possible test factors or control variables that can be used to uncover spurious relationships in cross-tabulations (Labovitz and Hagedorn 1981).
5. Provide narrative data to describe typical changes that appear to be related to program interventions. These data make the presentation of results more lively.
6. Use qualitative data to describe similarities and differences between comparison groups and between the research sample and the target population, and to describe the setting in which the social program is implemented.

All of the preceding procedures are used in evaluative research that attempts to develop cause-effect knowledge. Evaluative researchers use analysis of variance and covariance, multiple-regression techniques, and other conventional tests such as Scheffé's test for multiple comparisons (1953) and nonparametric statistics (Siegel 1956).

Statistical control procedures and the testing of equivalence between experimental and control groups are necessary for determining the validity of randomization in social experiments. Quantitative and qualitative data are used to indicate the extent to which the comparison groups are receiving social work or other interventions, as well as to describe the process of client and worker involvement in the social program.

Qualitative data are particularly necessary for describing unforeseen developments in social programs. For example, a social program aimed at providing an educational center for children in Giugliano, Italy, was delayed because the building for the center was destroyed by a storm. A program aimed at reducing unemployment may be less successful than originally planned, due to the fact that an automobile factory that employed most of the residents shut down. Qualitative data are also used to develop further hypotheses about the effectiveness of social programs.

USES OF DATA FOR EVALUATING INDIVIDUALS

Combinations of qualitative and quantitative analyses are essential for evaluating individual clients. Clinical judgments are made by social workers and other professionals. Those judgments are made on the bases of interviews, observations, psychological tests, questionnaires and other types of data related to clients' problems, agency orientations, and worker-client expectations of change.

For the developing of hypothetical knowledge, data can be used as follows:

1. Unstructured and semi-structured interviews, logs kept by clients, and case records generate quantitative and qualitative data. Use these data to develop hypotheses about the clients' problems and provide tentative diagnostic assessments, noting such information as the clients' symptoms and factors apparently leading to the onset of symptoms. Analyses of these data are made easier by conceptual schemes and theories about social-work interventions, for theories of practice provide frameworks for defining relevant hypotheses.
2. Clients' self-reports provide data about their histories, experiences with previous interventions, significant social interactions, expectations, treatment goals, and so on.
3. Time-series data on variables for which clients seek change and the reporting of critical incidents that occur with changes in the time-series provide hypotheses about intervention (Gottman and Leiblum 1974).

Qualitative data are employed to describe worker-client interactions and progress, client deterioration, or no obvious changes in the individual client. In addition, the social worker describes the extent to which the client is similar or different from other clients who receive services from a particular social agency.

There are several uses of data for the development of quantitative-descriptive knowledge:

1. Tabulate and graph time-series data for repeated measures of effectiveness at baseline. In other words, quantitatively describe natural data patterns when measures are repeated over time. Use measures of central tendency and dispersion to describe the distributions.
2. When standardized tests are used, compare the client against normative groups. For example, an individual is described as anxious if his or her score on an anxiety test indicates more self-reported anxiety than 95% of the population on which the test was standardized.
3. Describe worker and client actions and interactions. For example, perform content analyses of interviews to describe the themes covered in social-work interviews, the relative amounts of time the worker and client speak, and so forth (Tripodi and Epstein 1980).
4. Describe the extent to which a sample of interactions is representative of some designated target population of interactions. To illustrate, there are groupings of worker statements as observed in ten tape-recorded interviews with a particular client; for example, exhortative, supportive, and confrontative statements. The degree to which the proportion of confrontative statements in a particular interview is similar to (representative) or different from (nonrepresentative) the average of the nine other interviews is determined by statistical-significance testing. Representativeness is regarded as important for testing the effectiveness of the intervention, which requires that the worker be consistent in his or her use of confrontative statements.

Correlational knowledge showing the relationship between changes in states of the social-work intervention and the dependent variables is produced by qualitative or quantitative data, or combinations of both. Changes in intervention are described in terms of their presence or absence, while a change in the dependent variable is described in relation to satisfying the client's objective. If a client describes himself or herself as feeling less depressed after the onset of intervention, there is qualitative evidence of an association between the intervention and the degree of client depression.

Quantitative indications of correlation are possible with repeated measures. There must be either qualitative or quantitative information indicating changes of intervention status. Statistically significant shifts in time-series data should occur simultaneously with the presentation of the intervention. As indicated in chapter 7, Shewart Chart Analyses and the binomial and other statistical techniques are used to detect changes in time-series patterns for the dependent variables.

Cause-effect knowledge can only be approximated in evaluating the effectiveness of intervention on an individual client. Graduated withdrawal-reversal, and multiple-baseline designs are used to make causal inferences (Hersen and Barlow 1976). The evaluator uses a plausibility criterion. On the basis of the principle of unlikely successive coincidences (Jayaratne and Levy 1979), she or he interprets ideal data patterns as sufficient for ruling out all internal validity factors as explanations of change. There are two procedures the evaluator can use to support the assertion that historical and maturational factors are not responsible for observed changes in dependent variables. First, through semistructured interviews and participant observation, she or he gathers information about the extent to which new, additional events have occurred in the client's life, and whether they appear to be responsible for observed changes in that client. Second, she or he performs replications of the interventions with other clients who have similar problems, using multiple-baseline designs. Replications with similar results increase the possibility that historical and maturational factors are controlled.

Qualitative data are used to indicate the degree to which the implementation of the social-work intervention is consistent, as perceived by the worker and the client. Narrative data provide a thorough description of the clients' situations; in so doing, these data furnish hypotheses about what aspects of intervention led to unanticipated positive or negative client changes. Moreover, factors can be located that might show the apparent correlations to be false. For example, a client has the objective of reducing his or her alcoholic intake. Intervention is applied, and the client reduces his or her consumption of alcohol, but is also physically sick. When the illness subsides, he or she may revert to pre-intervention drinking behavior.

COMMUNICATION

Evaluative research results should be pertinent to the program and practice decisions that social workers make (Tripodi, Fellin, and Epstein 1978; Shortell and Richardson 1978). Communication is much easier when evaluators' reports are clear and understandable. The evaluator should carefully note who the consumers of evaluation are and write the report so that it can be understood by them. Consumers are more likely to be practitioners and administrators than researchers, for they are in positions in which they make decisions affecting programs and individual clients.

Communication is made more effective by planning for it in the early stages of the evaluative research. The evaluator should consider the format in which results will be presented. Questions such as these should be answered in deliberations with relevant consumers: How long should the report be? Should the more technical aspects be included in an appendix rather than in the basic text? How sophisticated are the consumers in terms of their understanding of research and statistical concepts? The evaluator assesses the consumer's understanding in two ways. First, she or he presents dummy data that are representative of the kinds of data analyses that might be performed, and discusses them with the consumer. Second, she or he shares with the consumer samples of evaluative research ranging in length and amount of technical reporting. Subsequently, the consumer states his or her preference for the particular format that he or she understands most easily.

The evaluator's report should be written in a language and style compatible with the consumer's. In addition to a full-length report with appendices, there should be a compact summary that highlights the findings, limitations, and implications of the research. This saves time for those consumers who do not wish to read an entire report. Since there are persons who might read only the evaluation summary, it is most important that the evaluator accurately summarize the results. In the summary, as well as in the text, there should be direct statements about whether or not recommendations are based on data. Moreover, the degree to which the results are valid should be clearly communicated, so that they can be considered within the limitations of the research. There should be effective communication about the types and levels of knowledge, the control of contaminating factors, and the extent to which the results can be generalized and used for formative or summative evaluations. This is not to say that the evaluator should not present hypothetical and impressionistic speculations. On the contrary, much insight is acquired by speculation grounded on experience; however, the evaluator should indicate whether or not his or her notions are based on data obtained directly from the research.

According to Reid the text of a research report should be organized in sequence: the research problem, the method, the findings, and the results. The contents of the research report are:

1. *Problem* — "Background, rationale, and significance of the study; review of relevant research and theory; presentation and explanation of the research problem and variables"
2. *Method* — "Delineation of the strategy (design) and methods of the investigation, including a description of the setting and the sampling plan; description of data collection procedures, instruments, and measurement approach"

3. *Findings*—"Presentation of findings, including data displays (tables, graphs, etc.); textual exposition of data; description of relevant analytic procedures
4. *Discussion*—"Discussion of findings, including interpretation of data, implications for theory, practice, education and research; limitations of study; relationship to other research; summary and conclusions" (1981, p. 556)

The appendix should include instructions to research participants, sampling procedures, and copies of all instruments used for data collection. They can also include detailed analyses that are not directly pertinent to the major findings of the research; for instance, analyses pertaining to the reliability and validity of the research variables, equivalence of comparison groups, and representativeness of research samples.

There are modes of communication other than the written research report, including oral presentations, seminars, and workshops. To enhance communication, program evaluators often set up advisory groups comprised of evaluation consumers, sponsors, and researchers. Those groups can stimulate inquiry, locate potential communication problems, discuss possible solutions, and advise on effective implementation of evaluative research.

The consumer, of course, has to be committed to paying attention to the evaluative research results, otherwise communications are ineffective. Just as there should be clear transmission of research results by evaluators, consumers should be open to receiving those messages. Both administrators and social-work practitioners should seek to improve their receptivity to information from evaluative research (Tripodi 1974). Administrators, in particular, should ensure that research results are distributed throughout the social agency or organization and understood by all relevant personnel. A useful mechanism for spreading research knowledge is to distribute the report so that personnel can read it and pose questions about it. Then the evaluator orally summarizes the results in a meeting with administration and staff. Finally, questions are answered, and results are clarified and modified, if necessary. The implications of the results for program or practice decisions should be thoroughly discussed so they are understood before their possible implementation.

TIMING OF INFORMATION FEEDBACK

An issue that evaluators and evaluation consumers must deal with is the timing of information feedback. At what point in the evaluation should the consumer receive data from evaluative research? Evaluative information can be given out while the evaluation is in progress or after it is completed, that is, it can be formative or summative.

There is a need for continuous feedback in evaluations of individual clients. Formative information should relate to the assessment, the intervention plans, and the client's progress. Especially in times of emergency, evaluative data should be immediately available as input for the social-worker's clinical decisions. In contrast, summative information is recorded after a case is completed or when replicated information regarding particular techniques is produced.

It is exceedingly difficult and costly to provide continuous feedback on each client in program evaluation. However, periodic evaluations of different stages of a program's development can be efficiently managed. There can be evaluative research directed toward recruiting and referral processes, program contacts and their barriers, and so forth. This information is formative in that it relates to a program's development. Summative evaluations require the completion of a program for representative samples of clients.

Whether the evaluation is directed toward an individual client or program or is formative or summative, the results should be fed back to the consumer in time for her or him to consider them when making decisions about changes in policies, programs, or practices (Murrell 1977). Therefore, it is recommended that evaluators and evaluation consumers plan which decisions the evaluation is to provide inputs for and when the evaluation data should be disseminated (Weiss 1972).

It is also necessary for the evaluator to convey when it is important to delay the dissemination of information. For example, in the production of cause-effect knowledge by means of a social experiment, it is necessary to keep the intervention in a relatively constant state for a prescribed period of time. Data must not be fed back until the experiment is completed; otherwise the constancy of the experimental stimulus is threatened, with the possibility of program staff changing the intervention as a direct result of feedback. On the other hand, in the pursuit of lower levels of knowledge, there is less need for a constant, unchanging program stimulus. Hypothetical and descriptive knowledge of a formative nature can be fed back continuously and immediately, while summative data must await the completion of the program or practice.

The evaluation consumer should understand that, in general, the higher the level of knowledge desired, the longer the period of time before information can be distributed. Moreover, the degree of generality is proportional to the length of time before the results from evaluative research can be fed back to the consumer. Ideally for maximum communication, the consumer should at least be involved in the planning and implementation of the evaluation. Participation in the evaluation tends to increase a person's understanding of the process and the results obtained (Coursey, Mitchell, and Friedman 1977).

IMPLEMENTATION

There are a number of writers who have developed hypotheses and ideas about factors related to the implementation of evaluative research results (e.g., Havelock 1971; Weiss 1972; Davis and Salasin 1975; Posavac and Carey 1980; Rothman 1980). The basic issue involved in implementation is whether or not the results of evaluation will be adopted in the practice setting.

Tripodi specifies several factors related to the utilization of research results in social-work practice: communication, relevance, accessibility, receptivity, compatibility, and implementation potential (1974). Since evaluative research can be considered a subtype of social research (Tripodi, Fellin, and Meyer 1969), these factors are pertinent to the implementation of evaluative research results.

As previously indicated, it is important to faithfully communicate evaluative research results and to specify what level of knowledge is actually achieved. Obviously, if the knowledge is not new, or if it is not sound regarding the level of knowledge sought in the evaluation, the results should not be implemented. It is an abuse of an evaluation to implement invalid knowledge.

The findings of evaluative research should be relevant to decisions made by individuals or groups, whether they are practitioners, administrators, or sponsors. The results should relate to and inform about the policies, tasks, or procedures engaged in by staff, clientele, administrators, and sponsors. The more related the information is to practice and administrative decisions, the more relevant it is. Basically, what is relevant is in the "eyes of the beholder"—the evaluation consumer.

Accessibility is another key factor related to implementation. It is the extent to which variables can be manipulated or new ideas implemented to change practice. The manipulation of variables is regarded as their engineerability (Tripodi, Fellin, and Meyer 1969). For example, a technology can be introduced or modified. Variables related to the technology (how often it is provided, where it is delivered, etc.) are manipulable variables. Variables that may or may not be manipulable are those that refer to client characteristics such as gender and previous experience with social programs. Client eligibility is often related to political decisions, and whether particular client groups should receive social-work services is a matter of their rights and the ethical responsibilities of social workers. Therefore, variables may be theoretically but not practically manipulable, due to sociopolitical and ethical constraints.

The strategic value of knowledge is the degree to which it can influence decisions indirectly. There may be concepts, ideas, or analogies from other disciplines that are applicable to social-work practice. For example, there is a notion that client participation can make information gathering easier. This idea can influence decisions in a social program, for example, client participation may be requested in more phases of program operation.

Certainly, evaluative research results cannot be implemented if there are barriers such as individual or organizational resistance. Conflicts appear when there are disagreements among consumers as to whether or not it is necessary to implement new knowledge. The evaluator should consider who the primary evaluation consumers are and whether they are receptive to evaluative research results that might indicate program or practice changes. If it appears the consumer is not receptive to change, then the motivation for evaluative research, and its utility, should be questioned.

Compatibility is a factor that refers to the agreement between the contents of the evaluative research knowledge and the ideologies and values of the evaluation consumer (Weiss 1972). Some schemes for producing change may be effective and efficient but inhumane and unethically suitable for social-work practice. Or, knowledge may not be implemented in a particular agency because it is not compatible with the theoretical orientation of the practicing social workers. It may only be implemented if there are changes in the workers' orientations.

Finally, evaluative research results cannot be implemented unless there is an implementation potential in the evaluation consumer. Implementation potential involves a variety of practical considerations. In addition to needing appropriate timing and feedback of results, the consumer must be able to afford adoption of the new knowledge. Costs may include hiring of new personnel, training staff, and buying special equipment and supplies. Costs can be reduced if the consumer has a sufficient amount of resources, including supplies, time for staff to receive training, and volunteer workers.

Coordination is necessary for implementing knowledge in a large organization. Procedures for implementation need to be developed by social-work administration and staff, and these procedures must be clearly communicated and enforced.

Probably the most vital aspect in implementation is the decision-making power of the consumer. The greater his or her ability to influence decisions that affect social-work policies, programs, and practices, the greater the likelihood that evaluative research results will be implemented.

In conclusion, the implementation of evaluative research results depends on careful planning between the evaluator and the evaluation consumer. Therefore, the evaluator should think of the potential utilization of results at the beginning of an evaluative research study. With careful, cooperative planning, evaluative research results can be effectively implemented in social-work practice.

REFERENCES

ANDRIEU, M. "Benefit Cost Evaluation." In *Evaluation Research Methods: A Basic Guide*, edited by Leonard Rutman, Beverly Hills, Calif.: Sage Publications, Inc., 1977, pp. 219–32.
AUSTIN, M.J., AND J. CROWELL. "Survey Research." In *Social Work Research and Evaluation*, edited by R.M. Grinnell, Jr. Itasca, Ill.: F.E. Peacock, 1981, pp. 226–54.
BABBIE, E.R. *Survey Research Methods*, Belmont, Calif., Wadsworth, 1973.
BALES, R.F., "A Set of Categories for the Analysis of Small Group Intervention." In *Stages of Social Research: Contemporary Perspectives*, edited by D.P. Forcese and S. Richer, Englewood Cliffs, N.J.: Prentice-Hall, 1970, pp. 216–24.
BELL, R.; G. WARHEIT; AND J. SCHWAB. "Need Assessment: A Strategy for Structuring Change." In *Program Evaluation for Mental Health: Method, Strategies and Participants*, edited by R.D. Coursey and others. New York: Grune & Stratton, 1977, pp. 67–76.
BENTLER, P.M. AND J.A. WOODWARD. "Nonexperimental Evaluation Research Contributions of Causal Modeling." In *Improving Evaluations*, edited by L.E. Datta and R. Perloff. Beverly Hills, Calif.: Sage Publications, Inc., 1979, pp. 71–102.
BERGIN, A.E. AND S. GARFIELD, EDS. *Handbook for Psychotherapy and Behavior Change*. New York: John Wiley, 1971.
BERGIN, A.E. AND H.H. STRUPP. *Changing Frontiers in the Science of Psychotherapy*. New York: Aldine, 1972.

BLALOCK, H.M., JR. *Causal Inference in Non-Experimental Research.* Chapel Hill, N.C.: University of North Carolina Press, 1967.
——. *Social Statistics.* 2d ed. New York: McGraw-Hill, 1972.
BUROS, O.K. *Personality Tests and Reviews II.* Highland Park, N.J.: Gryphon Press, 1975.
——. *The Seventh Mental Measurements Yearbook.* Highland Park, N.J.: Gryphon Press, 1972.
CAMPBELL, D.T. "Reforms as Experiments" In *Handbook of Evaluation Research*, vol. 1, edited by E.L. Struening and M. Guttentag. Beverly Hills, Calif.: Sage Publications, Inc., 1975, pp. 71-100.
CAMPBELL, D.T. AND J.C. STANLEY. *Experimental and Quasi-Experimental Designs for Research.* Skokie, Ill.: Rand McNally, 1966.
CAPORASO, J.A. "Quasi-Experimental Approaches to Social Science: Perspectives and Problems." In *Quasi-Experimental Approaches: Testing Theory and Evaluating Policy*, edited by Caporaso, J. and L.L. Roos, Jr. Evanston, Ill.: Northwestern University Press, 1973, pp. 3-38.
CAPORASO, J. AND L.L. ROOS, JR., EDS. *Quasi-Experimental Approaches: Testing Theory and Evaluating Policy.* Evanston, Ill.: Northwestern University Press, 1973.
CARRINO, L. *Medicina Critica in Italia.* Messina-Firenze: Casa Editrice G. D'Anna, 1977.
CARTER, R. "Internal Validity in Intensive Experimentation," and "Designs and Data Patterns in Intensive Experimentation (Part 1)" Course Monographs, Research in Interpersonal Influence. Mimeographed. Ann Arbor, Mich.: University of Michigan, School of Social Work, 1972.
CHASSAN, J.B. *Research Design in Clinical Psychology and Psychiatry.* New York: Appleton-Century-Crofts, 1967.
CIARLO, J. AND J. REIHMAN. "The Denver Community Mental Health Questionnaire: Development of a Multidimensional Program Evaluation Instrument." In *Program Evaluation for Mental Health: Method, Strategies and Participants*, edited by R.D. Coursey and others. New York: Grune & Stratton, 1977, pp. 131-68.
CIMINERO, A.R.; K.S. CALHOUN; AND H.E. ADAMS, EDS. *Handbook of Behavioral Assessment.* New York: John Wiley, 1977.
COCHRAN, W.G.; F. MOSTELLER; AND J.W. TUKEY. "Principles of Sampling." In *Stages of Social Research: Contemporary Perspectives*, edited by D.P. Forcese and S. Richer. Englewood Cliffs, N.J.: Prentice-Hall, 1970, pp. 168-85.
COHEN, J. *Statistical Power Analysis for the Behavioral Sciences.* New York: Academic Press, 1969.
COHEN, J. AND P. COHEN. *Applied Multiple Regression/Correlation Analysis for the Behavioral Sciences.* New York: Lawrence Erlbaum, 1975.
COMPTON, B. AND B. GALLOWAY, EDS. *Social Work Processes.* Homewood, Ill.: Dorsey Press, 1975.
COOK, T.D. AND CAMPBELL, D.T. *Quasi-Experimentation: Design and Analysis Issues for Field Settings.* Chicago: Rand McNally, 1979.
COOK, T.D. AND C.S. REICHARDT, EDS. *Qualitative and Quantitative Methods in Evaluation Research.* Beverly Hills, Calif.: Sage Publications, Inc., 1979.
COURSEY, R.D.; R. MITCHELL; AND J. FRIEDMAN. "Staff Participation in Program Evaluation." In *Program Evaluation for Mental Health: Method, Strategies and Participants*, edited by R.D. Coursey and others. New York: Grune & Stratton, 1977, pp. 297-312.

References

COURSEY, R.D.; G.A. SPECTER, S.A. MURRELL, AND B. HUNT, EDS. *Program Evaluation for Mental Health: Method, Strategies and Participants.* New York: Grune & Stratton, 1977.

DAVIDSON, P.O.; F.W. CLARK; AND L.A. HAMERLYNCK, EDS. *Evaluation of Behavioral Programs in Community, Residential and School Settings.* Champaign, Ill.: Research Press, 1974.

DAVIS, H. "Four Ways to Goal Attainment," Evaluation. Special Monograph No. 6, 1973.

DAVIS, H. AND S. SALASIN. "The Utilization of Evaluation." In *Handbook of Evaluation Research*, vol. 1, edited by E.L. Struening and M. Guttentag. Beverly Hills, Calif.: Sage Publications, Inc. 1975, pp. 621-66.

DILLMAN, D.A. *Mail and Telephone Surveys.* New York: John Wiley, 1978.

DONABEDIAN, A. "Evaluating the Quality of Medical Care." In *Program Evaluation in the Health Fields*, edited by H.C. Schulberg, A. Sheldon, and F. Baker. New York: Behavioral Publications, 1969, pp. 196-218.

ELLSWORTH, R. "Consumer Feedback in Measuring the Effectiveness of Mental Health Programs." In *Handbook of Evaluation Research*, vol. 2, edited by M. Guttentag and E.L. Struening. Beverly Hills, Calif.: Sage Publications, Inc., 1975, pp. 239-74.

EPSTEIN, I. AND T. TRIPODI *Research Techniques for Program Planning, Monitoring, and Evaluation.* New York: Columbia University Press, 1977.

ETZIONI, A. *Modern Organizations.* Englewood Cliffs, N.J.: Prentice-Hall, Inc., 1964.

FAIRWEATHER, G.W. *Methods for Experimental Social Innovation.* New York: John Wiley, 1967.

FERMAN, L.A., ED. "Evaluating the War on Poverty." *Annals of the American Academy of Political and Social Science.* vol. 385, (September 1969).

FILSTEAD, W.J., ED. *Qualitative Methodology.* Chicago: Markham, 1978.

FISCHER, J. Effective Casework Practice: An Eclectic Approach. New York: McGraw-Hill, 1978.

FISHER, R.A. *The Design of Experiments.* New York: Hafner, 1935.

FITZ-GIBBON, C.T. AND L.L. MORRIS. *How to Design a Program Evaluation.* Beverly Hills, Calif.: Sage Publications, Inc., 1978.

FITZPATRICK, R. "The Selection of Measures for Evaluating Programs." In *Evaluative Research.* Pittsburgh: American Institutes for Research, 1970.

FORCESE, D.P. AND S. RICHER, EDS. *Stages of Social Research: Contemporary Perspectives.* Englewood Cliffs, N.J.: Prentice-Hall, 1970.

FREEMAN, H.E. AND C.C. SHERWOOD. "Research in Large Scale Intervention Programs." In *Readings in Evaluation Research*, 2d ed., edited by F.C. Caro. New York: Russell Sage Foundation, 1977, pp. 205-20.

FRY, L.J. "Participant Observation and Program Evaluation." *Journal of Health and Social Behavior* 14 (September 1973): 274-78.

GLASER, B. AND A. Strauss. *The Discovery of Grounded Theory.* Chicago: Aldine, 1967.

GLASER, D. *Routenizing Evaluation: Getting Feedback on Effectiveness of Crime and Delinquency Programs.* Rockville, Md: National Institute of Mental Health, Center for Studies of Crime and Delinquency, 1973.

GOLDSTEIN, H.K. *Research Standards and Methods for Social Workers.* New Orleans: Hauser Press, 1963.

GORSUCH, R.L. "Bivariate Analysis: Analysis of Variance." In *Social Work Research and Evaluation*, edited by R.M. Grinnell, Jr. Itasca, Ill.: F.E. Peacock, 1981, pp. 500-29.

GOTTMAN, J.M. AND S.P. LEIBLUM *How to Do Psychotherapy and How to Evaluate It.* New York: Holt, Rinehart and Winston, 1974.

GRINNELL, R.M., JR., ED. *Social Work Research and Evaluation.* Itasca, Ill.: F.E. Peacock, 1981.

GUTTENTAG, M. AND E.L. STRUENING, EDS. *Handbook of Evaluation Research*, vol. 2. Beverly Hills, Calif.: Sage Publications, Inc., 1975.

HARRIS, P.; M. BLACKMORE; E. BLACKMORE; A. DAVIS; D. ROBINSON; J. SMITH; B. TAYLOR; AND G. WILLIAM. *Evaluation of Community Work.* London: London Council of Social Service, Calverts North Star Press, 1978.

HAVELOCK, R.G. *Planning for Innovation Through Dissemination and Utilization.* Ann Arbor, Mich.: University of Michigan, Center for Research on Utilization of Scientific Knowledge, Institute for Social Research, 1971.

HAYS, W.L. *Statistics for the Social Sciences.* New York: Holt, Rinehart and Winston, 1973.

HENKEL, R.E. *Tests of Significance.* Beverly Hills, Calif.: Sage Publications, Inc., 1976.

HERSEN, M. AND D.H. BARLOW *Single Case Experimental Designs.* New York: Pergamon Press, 1976.

HIEBERT, S. "Who Benefits from the Program? Criteria Selection." In *Evaluation of Behavioral Programs in Community, Residential and School Settings*, edited by Davidson, P.O., F.W. Clark and L.A. Hamerlynck. Champaign, Ill.: Research Press, 1974, pp. 33-54.

HIRSCHI, T. AND H.C. SELVIN *Delinquency Research: An Appraisal of Analytic Methods.* New York: Free Press, 1967.

HOLLIS, F. *Casework: A Psychosocial Therapy*, rev. ed., New York: Random House, 1972, pp. 57-86, 164-84.

HOSHINO, G. AND LYNCH, M.M. "Secondary Analysis of Existing Data." In *Social Work Research and Evaluation*, edited by R.M. Grinnell, Jr. Itasca, Ill.: F.E. Peacock, 1981.

HOWE, W. "Using Clients' Observations in Research." *Social Work* vol. 2, no. 1 (1976): 28-33.

HOWARD, S. "Response-Shift Bias: A Problem in Evaluating Interventions with Pre/Post Self-Reports," *Evaluation Review* vol. 4, no. 1, (1980): 93-106.

HUDSON, J. "Problems of Measurement in Criminal Justice." In *Evaluation Research Methods: A Basic Guide*, edited by Leonard Rutman. Beverly Hills, Calif.: Sage Publications, Inc., 1977, pp. 73-100.

HUDSON, W. AND ASSOCIATES. "Clinical Measurement Package for Social Workers." In *Social Work Research and Evaluation*, edited by R.M. Grinnell, Jr. Itasca, Ill.: F.E. Peacock, 1981, pp. 640-49.

HUNT, J. MCV. AND L. KOGAN *Measuring Results in Social Casework: A Manual on Judging Measurement*, rev. ed. New York: Family Service Association of America, 1952.

HYMAN, H. *Survey Design and Analysis.* New York: Free Press, 1955.

HYMAN, H.H.; C.R. WRIGHT; AND T.K. HOPKINS. *Applications of Methods of Evaluation: Four Studies of the Encampment for Citizenship.* Los Angeles: University of California Press, 1962.

ISAAC, S. in collaboration with William B. Michael. *Handbook in Research and Evaluation.* San Diego: Robert R. Knapp, 1971.

JAYARATNE, S. AND R. LEVY. *Empirical Clinical Practice.* New York: Columbia University Press, 1979.

JENKINS, S. "Collecting Data by Questionnaire and Interview." In *Social Work Research*, rev. ed., edited by N.A. Polansky. Chicago: University of Chicago Press, 1975, pp. 131-58.

KADUSHIN, A. *The Social Work Interview.* New York: Columbia University Press, 1972.
KAHN, A.J. *Theory and Practice of Social Planning.* New York: Russell Sage Foundation, 1969.
KAHN, R.L. AND CANNELL, C.F. *The Dynamics of Interviewing.* New York: John Wiley, 1952.
KAZDIN, A.E. *Behavior Modification in Applied Settings.* Homewood, Ill.: Dorsey Press, 1975.
——. "Methodological and Interpretive Problems of Single-Case Experimental Designs." *Journal of Consulting and Clinical Psychology* vol. 46, no. 4, (August 1978): 629–42.
KERLINGER, F.N. *Foundations of Behavioral Research.* New York: Holt, Rinehart and Winston, 1964.
KIRESUK, T.J. "A Reply to the Critique of Goal Attainment Scaling." *Social Work Research and Abstracts* vol. 13, no. 2 (1977): 9–11.
KIRESUK, T.J. AND R.E. SHERMAN. "Goal Attainment Scaling: A General Method for Evaluating Comprehensive Mental Health Programs." *Community Mental Health Journal* vol. 4, no. 6 (1968): 443–53.
KISH, L. *Survey Sampling.* New York: John Wiley, 1965.
KNAPP, M.S. "Applying Time Series Strategies: An Underutilized Solution." In *Improving Evaluations*, edited by L.E. Datta and R. Perloff. Beverly Hills, Calif.: Sage Publications, Inc., 1979, pp. 111–27.
KOGAN, L.S. "The Distress-relief Quotient (DRQ) in Dictated and Verbatim Social Casework Interviews." *Journal of Abnormal and Social Psychology* vol. 46 (1951): 236–39.
——. "Principles of Measurement." In *Social Work Research*, rev. ed., edited by N.A. Polansky. Chicago: University of Chicago Press, 1975, pp. 68–92.
LABOV, W. AND D. FANSHEL. *Therapeutic Discourse: Psychotherapy as Conversation.* New York: Academic Press, 1977.
LABOVITZ, S. AND R. HAGEDORN. *Introduction to Social Research.* New York: McGraw-Hill, 1971.
——. *Introduction to Social Research*, 3rd ed. New York: McGraw-Hill, 1981.
LAKE, D.G.; M.B. MILES; AND R.B. EARLE, JR., EDS. *Measuring Human Behavior: Tools for the Assessment of Social Functioning.* New York: Teachers College Press, Columbia University, 1973.
LARSEN, D.L.; C.C. ATTKISSON; W.A. HARGREAVES; AND T.D. NGUYEN. "Assessment of Client/Patient Satisfaction: Development of a General Scale." *Evaluation and Program Planning*, vol. 2, no. 3 (1979): 197–208.
LEVIN, H.M. "Cost-Effectiveness Analysis in Evaluation Research." In *Handbook of Evaluation Research*, vol. 2, edited by M. Guttentag and E.L. Struening. Beverly Hills, Calif.: Sage Publications, Inc., 1975, pp. 89–112.
LYERLY, S.B. AND P.S. ABBOTT. *Handbook of Psychiatric Rating Scales.* Public Health Service Publication, No. 1495. Bethesda, Md: National Institute of Mental Health, 1966.
MC CALL, G. AND J. SIMMONS, EDS. *Issues in Participant Observation.* Reading, Mass.: Addison-Wesley, 1969.
MAHONEY, M.J. "Experimental Methods and Outcome Evaluation." *Journal of Consulting and Clinical Psychology* vol. 46, no. 4, (August 1978): 660–72.
MARSDEN, G. "Content Analysis Studies of Therapeutic Interviews: 1954 to 1974." In *Psychotherapy Research*, edited by G.E. Stallak, B.G. Guerney, Jr., and M. Rothberg. Chicago: Rand McNally, 1966, pp. 336–64.
MARSH, J. "The Goal Oriented Approach to Evaluation: Critique and Case Study from Drug Abuse Treatment." *Evaluation and Program Planning* vol. 1, no. 1, 1978, pp. 51–64.

MAYER, R.R. AND E. GREENWOOD. *The Design of Social Policy Research.* Englewood Cliffs, N.J.: Prentice-Hall, Inc., 1980.
MILL, J.S. *A System of Logic.* London: Parker, Son and Bowin, 1850.
MILLS, T.M. "The Observer, the Experimenter and the Group." In *Stages of Social Research: Contemporary Perspectives*, edited by D.P. Forcese and S. Richer. Englewood Cliffs, N.J.: Prentice-Hall, 1970, pp. 132-41.
MOOS, R.H. *Evaluating Correctional and Community Settings.* New York: John Wiley, 1975.
MORRIS, L.L. AND C.T. FITZ-GIBBON. *Evaluator's Handbook*, Beverly Hills, Calif.: Sage Publications, Inc., 1978.
MOSER, C.A. *Survey Methods in Social Investigation.* London: Heinemann, 1965.
MOURSAND, J.P. *Evaluation: An Introduction to Research Design.* Monterey, Calif.: Brooks/Cole, 1973.
MULLEN, E.G.; J.R. DUMPSON; AND ASSOCIATES. *Evaluation of Social Intervention.* San Francisco: Jossey-Bass, 1972.
MURRELL, S. "Conducting a Program Evaluation: Collaboration, Feedback, and Open-System Perspectives." In *Evaluation for Mental Health: Methods, Strategies and Participants*, edited by R.D. Coursey and others. New York: Grune & Stratton, 1977, pp. 259-74.
NUNNALLY, J.C. AND R.L. DURHAM. "Validity, Reliability, and Special Problems of Measurement in Evaluation Research." In *Handbook of Evaluation Research*, vol. 1, edited by E.L. Struening and M. Guttentag. Beverly Hills, Calif.: Sage Publications, Inc., 1975, pp. 289-352.
NUNNALLY, J.C. AND W.H. WILSON. "Method and Theory for Developing Measures in Evaluation Research." In *Handbook of Evaluation Research*, vol. 1, edited by E.L. Struening and M. Guttentag. Beverly Hills, Calif.: Sage Publications, Inc., 1975, pp. 227-88.
OSTROM, C.W., JR. *Time Series Analysis: Regression Techniques.* Beverly Hills, Calif.: Sage Publications, Inc., 1978.
PATTON, M. *Utilization-Focussed Evaluation.* Beverly Hills, Calif.: Sage Publications, Inc., 1978.
PINCUS, A. AND A. MINAHAN *Social Work Practice: Model and Method.* Itasca, Ill., F.E. Peacock, 1973.
POLANSKY, N.A., ED. *Social Work Research Methods for the Helping Professions.* Chicago: University of Chicago Press, 1975.
PORTER, W. "A Management by Objectives Approach to Program Evaluation." In *Program Evaluation for Mental Health: Method, Strategies and Participants*, edited by R.D. Coursey and others. New York: Grune & Stratton, 1977, pp. 93-104.
POSAVAC, E.J. AND R.G. CAREY. *Program Evaluation: Methods and Case Studies.* Englewood Cliffs, N.J.: Prentice-Hall, Inc., 1980.
POSER, E.G. "The Effect of Therapists' Training on Group Therapeutic Outcome." *Journal of Consulting Psychology* vol. 30, no. 4 (1966): 283-89.
REID, W.J. "Evaluation Research in Social Work." *Evaluation and Program Planning* vol. 2, no. 3 (1979): 209-18.
———. "Research Reports and Publication Procedures." In *Social Work Research and Evaluation*, edited by R.M. Grinnell, Jr. Itasca, Ill.: F.E. Peacock, 1981, pp. 553-68.
RIECKEN, H.W.; R.F. BORUCH; D.T. CAMPBELL; N. CAPLAN; T.K. GLENRAN; J. PRATT; A. REES; AND W. WILLIAMS. *Social Experimentation.* New York: Academic Press, 1974.
RILEY, M.W. *Sociological Research*, vol. 1, New York: Harcourt Brace Jovanovich, Inc., 1963.

RIVLIN, A. *Systematic Thinking for Social Action.* Washington, D.C.: Brookings Institution, 1971.
ROBINSON, J.P. AND P.R. SHAVER. *Measures of Social Psychological Attitudes.* Ann Arbor, Mich.: University of Michigan, Institute for Social Research, 1969.
RODMAN, H. AND R. KOLODNY. "Organizational Strains in the Researcher-Practitioner Relationship." In *Readings in Evaluation Research*, 2d ed., edited by F.C. Caro. New York: Russell Sage Foundation, 1977, pp. 73-93.
ROSEN, S. AND N.A. POLANSKY. "Observation of Social Interaction." In *Social Work Research*, rev. ed., edited by N.A. Polansky. Chicago: Univ. of Chicago Press, 1975, pp. 154-81.
ROSENTHAL, D. AND J.D. FRANK. "Psychotherapy and Placebo Effect." *Psychological Bulletin*, vol. 53 (1956): 294-302.
ROSSI, P.H.; H.E. FREEMAN; AND S.R. WRIGHT. *Evaluation: A Systematic Approach.* Beverly Hills, Calif.: Sage Publications, Inc., 1979.
ROSSI, P. AND W. WILLIAMS. *Evaluating Social Programs: Theory, Practice and Politics.* New York: Seminar Press, 1972.
ROTHMAN, J. *Social R & D: Research and Development in the Human Services.* Englewood Cliffs, N.J.: Prentice-Hall, 1980.
RUBIN, A. AND A. ROSENBLATT. *Sourcebook on Research Utilization.* New York, Council on Social Work Education, 1979.
RUTMAN, L. "Formative Research and Program Evaluability." In *Evaluation Research Methods: A Basic Guide*, edited by L. Rutman, Beverly Hills, Calif.: Sage Publications, Inc., 1977, pp. 47-72.
SAXE, L. AND M. FINE. "Expanding Our View of Control Groups in Evaluations." In *Improving Evaluations*, edited by L.E. Datta and R. Perloff. Beverly Hills, Calif.: Sage Publications, Inc., 1979, pp. 61-70.
SCHEFFÉ, H. "A Method for Judging All Contrasts in the Analysis of Variance." *Biometrika* (1953): 87-104.
SCHULBERG, H.C. AND J.M. JERRELL, EDS. *The Evaluator and Management.* Beverly Hills, Calif.: Sage Publications, Inc., 1979.
SCHULBERG, H.C.; A. SHELDEN; AND F. BAKER, EDS. *Program Evaluation in the Health Fields.* New York: Behavioral Publications, 1969.
SCHUERMAN, J.R. "Bivariate Analysis: Cross Tabulation." In *Social Work Research and Evaluation*, edited by R.M. Grinnell, Jr. Itasca, Ill.: F.E. Peacock, 1981, pp. 461-99.
SCRIVEN, M. "The Methodology of Evaluation." In *Perspectives of Curriculum Evaluation*, AERA, Monograph Series on Curriculum Evaluation, no. 1, edited by R.W. Tyler, R.M. Gagne, and M. Scriven. Chicago: Rand McNally, 1967, pp. 39-83.
SEABERG, J.R. AND D.F. GILLESPIE. "Goal Attainment Scaling: A Critique." *Social Work Research and Abstracts*, vol. 13, no. 2 (1977): 4-9.
SHAW, M.E. AND J.M. WRIGHT. *Scales for the Measurement of Attitudes.* New York: McGraw-Hill, 1967.
SHERMAN, R. "Will Goal Attainment Scaling Solve the Problems of Program Evaluation in the Health Field?" In *Program Evaluation for Mental Health: Method, Strategies and Participants*, edited by R.D. Coursey and others. New York: Grune & Stratton, 1977, pp. 105-17.
SHORTELL, S.M. AND W.C. RICHARDSON. *Health Program Evaluation.* St. Louis: C.V. Mosby, 1978.
SHYNE, W. "Use of Available Data." In *Social Work Research*, edited by N.A. Polansky, Chicago: University of Chicago Press, 1960, pp. 106-24.
SIEGEL, S. *Nonparametric Statistics for the Behavioral Sciences.* New York: McGraw-Hill, 1956.

References

SJOBERG, G. "Politics, Ethics and Evaluation Research." In *Handbook of Evaluation Research*, vol. 2, edited by M. Guttentag and E.L. Struening. Sage Publications, Inc., 1975, pp. 29-51.

SOLOMON, R.L. "An Extension of Control Group Design." *Psychological Bulletin*, vol. 46 (1949): 137-50.

STEELE, M. *Contemporary Approaches to Program Evaluation.* Washington, D.C.: Capitol Publications, 1977.

STEPHAN, F.J. AND P.J. MCCARTHY. *Sampling Opinions*, Science Editions. New York: John Wiley, 1963.

STRAUSS, M.A. *Family Measurement Techniques.* Minneapolis: University of Minnesota Press, 1969.

STRUENING, E.L. AND M. GUTTENTAG, EDS. *Handbook of Evaluation Research*, vol. 1, Beverly Hills, Calif.: Sage Publications, Inc., 1975.

SUCHMAN, E.A. *Evaluative Research.* New York: Russell Sage Foundation, 1967.

SUDMAN, S. *Reducing the Cost of Surveys.* Chicago: Aldine, 1967.

SUSSER, M. *Causal Thinking in the Health Sciences*, New York: Oxford University Press, 1973.

THOMAS, E.J. "Uses of Research Methods in Interpersonal Practice." In *Social Work Research*, rev. ed., edited by N.A. Polansky. Chicago: University of Chicago Press, 1975, pp. 254-83.

TRIPODI, T. "An Evaluation of Social Centres for Children, Women and the Elderly: Center for Social Medicine, Giugliano, Italy." *Report of the European Programme of Pilot Schemes and Studies to Combat Poverty.* Brussels, 1980.

———. "The Logic of Research Design." In *Applied Social Work Research Evaluation*, edited by R.M. Grinnell, Jr. Itasca, Ill.: F.E. Peacock, 1981, pp. 198-25.

———. "Replication in Clinical Experimentation." *Social Work Research and Abstracts* vol. 16, no. 4 (Winter 1980): p. 35.

———. *Uses and Abuses of Social Research in Social Work.* New York: Columbia University Press, 1974.

TRIPODI, T. AND EPSTEIN, I. *Research Techniques for Clinical Social Workers.* New York: Columbia University Press, 1980.

TRIPODI, T.; P. FELLIN; I. EPSTEIN. *Differential Social Program Evaluation.* Itasca, Ill.: F.E. Peacock, 1978.

TRIPODI, T.; P. FELLIN; I. EPSTEIN; R. LIND, EDS. *Social Workers at Work*, 2d ed. Itasca, Ill.: F.E. Peacock Publishers, 1977.

TRIPODI, T.; P. FELLIN; H.J. MEYER. *The Assessment of Social Research.* Itasca, Ill. F.E. Peacock, 1969.

TRIPODI, T. AND J. HARRINGTON. "Uses of Time-Series Designs for Formative Program Evaluation." *Journal of Social Service Research* (Fall 1979): pp. 67-78.

TURNER, F.J., ED. *Social Work Treatment: Interlocking Theoretical Approaches.* New York: Free Press, 1974.

WALIZER, M.H. AND P.L. WEINER. *Research Methods and Analysis.* New York: Harper & Row, Pub. 1978.

WALKER, H.M. AND J. LEV. *Statistical Inference.* New York: Holt, Rinehart and Winston, 1953.

WECHSLER, H.; H.Z. REINHERZ; AND D.D. DOBBIN. *Social Work Research in the Human Services.* New York: Human Sciences, 1976.

WEISS, C.H. *Evaluation Research: Methods of Assessing Program Effectiveness.* Englewood Cliffs, N.J.: Prentice-Hall, 1972.

———. "Interviewing in Evaluation Research." In *Handbook of Evaluation Research*, vol. 1, edited by E.L. Struening and M. Guttentag. Beverly Hills, Calif.: Sage Publications, Inc., 1975, pp. 355-95.

WEISS, R.S. AND M. REIN. "The Evaluation of Broad-Aim Program: A Cautionary Case and a Moral." *Annals of the American Academy of Political and Social Science*, no. 385 (September 1969): 133-42.

WINER, B.J. *Statistical Principles in Experimental Design*, 2d ed. New York: McGraw-Hill, 1971.

YEAKEL, M. AND G. GANTER. "Some Principles and Methods of Sampling." In *Social Work Research*, rev. ed., edited by N.A. Polansky, Chicago: University of Chicago, 1975, pp. 93-108.

ZINOBER, J.W. "Starting an Internal Evaluation Program: Initial Steps." In *Program Evaluation for Mental Health: Method, Strategies and Participant*, edited by R.D. Coursey and others. New York: Grune & Stratton, 1977, pp. 253-59.

INDEX

Accessibility, of data, 57, 60, 158
Accountability, for program
 effectiveness, 13
Accuracy, of measurement, 86
Acquiescent-response tendency, 78
After-intervention measurement design,
 105-6, 107, 127
Aggregate matching, of control groups,
 137
Anchoring illustrations, 77
Annotated records, in case studies, 103
A posteriori judgments, 115, 149
"Applying Time-Series Designs"
 (Knapp), 135
A priori objectives, 114-15, 149
Aptitude tests, 61, 65
Area sampling, 93
Assessment, 18
 and expected change, 29-30
 initiation stage, 21-22
 statistical methods, 42
Attitude changes, in clients, 28-29

Bales, R. F., 82
Barlow, D. H., 27, 90, 94, 95, 147
Baseline measures, 53-54, 87, 89
 differential treatment focus, 111
 in interrupted time-series designs,
  110 & *f*, 111, 112 & *f*, 113 & *f*,
  134
 lengthy assessment of, 111
 Multiple-Baseline designs, 118-20
 reconstruction of, 111
 stabilizing of, 110, 135
Behavioral changes, in clients, 29, 31
Behavior Therapy (journal), 52
Benefit-cost analyses, 40
Bias, 62
 in comparison groups, 88, 91 (*see
  also* Selection bias)
 in interviews, 73
 in observational data, 82
 in rating scales, 78
Binomial tests, 54, 95, 110-11
Bivariate analyses, 151

172 Index

Blalock, H. M., Jr., 87, 146
Buros, O. K., 52

Campbell, D. T., 87, 88, 89, 91, 121, 135, 146
Caporaso, J., 135
Carey, R. G., 136
Case studies, 55 (*see also* Single-subject designs)
Catchment areas, 41-42
Causal Inference in Non-Experimental Research (Blalock), 87, 146
Causal Thinking in the Health Sciences (Susser), 87
Cause-effect knowledge, 6, 9-10, 84, 85, 145, 152, 154
   consumer information on, 157
   and empirical relationship, 86-87
   and generality types, 90-91
   and internal validity, 88-89
   research designs:
      group, 122*t*, 131, 139-44
      single-case, 101*t*, 114-20
Ceiling-basement effect, 117
Census data, 51, 92, 127
Central tendency measure, 151
   rating scale errors, 78, 79
Change
   in clients, 28-30, 145-46
   criteria of, 149-50
   in operational definitions, 55-56
   in variables, 29-30, 37
Change data, 54
Change variables (*see* Dependent variables)
Chi square test, 8, 54, 87, 94, 130, 131, 137, 142, 146
Clients (*see also* Contacts)
   contracts with, 12, 24
   dependency in, 38
   eligibility, 28, 53, 125-26, 158
   expected change in, 28-30, 145-46
Client Satisfaction Questionnaire, 98
Clinical replication, 94-95
Closed-ended responses, on questionnaires, 67, 68, 69, 70
Cochran, W. G., 92
Coefficient-alpha test, 56, 98, 151
Coefficients (*see* Correlation coefficients)
Coefficients of reliability, 56-57
Cohen, J., 146

Cohen, P., 146
Cohort studies (*see* Longitudinal group studies)
Community variables, 137
Comparative Intensity Design, 131, 132-33
Comparative questions, on questionnaires, 67-68
Compensatory equalization, of treatment, 89
Comprehensive evaluation, 5, 41 & *n*
Concepts
   nominal definition, 6
   operational definition, 6-7 (*see also* main entry)
   and validity, 47
Conceptual generality, 90
Concomitant variation, in case studies, 103-4
Concurrent validity, 47*n*
Consistent availability, of qualitative data, 59
Construct validity, 47*n*, 91*n*
Consumers, of evaluation research, 10-12, 145-46, 149, 154-55
   and implementation of results, 158-59
   information feedback to, 156-57
Contacts
   descriptions of, 148
   and program objectives, 27-28
   in social-work practice, 22-23
Contact stage, in program development, 20, 97-98
   variables in, 35-36, 39, 39*t*
Content analysis, 103, 153
Content relevance, 59
Content validity, 47
Contracts, with clients, 12, 24
Control (comparison) groups (*see also* Internal validity; Experimental groups), 89, 132, 146, 152
   biases in, 88, 91 (*see also* Selection bias)
   choosing variables for, 137
   compensatory treatment, 89
   nonequivalent controls for, 136-38
   and randomization procedures, 141, 142
   time-lagged, 144
Controlled Time-Series Designs, 139-40
Control variables, 136-37, 138, 148
Cook, T. D., 87, 89, 121, 135, 146

Correlational analysis, 147, 148
Correlational knowledge, 6, 8-9, 84, 145
  and causality, 9, 85
  and data analysis, 153-54
  and generality, 90
  negative, 9
  positive, 9
  presentation of, 148
  research designs
    group, 122t, 130-39
    single-case, 101t, 108-14
Correlation coefficients, 8, 151
  and empirical relationship, 86, 87
  and replication, 95-96
  and split-half reliability, 46
Cost effectiveness, 40
Cost ratios, 40
County and City Data Book, 51
Court records, 51
Covariates, in test groups, 141, 146, 152
Crossover Design, 144
Cross-sectional research designs
  case studies, 101-2
  groups, 122-24
  surveys, 98-99, 126-28, 151
    replicated, 128-29

Data, 3, 146 (*see also* Primary data; Secondary data)
  accessibility of, 57, 60, 158
  on social need, 5, 43, 123-24
  for time-series designs, 111, 135
Data analysis, 146-59
  communication of results, 154-56
  consumer information, 156-57
  general considerations, 147-48
  individuals, evaluation of, 152-54
  qualitative vs. quantitative data, 150-52
  textbooks on, 146-47
Definition, control by, 137, 138
Demoralization, of control groups, 89
Dependent variables, 7
  and causality, 9-10, 85
  and concomitant variation, 103-4
Development, stages of (*see* Initiation; Contact; Implementation)
Developmental studies (*see* Longitudinal studies)
Deviant cases, 123, 125
Differential evaluation, 21, 23

Differential treatment focus, in baseline measures, 111
Diffusion of treatment, 89
Dillman, D. A., 127
Direct advice, 117
Direct replication, 94, 95
Direct-service workers, 17
Dropouts, from programs (*see* Experimental mortality)
Durham, R. L., 46, 47n
Dynamic studies (*see* Longitudinal group studies)

Earle, R. B., 52
Effectiveness
  contact stage, 35, 36
  as an evaluation criterion, 33, 34
  implementation stage, 37
  initiation stage, 34
  in social-work practice, 38
Efficiency, 5
  contact stage, 35, 36
  as an evaluation critrion, 33, 34
  implementation stage, 37
  initiation stage, 34, 35
  and program magnitude, 42
  in social-work practice, 38
  between stages, 40-42
Efforts, 33
  contact stage, 35-36
  implementation stage, 37
  initiation stage, 34-35
  in social-work practice, 38
Eligibility for services, 28, 158
  secondary data on, 53
  variables, 125-26
Ellsworth, R., 76, 77
Empirical estimates, of reliability, 56-57
Empirical generalizations, 8, 118, 119, 143
Empirical relationships, 86-87, 151
Empirical validity, 47 & n, 48
Epstein, I., 27, 33, 35-36, 62, 66, 135
Etzioni, A., 26
European Economic Commission, 123
Evaluation (Rossi, Freeman, & Wright), 121-22
Evaluations
  consumer information, 156-57
  criteria for, 33-34
  histories of past, 148

Evaluations (*continued*)
  from quantitative data, 58
  in social-work practice, 18
Evaluation research (*see also* Research designs; Single-subject designs; Group research designs)
  applications, 1-2
  consumers of, 10-12, 145-46
  decision factors, 12-14
  defined, 1
  implementation results, 157-59
  knowledge levels, 6-10, 84
  major focuses, 3-5
  resources for, 14
  seven-step process, 2-3
  sponsors, 12-13
Evaluators, inside vs. outside, 14
Expected change, in clients, 28-30, 145-46
Experimental mortality, 89, 136, 141
Experimental research designs, 96-97, 148 (*see also* Quasi-experiments; Randomized Control Group Designs; Solomon Four-Group Design; Crossover Design)
External validity, 91 & *n*, 96, 142, 143

Face-sheet information, 58
Facts, 7, 8
Family Measurement Techniques (Strauss), 52
Family variables, 137
Fatigue
  and internal validity, 88, 89
  and rater errors, 79
Feasibility, of variables, 49
Federal Probation (journal), 52
Fellin, P., 33, 35-36
Focused interviews, 71-72
Follow-up studies, 30
  interviews, 74-75
  longitudinal group studies, 125
  replicated surveys, 128
  single-case designs, 107, 112-14, 112*f*, 113*f*
Formative evaluation, 4, 84, 101, 102, 156-57
Freeman, H. E., 42*n*, 121, 136, 137
F statistics, 8, 146

Ganter, G., 92
Generalizability, 4-5, 84, 89-97, 146
  conceptual, 90
  experimental procedures, 96-97
  external validity control, 91
  qualitative judgment, 91-92
  replication, 90-91, 94-96, 114
  representativeness, 90, 92
  sampling procedures, 92-94
Generalizations, 8
Geographic areas (*see* Catchment areas)
Gillespie, D. F., 79
Giugliano (Italy), social medicine project, 123, 152
Glasser, B., 146
Goal-attainment scales, 77, 79, 127
  in after-intervention designs, 105-6
Goldstein, H. K., 77
Gottman, J. M., 103, 110, 111, 147
Government agencies, as data resources, 51, 52
Graduated-Intensity Design, 117-18
Graphing patterns, 103-4, 104*f*, 110 & *f*, 149
Grinnell, R. M., 147
Group Comparative Design, 131-33
Group research designs, 83, 84, 121-44
  cause-effect, 122*t*, 139-44
  correlational, 122*t*, 130-39
  hypothetical-deductive, 122*t*, 122-26
  placebo effects, 97
  quantitative-descriptive, 122*t*, 126-29
  reactive effects, 91, 97
  statistical significance in, 87
  units of analysis, 121
  validity, threats to, 88-89, 96
  variables, 121
Groups, organizations, 4 (*see also* Programs evaluation)

Halo effects, 71, 78
Handbook of Basic Economic Statistics (Dept. of Labor), 51
Handbook of Psychiatric Rating Scales (N.I.M.H.), 52
Hersen, M., 27, 90, 94, 95, 147
Hiebert, S., 27
Hirschi, T., 147
Historical information, and group designs, 123

History, as a threat to validity, 88
Hollis, F., 47
Hopkins, T. K., 25, 33, 37
Hoshino, G., 50
Hospital records, 51
Howard, S., 106
Howe, W., 80
Hudson, Walter, 127
Hyman, H. H., 25, 33, 37
Hypotheses, 7
   practice, 41
   of previous studies, 54–55
   from qualitative data, 58, 153
   researchability of, 84–85, 91–92, 105, 145
   specific, 85
Hypothetical-developmental knowledge, 6–7, 84, 145
   and consumer information, 157
   and generality, 90, 91–92
   research designs
      group, 122t, 122–26
      single-case, 100–104, 152–53

Identification responses, 67
Impacts, 42n
Implementation
   of intervention, 18
   in program development, 20–21
   of research results, 157–59
   in social-work practice, 23
Implementation stage, 36–40, 39t
Incremental control, in time-series designs, 135
Independent variables, 7, 9–10, 85
Individual matching, in control groups, 137
Individuals, research designs for (*see* Single-subject designs)
Individual variables, 137
Initiation stage, 19–20
   effectiveness, 34, 35
   efficiency, 34, 35
   efforts, 34–35, 39t
   in social-work practice, 21–22
   unanticipated consequences, 34, 35
Inputs, 38–39, 39t, 40
Instrumentation, as a threat to validity, 88
Instruments, 3, 52, 64–65 (*see also* Questionnaires; Interviews; Observation forms; Rating scales)
   criteria for use, 62–63
   and needs assessment, 58
   types, 65
   uses, 61–62
Intensity-of-response scales, 67, 76
Interaction effects
   in comparison groups, 89, 96-97
   and external validity, 91, 96
Internal validity, 88–89, 96, 148
   group designs, 131, 134–35
   single-subject designs
      before/after, 108–9
      cause-effect, 114–15, 116
      interrupted time-series, 111, 113–14
      Multiple-Baseline, 118
Inter-observer reliability, 45–46, 63, 81, 86, 149–50
Inter-rater reliability, 77, 78
Interrupted time-series designs, 54
   group, 122t, 133–35, 139
   single-subject, 109–11
      with follow-up, 112–14, 112f, 113f
Interval scales, 44, 46, 48, 60
Intervention
   and effectiveness variables, 41
   implementation, 18
   multiple-treatment effects, 91 (*see also* External validity; Internal validity*)
   plan formulation, 18
Interview error, 73–74
Interviews, 71–75 (*see also* Rating scales)
   advantages, disadvantages, 75
   and data analysis, 153, 154
   evelution vs. intervention in, 74
   format, 72
   questionnaires in, 65, 69, 70, 71
   response errors, 70, 73–74
   semistructured, 71–72
   structured, 71
   telephone, 75
   unstructured, 72, 75
Interview schedules, 71, 72
Isaac, S., 30–31

Jayaratne, S., 27, 116
Journal of Alcoholism & Drug Abuse, 52
Journals, as data resources, 51, 52

Kadushin, A., 73
Kazdin, A., 147
Kiresuk, T. J., 79
Knapp, M. S., 135
Knowledge levels, 6, 13-14, 145
   and research designs, 84, 100, 101*t*,
      122*t*, 145
Kurtosis, 147

Lake, D. G., 52
Leiblum, S. P., 103, 110, 111, 147
Lengthy assessment procedure, 111
Levy, R., 27, 116
Likert-type scales, 68, 69, 76, 78
Longitudinal research designs (*see also*
      Time-series designs)
   case studies, 102-4, 104*f*, 106-7
   group studies, 124-26
Lynch, M. M., 50

Mailed questionnaires, 65, 68
   return rate, 69-70
   second mailings, 69-70
Marsh, J., 77
Mass media, as a data resource, 51-52
Matched-pairs *t* test, 8, 54, 130, 131,
      144
Maturation, as a threat to validity, 88
McCarthy, P. J., 92
McNemar, Q., 130, 147
Measurability, of variables, 44, 59, 60
   (*see also* Operational
      definition; Reliability;
      Validity)
Measurement
   accuracy, 86
   in research designs (O), 102, 106-7,
      115*n*
   validity, 86, 88
Measures of Social Psychological
      Attitudes (U. of Mich.), 52
Miles, M. B., 52
Minahan, A., 17
Minnesota Multiphasic Personality
      Inventory, 61
Modalities, 16
Money payments, to subjects, 140
Mosteller, F., 92
Multiple-Baseline Designs, 118-20,
      117*f*, 154
Multiple comparison tests, 152

Multiple regression techniques, 151, 152
Multiple-treatment interference, 91, 96
Multistage sampling, 93
Multivariate relationships, 10

Narrative accounts, 80, 148, 152, 154
Needs assessment (*see* Social needs)
Net inputs, thruputs, outputs, 39
Newspapers, as a data source, 51-52
Nominal definition, of concepts, 6
Nominal scales, 44, 48
Nonequivalent Control Group Design,
      136-39, 141
Nonprobability sampling, 92, 94
Norms, use of, in instruments, 63, 153
Nunnally, J. C., 46, 47*n*

O (*see* Observations)
Objectives, 2, 24-32
   choosing among, 26-27
   common vs. nonequivalent, 24
   defined, 24
   detailed, criteria for 27-30, 149
   in evaluation research, 2, 84
   examples, 31-32
   and knowledge levels, 13-14
   and practical significance, 149
   a priori, a posteriori, 114-15, 149
   program vs. practice, 24, 25
   writing specific, 30-31
Object of analysis, 4
Objects of practice, 16
Observational data, 3, 79-82
   advantages, disadvantages, 82
   format, 80-81
   participant influences, 81, 82
   time periods for gathering, 81-82
   units of analysis, 81
Observations (O), 102, 106-7, 115*n*
One Case Before/After Designs, 108-9,
      111
One Group Before/After (Pretest-
      Posttest) Design, 130-31
Open-ended responses
   in interviews, 71, 72, 74
   on questionnaires, 66-67, 68, 70
Operational definitions, 6-7, 44-45
   consistency in, 55-56
   formation of, 44-45
   and hypotheses, 85
Ordinal scales, 44, 46, 48, 60

Organizational variables, 121, 133, 137
Outputs, 38-39, 39t, 40
   and social need, 42 & n

Panel studies (*see* Longitudinal group studies)
Partial evaluation, 5
Participant observation, 75, 81, 82, 154
Periodicals, 51, 52
Pertinence, of variables, 43-44
Phenomena, frequency of occurrence, 85
Pincus, A., 17
Placebo effects, 91, 97
Planning, program and practice, 41-42
Polansky, N. A., 80
Police department records, 51
Population characteristics, 53, 148 (*see also* Sampling procedures)
Posavac, E. J., 136
Postrating, in single-case studies, 105, 106
Posttest-Only Control Group Design, 142-43 (*see also* Solomon Four-Group Design)
Practical constraints, in instruments, 63
Practical significance, 149
Practice hypotheses, 41
Predictability
   of data, 57
   and empirical relationship, 86, 87
Predictive validity, 47n
Pre-evaluative information, 123
Presence-of-trait scales, 76
Pretest-posttest Control Group Design, 141-42
Primary data, 50
Private agencies, as data sources, 51
Probability sampling, 92-93
Programs, 15-16
   descriptions of, 147-48
   developmental stages, 19-21
   evaluation, 4, 54
   histories of, 148
   objectives, 2, 5, 24-25 (*see also* main entry)
   research designs (*see* Group research designs)
Projective tests, 65
Purposive sampling, 94, 150

Qualitative data, 57-59
   analysis, 150-51
   descriptive function, 58-59, 150
   hypotheses from, 58
   into quantitative data, 59-60
   testing function, 59
Qualitative judgment, 91-92
Quantitative-descriptive knowledge, 6, 7-8, 84, 145
   analysis, 150, 151-52, 153
   and generality, 90
   research designs
      group 122t, 126-29
      single-case, 101t, 104-7
Quasi-Experimental Approaches (Caporaso & Roos), 135
Quasi-Experimentation (Cook & Campbell), 89, 121-22, 135, 146
Quasi-experiments, 135, 136
Questionnaires, 3, 65-71, 85 (*see also* Interviews; Rating scales)
   administration of, 65, 69-70
   advantages, disadvantages, 70-71
   and after-intervention designs, 105
   Client Satisfaction, 98
   construction, 68-69
   format, 66-68
      introduction, 66
      instructions, 66
      types of questions, 66-68
   language, 63
   mailed, 65, 68-70
   modified uses, 61-62
   pretesting, 70
   response rates, 69-70, 148
   split-half reliability, 46
Questions, and program effectiveness, 7
Quota sampling, 94

Randomization, of test groups, 141, 143, 146, 148 (*see also* Control groups; Experimental groups)
Randomized After Only Control Group Design, 142-43 (*see also* Solomon Four-Group Design)
Randomized Before/After Control Group Design, 141-42, 143
Random sampling, 92-93
   simple, 92, 93
   stratified, 92, 93

Index

Rating scales, 76-79, 85
  advantages, disadvantages, 79
  construction, 77-78
  format, 76-77
  goal attainment, 105-6
  in observational methods, 80, 81
  response errors, 78-79
Ratio scales, 44, 46
Reconstruction procedure, for baseline measurements, 111
Records, of social agencies, 51
Recruitment, of clients, 22
Reichert, C. S., 146
Reid, W. J., 155-56
Reliability, 45-47, 151
  empirical estimates, 56-57, 151
  of instruments, 62-63
  inter-observer, 45-46, 63, 81, 86, 149-50, 151
  in interviews, 74
  of measurement, 86, 87
  of qualitative data, 60
  of rating scales, 77, 78
  split-half, 45, 46, 56, 86
  test-retest, 46-47, 56, 86, 125
  (*see also* Replication)
Replicated Cross-Sectional Surveys, 128-29, 130
Replicated time-series designs, 114, 120, single-case, 114, 120
Replication, 90, 94-96, 146, 154
  clinical, 94-95
  direct, 94, 95
  in randomized group designs, 143
  systematic, 94, 95
Representative sampling, 54, 90, 92, 96, 146
  and group survey designs, 126, 127, 129
Research designs, 3, 83-99 (*see also* Single-subject designs; Quasi-experimental designs; Group research designs)
  formulation process, 83-84
  generality, procedures for, 89-97
    (*see also* main entry)
  knowledge development criteria, 84-89
    empirical relationship, 86-87
    hypotheses, 84-85
    internal validity, 87-88
    measurement, 86
    time order, 87
  selection of, 97-99
Research reports, 154-56
Research Techniques for Program Planning (Epstein & Tripodi), 135
Response errors
  in interview, 70, 73-74
  in questionnaires, 71
  in rating scales, 78-79
Response rates, to questionnaires, 69-70, 148
Responses, rating of (*see* Rating scales)
Richardson, W. C., 25, 27, 33, 143, 147
Riecken, H. W., 141
Roos, L. L., 135
Rorschach tests, 61, 63
Rosen, S., 80
Rossi, P. H., 42*n*, 121, 136, 137

Sampling procedures, 54, 92-94
  nonprobability, 92, 94
  probability, 92-93
  representativeness criterion, 90
Scalar responses, 67, 68, 69 (*see also* Rating scales)
Scales of measurement, 44, 60
Scheffé, H., 152
School records, 51
Seaberg, J. R., 79
Secondary data, 50-63, 64
  categorized, 53-57
    criteria for use, 55-57
    potential uses, 53-55
  instruments, 52, 60-63
    criteria for use, 62-63
    potential uses, 61-62
  location, 51-52
  uncategorized, 57-60
    criteria for use, 59-60
    potential uses, 58-59
Selection biases, 88, 91, 96, 131, 132, 136
  aggregate matching, 137
  control by definition, 136-37
  individual matching, 137
Self-reports, of clients, 61, 65, 78, 153
  (*see also* Rating scales)
Selvin, H. C., 147
Semistructured interviews, 71-72
Sensitivity, of variables, 48-49
Shaw, M. E., 77
Sherman, R. E., 79

Shewart control charts, 111, 134, 154
Shortell, S. M., 25, 27, 33, 143, 147
Side effects, of intervention (*see* Unanticipated consequences)
Siegel, S., 147
Significant others, 75, 86
Simple random sampling, 92, 93
Single-subject designs, 3, 4, 54, 83, 84, 100-120
  cause-effect, 114-20
  correlational, 108-14
  and data analysis, 152-54
  hypothetical-developmental, 100-104
  quantitative-descriptive, 104-7
  reliability, 78
  replication, 90
  placebo effects, 97
Single-mood tests, 134
Social agencies, as data sources, 51, 52
Social Casework (journal), 52
Social needs
  assessment, 42, 43
  data on, 5, 43, 53, 58
  and program effectiveness, 41-42
Social-work practice, 16-17
  defined, 16
  development stages, 21-23, 38-39, 39*t*
    contact, 22-23
    implementation, 23
    initiation, 21-22
  effectiveness, efforts, efficiency, 38
  five components, 18-19
  modalities, 16
  objectives, 24-25
  objects of, 16
  planning, 41
  theoretic orientation, 16
Social-work tasks, 17-19
Solomon Four-Group Design, 97, 143-44
Split-half reliability, 45, 46, 56, 86
Sponsors, of evaluation research, 12-13
Staff characteristics, 27
Stanley, J. C., 88, 91, 146
Static Group Comparison (Correlational) Design, 131-32
Statistical Abstract of the U.S., 51
Statistical analysis, 147
Statistical consultants, 147
Statistical regression, 58

Statistical significance, 8, 149
  and data analysis, 149-50, 154
  and empirical relationship, 86-87
  vs. practical significance, 149-50
  and program objectives, 29-30
Statistical tests, 54, 146, 150 (*see also* Sampling procedures)
Statistical trend, 88
Statistics
  location of, 51
  and need assessment, 42
Stephan, F. J., 92
Stratified random allocation, 141
Stratified random sampling, 92, 93, 98, 127-28
Strauss, A., 146
Strauss, M. A., 52
Structured interviews, 71, 128, 154
Structured questions, 66-67
Suchman, E. A., 2, 27, 28, 29, 33, 41*n*
Sudman, S., 127
Summaries, in research reports, 155
Summated scales, 76-77, 78
Summative evaluation, 4-5, 84, 138, 157
  and generality of results, 90
  and single-case designs, 101
Survey methodology, 98-99, 126-28, 151
Susser, M., 87, 147
Systematic replication, 94, 95
Systematic sampling, 94

Telephone interviews, 75
Termination, of practices, programs, 18-19
Test-retest reliability, 46-47, 56, 86, 125
Thematic Apperception Tests, 61
Then & Now rating
  in group designs, 127
  in single-subject designs, 105, 106
Theoretical expectation, 48
Theoretic orientation, 16
Theory failure, 41 & *n*
Thruputs, 38-39, 39*t*, 40
Time-Lagged Control Design, 119-20
Time-order criteria, 87, 89
Time sampling, for observational data, 81-82
Time-series designs (*see also* Interrupted time-series designs)

Time-series designs (*continued*)
  and data analysis, 149, 151, 153
  group, 139–40
  reliability, 78
  single-subject
    graduated intensity, 117–18
    replicated, 114
    Withdrawal/Reversal, 115–17
Tripodi, T., 27, 33, 35–36, 62, 66, 135, 158
t tests, 8, 54, 130, 131, 144, 146
Tukey, J. W., 92

Unanticipated consequences, 5, 25–26, 34, 37–38, 145, 148, 152
  contact stage, 35, 36
  implementation stage, 37
  initiation stage, 34, 35
  and present intervention, 55
  and qualitative data, 152
Unbalanced scales, 78
Undecided responses, to questionnaires, 69
Units of analysis
  group designs, 100
  in observational data, 81
  single-subject designs, 100
Unlikely successive coincidence, 116, 117–18, 119, 154
Unstructured interviews, 72, 75

Validity (*see also* Internal validity; External validity)
  content, 47, 62
  of data, 57, 60
  empirical, 48
  of instruments, 62–63
    interview responses, 72, 75
    questionnaire responses, 70
  of measurements, 86
  threats to, 87, 88–89
  of variables, 47–48, 151
Variables, 3, 33–49 (*see also* Dependent variables; Independent variables)

  and causality, 9–10
  changes in, 29–30, 37
  choosing, 42–43
  concomitant variation in, 103–4
  in data analysis, 147
  definitions (*see* Operational definitions)
  evaluation criteria, 33–34
  in group designs, 121, 136–37, 138
  and hypotheses, 7
  manipulable, 158
  properties, 43–49
    feasibility, 49
    measureability, 44
    operational definitions, 44–45
    pertinence, 43–44
    reliability, 45–47
    sensitivity, 48–49
    validity, 47–48
  in representative sampling, 54
  between stages of development, 40–42
  within stages of development, 34–40, 39*t*
    contact, 35–36, 38
    implementation, 36–38
    initiation, 34–35
    vs. inputs, thruputs, outputs, 38–39

Walker-Liv tests, 134
Weiss, C. H., 24, 26, 41*n*, 73, 123
Winer, B. J., 147
Withdrawal/Reversal Designs, 115–17, 115*f*, 154
Wright, C. R., 25, 33, 37
Wright, J. M., 77
Wright, S. R., 42*n*, 121, 136, 137

X (independent variable), 102, 115*n*

Yeakel, M., 92
Yes–no responses, on questionnaires, 67, 68